American Political Radicalism

❧❧❧American

CONTEMPORARY

EDITED BY
Gilbert Abcarian FLORIDA STATE UNIVERSITY

Political Radicalism

ISSUES AND ORIENTATIONS

Xerox College Publishing

Waltham, Massachusetts / Toronto

Copyright © 1971 by Ginn and Company.
All rights reserved. No part of the material covered by this copyright may be produced in any form or by any means of reproduction.
Library of Congress Catalog Card Number: 71-125638
Printed in the United States of America.

To my sons
MIKE AND STEVE

Preface

"Radical" political perspectives tend to be scorned by most Americans even though such perspectives are in part products of the system they support and often serve as barometers of the relative health of the body politic. Some of the selections incorporated in this volume are also tinged by scorn or contempt: on the part of radical spokesmen condemning "the system," or of critics who dismiss radical views as abhorrent, paranoid, or unworthy of serious consideration. While I am in occasional agreement with both types of attribution, I firmly believe that all are worthy of study, for radicalism is as "American" as the views of its severest critics. In short, the "problem" of radicalism in contemporary American society embraces not only the unpopular orthodoxies of various True Believers, but also the responses of their most passionate critics and debunkers.

If conflict is the heart of politics, radicalism is one of the taproots of contemporary American political conflict and is therefore a subject of paramount importance. That, at any rate, has been a key assumption in the shaping of this book.

On a practical level, this volume has developed in response to the unavailability of a single, general work for assignment in a class on current political radicalism. While a sizable body of literature on that topic is in existence, most of what I, as a teacher, have wished to assign is so widely dispersed as to create serious or unmanageable problems of availability to students. Also, my desire to portray the wide range and diversity of American political radicalism has dictated the use of materials found only in obscure sources or previously unavailable in reprinted form.

Needless to say, I regard the study of political radicalism as important not for the purpose of radicalizing or de-radicalizing the student or popularizing particular belief systems, but because I believe that we ignore the political impact and issue orientations of radicals and antiradicals only at considerable cost to rational political discourse in a democratic society. Accordingly, my intent has been to bring together a group of readings that convey the political *generality* and *relevance* of radical orientations as well as prescriptions for the political arena. I have decided not to include selections primarily because of their reference to immediate events or issues, such as the Vietnam war or campus protest; doing so would result in a loss of the desired broad focus, whatever the gain in terms of attention to important but short-run concerns.

As to the choice of specific selections, right–left source materials were chosen with an eye to such criteria as the relative prominence of each author, viewpoints reflecting the sentiments of organized political constituencies, and reference to such recurrent and sensitive areas of public concern as dissent, the social system, and foreign relations.

As to the commentaries, the basic intent is to include selections, some sympathetic and others antagonistic toward radicalism, that are authored by writers of scholarly or popular repute, and which themselves are provocative enough to elicit intellectual and political responses on their own merits.

The readings are diverse enough to suggest that terms such as "new left" and "radical right" cover a multitude of sins, virtues, and perceptions, as the case may be. Hopefully, these readings will also discourage the notion that radicals are "all the same," and that left and right are mere semantic variations on a single, well-standardized political theme.

The above is an obvious warning against oversimplification, but it is not meant to deny the existence of overlapping characteristics between left and right. In his *The Crisis of Confidence,* Arthur M. Schlesinger, Jr., points to one of these common dimensions. The new left and the right agree, he says, that ". . . the American democratic process is corrupt and phony, that it cannot identify or solve the urgent problems and that American society as at present organized is inherently incapable of providing justice to the alienated groups—for the New Left, the poor, the lower-middle-class whites." But as we shall see, the imputations of corruption made in common by left and right do not necessarily lead to common political diagnoses and prescriptions.

Four concepts provide the conceptual framework for this book: Roots, Sources, Profiles, and Perspectives.

Roots. Initially, several essays are presented each of which probes social, political, cultural, and psychological roots—objective and subjective—of political radicalism. The basic purpose of this section is to sketch the generative conditions as well as structural contexts in which radicalism of both right and left has become resurgent in the past decade. Attention is appropriately drawn to the larger society as a source of strain, cleavage, protest, alienation, and conflict, to which radicalism is a response.

Sources. Having provided the reader with a general grasp of the social matrix out of which radicalism emerges, we turn next to the viewpoints of radical spokesmen through publications that reflect the most salient levels and objects of political protest and analysis. The basic objective of these two sections is portrayal of the broad range and the issue intensity that typify each general form of radicalism. In brief, the intent here is to allow each movement to "make its case" through a choice of some of the most articulate and characteristic literature presently available.

Profiles. The purpose of this group of readings is to present a series of analytical—and occasionally opinionated—portraits of each movement and some of the principal aspects and implications of each. The major question to which these portraits may be considered a response is this: What have scholarly students of contemporary radicalism to say about each movement and its significance in and for American society? The reader will sense the need to place these evaluations, in turn, into the context of his own analytic perspectives.

Perspectives. Here, finally, is presented a small group of essays that explore the significance of radical viewpoints *and* the profiles themselves in the larger context of ideology, both radical and nonradical. These essays are distinguished from the preceding commentaries in that they assess the significance of the debate itself between friends and enemies of the right and the left. Thus radicals and their observers are scrutinized in a manner that encompasses both, one in which the nature and the credibility of radical political postures are explored.

In several selections, certain errors or inconsistencies in style, construction, or analysis are to be found. These have been retained and should be attributed to the specific author rather than to the editor or publisher. We have been reluctant to tamper with the contributors' original language for understandable reasons of textual responsibility.

Since this volume offers a broad portrait of political radicalism and antiradicalism relevant to American politics in the 1960s and 1970s, certain dated references (to elections, political personalities, defunct organizations, etc.) have been retained in order to assist the reader in following the types of relationship particular authors have established between specific issues, events, or personalities and the larger analytical perspectives.

G. A.

Contents

1. *American Political Radicalism:*
   Context and Perspectives   **Gilbert Abcarian**   1

PART ONE
Roots—Societal Contexts of Radical Politics   19

2. *Radicalism in American History*   **Victor C. Ferkiss**   21
3. *Faith of the Fanatic*   **Eric Hoffer**   37
4. *The Conflict of Generations*   **Lewis S. Feuer**   45

PART TWO
Sources—The Radical Right   51

5. *Democracy Is a Fraud*   **Robert Welch**   53
6. *The Rise of Soviet America*   **Billy James Hargis**   57
7. *Danger from the Supreme Court*   **G. Edward Griffin**   67
8. *Communists Can Be Trusted*   **Fred Schwarz**   72
9. *Who Killed John F. Kennedy?*   **Revilo P. Oliver**   86
10. *To the Negroes of America*   **Robert Welch**   94

PART THREE
Sources—The New Left   101

11. *To the British Left: The Need for Utopianism*   **C. Wright Mills**   103
12. *Fascism and Imperialism*   **Mark Rudd**   115
13. *The Black Manifesto*   **James Forman**   121
14. *Succeeding at Revolution*   **Huey Newton**   128
15. *Free the People*   **Carl Oglesby**   133
16. *Dehumanization and Repression*   **Herbert Marcuse**   144

PART FOUR
Profiles—Assessments of Right and Left — 159

17. *Paranoid Politics*   **Richard Hofstadter** — 161
18. *The Politics of Right-wing Fundamentalism*   **David Danzig** — 170
19. *America Moves to the Right*   **David Riesman** — 182
20. *Supporters of the Birch Society*   **Seymour M. Lipset** — 195
21. *A Prophetic Minority*   **Jack Newfield** — 211
22. *Studies in Radical Commitment*   **Kenneth Keniston** — 220
23. *New Styles in "Leftism"*   **Irving Howe** — 231
24. *The New Left and Its Limits*   **Nathan Glazer** — 244

PART FIVE
Perspectives—Radicalism in American Society — 263

25. *The Radical Intellectual*   **Clarence B. Carson** — 265
26. *Deadly Parallels: Left and Right*   **Alan Westin** — 278
27. *The Curse of Conformity*   **Robert M. Lindner** — 292

American Political Radicalism

1

*American Political Radicalism:
Context and Perspectives*

Gilbert Abcarian

This book is about radical politics, its exponents and its critics. It explores the nature, functions, and implications of "extremist" perspectives as found in contemporary American society.

By formal definition, "radicalism" refers to the process by which the center, foundation, or source of certain phenomena is explored, as in the sense of going to the "root" of a problem. In popular usage the term has taken on a variety of meanings. Yet the formal definition may not be so different from these meanings if it is borne in mind that radicals are often perceived as persons who threaten to alter or undermine the foundations of society.

Political radicalism involves three interrelated functional dimensions: *perceptions* (descriptions or definitions), *prescriptions* (demands or expectations), and *norms* (style or fashion). The first two constitute the major preoccupation of this book; lesser attention is focused on the norms that influence radical organization and behavior in specific political situations.

Political radicalism is customarily studied at either the intrinsic or the extrinsic level. The difference is one of focus and objective. An intrinsic orientation calls attention to internal characteristics and events of radicalism. The extrinsic focus seeks to relate knowledge of radicalism to the social system or to specific public issues. This volume incorporates material relevant to observances at both levels. However, the greater emphasis is upon the extrinsic dimension, for a basic objective is to probe the relevance of political radicalism for the larger society, rather than to provide a forum for argumentative assessments about the merits of one or another kind of radicalism.

Whether radicalism is most accurately defined as an outgrowth or perversion of American culture is a hotly debated question. Our purpose here, however, is to provide a serious forum for the study of radicalism, not one devoted to mere polemical judgments about the quality and political relevance of American culture. A receptive rather than close-minded intellectual spirit is essential if study of political radicalism is to yield useful perspectives about its own political orientations and about the crucial processes of social control and social change. Study of radicalism is especially useful for understanding the ways in which patterns of social control affect and are affected by "deviant" groups and individuals. Similarly, such study helps to account for some of the characteristic ways in which social change influences and is influenced by social groups that are marginal to the mainstream of society.

Radicalism is a political and sometimes also an intellectual life style for many citizens. But since politics is only one among many roles of the average individual, we find that with rare exceptions the "pure" radical is a creature of fiction. Accordingly, one should avoid the notion that the study of radicalism is in essence the study of rampant disease or evil.

Are Radicals Interchangeable?

There is a popular though vague notion that in essentials "extremists" or "radicals" are interchangeable, that there is, in effect, a basic similarity of intent, values, and consequences among radical political movements. This view is held not only by members of the general public but also by a sizable group of social scientists. It is worthwhile recalling two recent expressions of the interchangeability perspective: first, the literature developed before and during World War II, in which Fascism and Communism were presented as twin evils sharing in a common set of reality misconceptions and institutional perversions; and second, Eric Hoffer's development of the thesis that "when people are ripe for a mass movement, they are usually ripe for any effective movement, and not solely for one with a particular doctrine or program."

As applied to political radicalism, the idea of interchangeability represents a cluster of specific theories operating on several different levels of analysis. It will be useful to identify these theoretical components before assessing the relevance of this idea for comparative analysis of the radical right and the new left.

The *theory of personality* holds that radical movements indiscriminately attract persons suffering identity crises, persons who seek attenuation of feelings of estrangement and inauthenticity through identification with groups bent on transforming society or the world. A common experience is presumed to be that of "conversion" from a lower to a higher self, a transcendence from experiences of frustration and meaninglessness to experiences of dedication, integration, and normative certitude.

The *theory of authoritarianism* suggests that radical movements are functional equivalents of one another with respect to the antidemocratic orientation of their doctrines, structures, leaders, and programs. In this perspective, radicals of all hues, despite superficial distinctions, possess a common authoritarian denominator. That is, each is believed to embody the underlying unidimensionality of all radical movements.

The *theory of pathology* centers on a clinical interpretation of radicalism. Its most characteristic form is the imputation of paranoia to those who allegedly have lost touch with "reality" and hence live in a fantasy world of mysterious forces, perpetual evil, betrayal, and martyrdom.

The *theory of extremism* emphasizes the adoption by all radical groups of a common style of public protest typified by contempt for existing forms of authority and communication, rejection of the ameliorative approach to problem solving, and a strong inclination toward the adoption of illegal or immoral means of goal attainment.

The *theory of defection,* finally, stresses the transient nature of radical affiliation patterns, particularly the rather free migration from one radical group to another. The classic instance cited is the defection of some left-wingers to right-wing extremist values and organizations.

How do these theoretical components of the interchangeability perspective apply to radical right and new left? Do they apply more or less uniformly to right and left? From the standpoint of published empirical evidence, the following highly tentative observations seem warranted:

Regarding the theory of personality, there is little evidence of unusual gravitation of persons suffering identity crises to one movement rather than another. Since the incidence of such crises appears to be just as high, or low, in nonradical strata of society, the distribution seems random.

Comparison on the basis of authoritarian predilections suggests a higher incidence within the radical right than the new left. In the context previously suggested, the new left manifests fewer of the authoritarian features associated with the radical right.

As to pathological dimensions, no one has established that the members of either movement possess a unique monopoly of delusions so serious as to justify one-sided clinical inferences.

In the extremist context, it appears that while both movements occasionlly engage in extralegal, illegal, or immoral activity, the new left exhibits a significantly greater tendency toward such activity.

Finally, the type of freewheeling political migration suggested by the defection theory of radical movements is not to be observed to any appreciable degree to or from either movement.

We conclude, then, that the idea of interchangeability largely fails to demonstrate the functional equivalence of the radical movements under discussion, though that conclusion must be qualified with respect to apparent confirmation of the personality and pathology theories.

The persistent notion that radicals are all "basically the same" would appear to involve some combination of these, and possibly other, components of the interchangeability idea. But if we shift our analysis from radicals to those employing the idea, we find that it may express the serious concern of the moderate intellectual who regards all radicals as threats to the prevailing system of social control with which he has generally identified himself. There is considerable evidence that variations in ideological commitment among radicals lead to variations in behavior systems and political consequences. If this is so, we must conclude that the consequences of radical ideologies for the social system are by no means equivalent. This is particularly evident if one undertakes to trace out the somewhat different emphases that the radical right and new left place on the specific features and tactical uses of ideology discussed below. Thus the standardized portrait of the radical expressed in the idea of interchangeability has several serious flaws: it fails to account for variations in those aspects of the social system under attack; it obscures the political potential and impact of specific movements; and it minimizes the degrees and sources of public sympathy and hostility. The persistence of the portrait may be understood, then, as itself performing an ideological function in principle hardly distinguishable from the movements under attack. A classic illustration of antiradicalism as ideology is the regrettable tendency among some social scientists to reduce all political movements and ideologies to simple "democratic" and "totalitarian" archetypes.

Functions of Radical Ideologies

Imputations about right and left radicalism frequently reflect and serve ideological purposes, though such imputations may originate with persons and groups that consider themselves "nonideological," "moderate," or "pragmatic." In terms of ideological tactics, could it be that the repudiation of "radicals" often serves to maximize efforts toward a middle-of-the-road political ideology that is not "radical" in the sense of providing its adherents with a root interpretation of political life? Probably not. Perhaps certain ideologies are described as radical in the sense of assuming that commitment to them results in deviant behavior patterns and disruptive social consequences. The weakness in this interpretation is the assumption of predictable congruence between political ideas and political behavior, an assumption not sustained by the available evidence. To say that ideology influences behavior is a tenable proposition; to say that ideology determines behavior is not.

A distinctive feature of contemporary political radicalism is its ideological protest against the direction and morality of the existing political system. In the case of the radical right, what began in the 1950s as a schism within the Republican Party has by now assumed the proportions of a national protest phenomenon that openly challenges the normative and structural control systems of American society. With respect to the new left, disillusionment with progress in civil rights triggered approximately the same challenge. Nonradicals, in reply, often refer to radicals variously as "extremist," "paranoid," "irrational," or "nihilistic," in themselves terms of no little ideological import.

Radical right and new left ideologies are mechanisms for organizing and routinizing political beliefs and behavior patterns of members and supporters. Through zealous propagation of its basic values, each movement seeks to influence strategically placed individuals and groups in order to modify the political system. Ideology promotes that goal by providing radicals with verbal systems of action-oriented communication.

Ideology in the broadest sense is an integrated system of observations and prescriptions whose ultimate intent is to provide individuals with a conceptual basis for faith, evaluation, and action in life.

Political ideology refers to a coherent system of values, definitions, and imperatives. That system contains diagnostic and prescriptive statements that undertake to interpret, conceal, defend, or alter the political order by inspiring action-oriented movements or organizations. Thus, political ideology encompasses (1) symbolic unity, (2) social perspectives, (3) power preferences, and (4) public strategies.

Though different in specific content, radical belief systems exhibit certain common features that characterize each as "ideology."

Perceptual selectivity refers to the tendency of radical ideologies to incorporate certain limited, incomplete aspects of life. Political ideologies are hence highly selective sets of perceptions drawn out of a much larger political universe, though they customarily are presented as valid representations of political realities. Adherents of a given ideology tend to believe that their perceptions and the political principles derived from them constitute objective knowledge. Because of their selectivity, ideologies tend to "manage" events by a certain degree of distortion. Nevertheless, the capacity of an ideology to present a unified, coherent account of political life may strengthen the movement by intensifying the faith of its members and attracting new followers who crave formalized interpretations.

Rationalization is characteristic of radical ideologies in that they offer elaborate justifications for proposed political changes. These justifications serve as abstract public explanations for political preferences by investing them with legitimacy and objective merit. Such rationalization is rarely on the level of conscious motivation; it is typical for radicals to believe themselves guided by the requirements of loyalty, law and order, God, justice, class, or humanity.

Scripturalism is encountered in the form of appeal to a special body of literature believed to contain propositions of absolute validity. The basic "scripture" of a radical ideology frequently evokes a quasi-religious response from its adherents, who tend to regard its content and author(s) as unique or even sacred.

Normative certitude signifies the moral sense of purity and validity that is associated with the various components of ideology. Radical ideology may confer on the believer a feeling of commitment to principles whose validity is beyond challenge. This sense of certitude may be described alternatively as political fundamentalism in the sense that certain religious writings are believed to contain "fundamentals" of literal validity in the spiritual life of the individual.

Transcendentalism is the process through which political supporters experience moral and political uplift, an elevation from disturbing aspects of prevailing life. The radical ideology thus provides a transcendent vision against which the existing order can be assessed.

In its milder form, this process may lead to reform efforts; in its more intensive expression, to utopian schemes or revolutionary acts.

The radical ideology may be viewed not only as a system of ideas but also as a vehicle for generating conditions that are conducive to success in the political arena. In this sense we may refer to several characteristic tactical operations of radical political ideologies.

The success or failure of a radical movement is influenced by the extent to which public receptivity is shaped through a program of *political socialization*. The social structure of any society contains a variety of institutions that exercise considerable influence in the formation of popular political attitudes. Such institutions may be said to "socialize" particular viewpoints when individuals are taught to accept some as authoritative and to reject others as deviant. Political socialization in desired directions depends upon the extent to which these institutions legitimize the basic tenets of the radical ideology, or at the very least permit a nonhostile atmosphere in which such tenets might thrive.

Acceptance of political ideology is closely linked to the intensity of personal faith it inspires. Radical leaders commonly attempt to maximize a movement's goals through propaganda programs aimed at *emotional arousal*. It is necessary to sustain and reinforce ideological orthodoxy on the part of members and to generate political emotions that promise eventual affiliation or support from others. Characteristically, emotional arousal consists in attacks on those individuals, groups, norms, agencies, and policies regarded as threats to the values and influence of the movement.

Radical ideologies must interpret events that for many persons appear overwhelmingly complex or meaningless. Successful propagation of an ideological position requires skill in presenting the public with a relatively simple framework of interpretation that will replace frustration and confusion with cognitive order. The employment of such an interpretive framework may be termed *reductionism*, the process through which a comparatively simple thesis, such as "conspiracy" or "exploitation," purports to "explain" political intricacies to the outsider through a theory whose meaning is easily grasped.

Radical movements frequently engage in *personification*. Certain spokesmen are presented to the public as symbols of ideological integrity. If those presented command great public prestige, credibility may be lent to the political ideas expounded and thereby induce others to adopt them. Some movements are able to call upon the services of leaders to whom charisma is imputed—powers of persuasion, knowledge, and wisdom denied ordinary persons.

To one degree or another, radical ideologies perceive the political sphere in terms of friendly and hostile forces. Accordingly, a crucial function is that of strategic assessment, the development of techniques that help distinguish between friends and enemies in the power arena. The ideology itself provides guidelines for making strategic assessments; persons supporting its doctrines are friends, while those opposing them are enemies.

The final tactical element is *political action,* the process through which abstract ideas inspire active involvement in the form of various political contests. That struggle invariably leads to competing demands for control of power roles.

Radical Right and New Left Ideologies

The political ideology of the radical right encompasses five principal dimensions:

1. *Conspiracy* reflects the belief that "communists," "fellow travelers," and "dupes" have penetrated, effectively control, and are systematically undermining "the American way of life." Virtually all top public leaders are presumed to be witting or unwitting accomplices in a variety of interrelated schemes. Political events that on the surface appear chaotic and meaningless to the average citizens are believed to "cloak" the designs of conspirators who are extraordinarily skilled at public deception and political betrayal.

2. *Failure of foreign policy* assumes that American calamities around the world are due to commitment to subversive and alien objectives at the highest levels of decision-making. The right wing sees the nation plunged into international humiliation and national dishonor through policies geared to appeasement and "surrender."

3. *Fundamentalism* expresses the conviction that the universe embodies norms of absolute moral validity, but norms that have been betrayed. Americans are implored to return to the eternal truths, divine and secular, that are embodied in the teachings of the Scriptures, regarded as a perfect reflection and "inerrant" source of truth. The secular version of fundamentalism takes the form of a call to "Americanism" by a small body of true patriots and moral leaders who will initiate a "return" to the universal moral principles that once guided the American "republic."

4. *Distrust of democracy* conveys the belief that the political sys-

tem is dominated by demagoguery, mob rule, ideological heresy, and vulgarizing mass values. Such distrust reveals the view that the masses are highly gullible and that their inclusion in the governing process, as with most interest groups, leads to erosion of "constitutional government." The ultimate expression of the democratic process is the omnipotent state, which "collectivizes" and "enslaves" the individual even while proclaiming the glories of individual freedom.

5. *Anticollectivism* completes the repertoire of right-wing ideological dimensions and is expressed typically in the warning that Americans face an either/or choice between a "free" and a "collectivistic" political destiny. It is believed that American individualism has virtually disappeared in proportion to the growth of governmental "regimentation" and "coddling" in nearly all aspects of national life. Through centralization, government ostensibly has grown remote from the genuine needs and aspirations of the people; by imposing alien ideals and programs, government has taken this nation into socialism, the stage leading "inevitably" to communistic "slavery."

The rightist ideological mood reflects intense feelings of estrangement from contemporary American society and from the political processes shaping the future. From the diagnostic perspective of rightist ideology, traditional "absolutes" have declined in modern life and as a consequence the likelihood of the individual's living a life of significance, worth, belongingness, and rootedness has been destroyed. The political system—perceived as alien, evil, punitive, intractable, and manipulated by an elite—is regarded as unresponsive to individual merit as defined in the nation's own heritage. With that heritage repudiated by the "forces" exercising "real power," impersonality, emptiness, and distrust appear the tragic price of modern life as the gulf widens between the defenders and the enemies of "our way of life."

The prescriptive aspect of rightist ideology reflects the conviction that politics require the simple extension of moral propositions possessing absolute and self-evident validity into government affairs. For at bottom, the rightists say, social problems are moral problems, which means that political understanding cannot be attained nor political solutions devised through primary reliance on science and intellect.

Political salvation accordingly lies in the hands of the few "natural" leaders possessing acute moral vision and selfless courage. This charismatic orientation derives in part from the idea that the political destiny of a nation is determined by epic struggles between the forces of good and evil as embodied in the political activities of a few great or evil men of power. All else in politics and political analysis is regarded as secondary and illusory. The final hope in politics is that a few men of divine charisma who possess extraordinary understanding and resources might assume their "rightful" positions of highest authority in order to crush those men of evil whose diabolic machinations threaten all that is sacred.

Political events are hence believed to derive from the clash of wills among a tiny number of powerful men. The exclusion of impersonal environmental circumstances as shaping forces in the political sphere leads the radical rightist to the view that the political process is dominated by superactivists through whose efforts the rest of society is led to either salvation or damnation.

The ideology of the radical right reinforces certain personal and organizational needs.

On the personal side, the *impulse for certainty* is supported. Rightist ideology provides a relatively simple framework of interpretation through which events on the personal, national, and world levels are invested with clarity, meaning, and directionality. The *image of self-righteousness* receives impetus, since, through ideological commitment, displacement of guilt feelings and a mood of self-gratification are achieved by dedication to a crusade to destroy the "enemy." Such commitment also reinforces the need for *compensatory superiority*. An individual may overcome status frustration through identification with a movement deemed on the "right" side of a universal struggle against evil and corruption. Finally, since the enemy must be treated mercilessly, the tendency toward *rationalized aggression* receives reinforcement through affiliation with a movement that has identified an absolute, intolerable adversary. All hostile measures against the adversary are sanctioned by the principles of morality and the requirements of the public interest.

On the organizational side, two needs served by right-wing ideology are worth noting. The ideology helps create *relational linkages* among actual and potential members. These are of sufficient importance to give the movement a sense of organic life and activity apart from the individuals constituting it. *Solidarity* of the group structure is buttressed by singling out leaders who are regarded as possessing charismatic powers that include an unexcelled, quasi-religious understanding of the ideology and a moral vision of the future to which the movement is dedicated.

The rhetorics of several traditional ideologies are intermingled in the new left movement. But if verbal style of the moment is distinguished from deeply rooted, recurrent concepts, a meaningful approximation of new left ideological tendencies is possible. The following appear noteworthy:

1. *Romanticism* reflects the view of politics as a venture in moral values rather than as power mechanics or calculating "realism." It springs from the leftists' deep faith in human nature, character, and aspirations, especially among the poor and the oppressed. Above all, romanticism is reflected in the demand for the strict adaptation of political resources and behavior to the implementation of a utopian vision, unencumbered by concessions to "practicality."

2. *Ahistoricism* is expressed in detachment from the past and from presumably spurious "lessons" of history. There is a refusal to adjudicate among or accept uncritically any of the traditional radical ideologies; there is a fundamental skepticism toward orthodoxies. The result is a considerable degree of both antidogmatic and antiintellectual feeling, but above all a vehement anti-anticommunism.

3. *Revitalization* expresses the demand for social reconstruction through a spirit of insurgency, through acts of disruption and detachment from practices or institutions deemed corruptive of one's normative commitments. Society must be radicalized by preventing cooptation of the young by corporate liberalism. It must be purified by avoiding the politics of coalition and by creating counterinstitutions that will precipitate authentic "confrontations."

4. *Communitarianism* calls for de-alienation through the creation of smaller communities and structures. These will offset the evils of mass society by making participatory democracy a reality for those at the bottom levels of the social system.

5. *Disengagement,* finally, conveys the belief that the United States is the great disturber and imperialist of the world, and should therefore withdraw from political, economic, and military intervention in the affairs of other countries. Before the United States can resume a constructive role in world politics, it must rebuild and humanize its own institutions.

According to Jack Newfield, a contributor to this volume and also from his contribution to this book, what seems new about the new left ". . . is its ecumenical mixture of political traditions that were once murderous rivals in Russia, Spain, France, and the U.S. It contains within it, and often within individuals, elements of anarchism, socialism, pacifism, existentialism, humanism, transcendentalism, bohemianism, Populism, mysticism, and black nationalism."

Fortunately, we may concentrate upon one group that encompasses most of the new left's relevant characteristics and tendencies, namely, Students for a Democratic Society.

SDS membership embraces several distinguishable but overlapping categories of persons: revolutionaries who seek transformation through violence; political idealists with a Populist outlook who view supermilitancy and apathy with equal disdain; organizational old guardists who performed the function of founding fathers; anarcho-hipsters skeptical of all organized power and decisions made by formal voting processes; ghetto workers who devote their entire time to programs aimed at alleviating the misery of the poor; and liberal intellectuals, a large group of career-oriented professionals scattered around the nation.

The closest approximation of an "official" statement of values of SDS is to be found in the now partially disavowed *Port Huron Statement* of 1962, which expressed its critique of university education, mass culture, party politics, the economic system, discrimination, anticommunism, and foreign policy. The following statements are typical:

> We regard men as infinitely precious and possessed of unfulfilled capacities for reason, freedom, and love. In affirming these principles we are aware of countering perhaps the dominant conceptions of man in the twentieth century: that he is a thing to be manipulated, and that he is inherently incapable of directing his own affairs. We oppose the depersonalization that reduces human beings to the status of things. . . .
>
> Loneliness, estrangement, isolation describe the vast distance between man and man today. These dominant tendencies cannot be overcome by personnel management, nor by improved gadgets, but only when a love of man overcomes the idolatrous worship of things by man. . . .
>
> As a social system we seek the establishment of a democracy of individual participation, governed by two central aims: that the individual share in those social decisions determining the quality and direction of his life; that society be organized to encourage independence in men and provide the media for their common participation. . . .

From its inception, SDS was an uneasy coalition of diverse groups and left-wing orientations. Whatever cohesiveness it possessed was less in the realm of a unifying belief system than in radical, and later prerevolutionary, action programs. At its 1969 national meeting, the breach between the Progressive Labor and Revolutionary Youth Movement factions erupted into a formal split; the former was expelled from the organization. Since then, further fissures of a sectarian nature intensified the pluralistic character of SDS.

The SDS analysis goes something like this: Supreme political power—for good or evil—rests in the hands of political liberals for whom the large corporation is taken as the desired model for organizing the entire social system. The liberals' presumed goal is to achieve harmony among the dominant strata of society by distributing just enough rewards throughout the system to discourage the lowest segments from weakening or destroying it. Except in rhetoric, however, redistribution never really occurs; hence millions of citizens are doomed to poverty, futility, and embitterment. For this reason, say SDS activists, the vanguard for restructuring society is the organized poor, for they alone constitute a force compelling basic structural change. It is believed that corporate liberals work diligently to prevent an alliance from developing between the very poor and the unorganized workers, since such an alliance might weaken the power of the trade unions and civil rights organizations, which the liberals control. Liberal leftists who fret because the SDS brand of radicalism disparages traditional electoral processes are reminded by one writer of "this quadrennial spasm of the body politic [presidential elections] that puts purchasable men in the low places and purchasers in the high. . . ."

The link between SDS diagnosis and action is provided by the concept of "participatory democracy," or decentralized decision-making, through which every man would have an "equal voice" in decisions that affect him. Democratic participation ostensibly will help the poor develop a sense of group solidarity that must precede legitimate demands for a role in making public policies. In a work from which his contribution to this volume is taken, Carl Oglesby observes that "it is neither in the nature of the state that it can give political freedom nor in the nature of political freedom that it can be given. . . . Political freedom is in political man, in his life, and it exists when he claims it. . . . *Any decision not made by the people in free association, whatever the content of that decision, cannot be good. . . .*"

SDS members exhibit intense hostility toward American political processes. That response derives from the experienced disparity between democratic ideology and social realities, from the conviction that the reigning credo promises far more than its guardians are willing to deliver. The disparity between promise and performance is bitter to endure, for the young radical tends to identify himself with moral imperatives rather than with the politics of practicality and gradualism. Hence, the "credibility gap" he experiences is not just a temporary loss of faith in the honesty of specific public officials, but also alienation from the structures they dominate.

The new left finds fault with conventional political values not so much because they have declined or become irrelevant, but because they continue to command widespread rhetorical support even while they refer loftily to problems their adherents have no intention of confronting. In this sense, these values are believed to have corrupted and undermined civic-mindedness, at least for the older generations, by breeding apathy, hypocrisy, and social insensitivity, qualities that have been passed off as moral responsibility and political "realism."

While the two sets of radical ideologies are significantly different from one another, they do point to several commonly held apprehensions worth noting.

Both express vehement protest against a social and political system presumably incapable of providing an integrative role for the individual. Such protest typifies one who feels like an outsider, a stranger who is acted upon as victim rather than beneficiary of the system.

The radical often experiences powerlessness, a sense of low subjective probability for mastery and control over the outcome of personal, national, and international events. The external social environment is looked upon as nonmanipulable and as unresponsive to personal needs and efforts.

Radical groups are highly volatile and often lacking in internal cohesion. Is it likely, then, that organized radical movements provide their members with substantial relief from feelings of political alienation? The available evidence, while not conclusive, suggests a negative answer. The search of such movements for internal stability and public influence more often than not has been a failure. Organizational volatility appears to be related to unsatisfactory and usually short-lived group attachments on the part of individual adherents. Accordingly, it may be conjectured that radical groups tend to attract some highly alienated persons without providing them long-range satisfaction.

Sources and Consequences of Radicalism

Rational responses to the political radical require understanding of the conditions or experiences that lead to radical commitment. While students of radical movements hardly agree on any single-cause interpretation, several theories have gained scholarly support and are frequently encountered in a variety of publications.

1. *Fundamentalism.* Since a stylistic similarity may be found between radical and religious movements, some observers have suggested that the radical is one who transfers his fervor for sacred principles to the political sphere. Given that inclination, he may be recognized by the ease with which he believes that social questions may be resolved by placing them in the context of absolutes whose meaning he perfectly understands and is anxious to articulate. The fundamentalist has a Manichean concept of life as a titanic struggle between absolute good and absolute evil. The exponents of this model believe that the fundamentalist is unable to approach political questions in any other framework than evangelical revivalism or moral crusading. The radicals' perennial diagnosis for the political ills of our times is to "get back to fundamentals."

2. *Anomie.* An anomic society is characterized by social disorganization produced by certain patterns of urban life. The big city, for example, is pointed to as the most likely context within which personal relationships perform a largely utilitarian rather than humanizing function. The city may be anomic because individuals within it pursue purely personal goals in face-to-face relations. Anomie, hence, means loss of spontaneous self-expression, morale, and the sense of community identification associated with life in an integrated society. In the anomic community interpersonal relations are pecuniary and predatory. Anomie presumably breeds the personal responses and organizational roles that encourage the emergence of the political radical. In this perspective, the radical is regarded as a response to a society in which older common values and meanings are no longer understood or accepted, but in which new common values and meanings have not been developed.

3. *Paranoia.* The paranoid is one who experiences delusions, the chief of which is often persecution. Numerous commentators regard radical movements as the collective manifestation of personal mental

disorders widely experienced among the population. Applied to politics, paranoia consists in the belief that a "gigantic" conspiracy governs major events, a demonic view of life in which "time is running out," "tomorrow may be too late," etc. Crisis for the paranoid is always at a cosmic level of significance. To the paranoid the enemy is a superforce possessed of extraordinary power, persistence, and evil. Indeed, the paranoid's (often unconscious) admiration for the enemy's style often leads to the adoption of his tactics, though the paranoid never realizes that the enemy he imitates is the product of his fantasies. According to its proponents, then, a basic explanation for radicalism is the persecution complex, one that is experienced, in many cases, on the paranoid level of social adaptation.

4. *Alienation.* The alienation theory emphasizes the severance of man from certain historic and moral certitudes in the age of the mass society. It is held that mass society has instrumentalized and depersonalized individual relationships in such a way as to produce highly estranged persons. Alienation suggests the loss of community and the sense of belongingness in an age of enveloping bureaucracy and technology. The alienated man supposedly feels unrelated to others in a world in which interpersonal relations have become mechanized. The end result is a loss of self, which in turn generates the compulsion to plunge into beliefs or movements promising "genuine" freedom.

In this fashion alienation is treated as a generative condition of radical political commitment. The alienated man feels unrelated to others in a brutalizing social system. His response may take the form of apathy or indifference, at one extreme, or, as in the case of some radical rightists or leftists, political obsessiveness and habitual protest at another.

5. *Authoritarianism.* Certain psychodynamic orientations are sufficiently powerful to motivate a person to adopt a radical belief system and behavior pattern. The origins of such orientations are usually complex and may include early socialization experiences, maladjustments to the outer world, painful family experiences, or personality disruptions. Whatever the origins, the suggestion is made that these orientations help produce an authoritarian personality who is attracted to radicalism.

What are the characteristics of the authoritarian as political radical? He is believed to display tendencies toward undiscriminating faith in leadership, intense distrust of presumed enemies, superconfidence in the objective rightness of his beliefs, absolute justification for imposing his views on others by any means including violence, and unwillingness to concede that there is any real ambiguity about how to solve outstanding problems. In short, the politics of the authoritarian are heavily colored by a set of deep emotional insecurities that lead him to the adoption of extreme viewpoints and behaviors.

Each of these theories has something of value to say about political radicalism in particular times and circumstances. None, however, is the ultimate explanation, since each provides answers to quite different questions about radicalism.

Antiradicalism in a Democratic Society

The radical's view of society is crisis oriented. But he is hardly alone in this. Many other strata of society also sense crisis in one form or another. Rare is the man who believes the times are "normal." It is not so much the orientation to crisis as it is the preferred mode of responding to it that characterizes conflict between radicals and nonradicals. The radical tends to react to crisis situations by demanding near-perfect congruence between reality and the prescriptive norms of his ideology. In similar circumstances, the nonradical tends to regard insistence on subordination of reality to ideological purity as an aggravation of the given problem rather than a contribution to its solution. Indeed, his immediate reaction is often that of attacking the radical rather than the problem. If sufficiently alarmed, the radical responds in kind, which leads to the intensification rather than attenuation of crisis situations.

Most behavioral scientists are inclined to regard political radicalism as the product of social structures and events, and not as the manifestation of "abnormal" individuals unable to adjust to an otherwise "healthy" environment. While the forces that lead to the adoption of deviant beliefs and actions are imperfectly understood, it is widely recognized that society itself is the locus of the experiences, tensions, and events that precipitate radical commitment. It is far wiser to cope with radicalism through social analysis and understanding than through mechanisms of repression that breed further discontent. Too often the antiradical postulates the myth of the "rational" man, a myth that serves the convenient purpose of justifying extreme treatment of the radical as a dangerous outsider who "deserves what he gets."

While essential to the continuation of democracy, moderation sometimes demands a political climate hostile to dissent. Dissenters are often confused with radicals because they are critical of the institutional structure which most people trust. What may begin as rational dialogue between radicals and moderates on specific issues sometimes acquires a dynamic that is destructive of normal, constitutionally protected dissent. That dynamic can create such intense conflict that immediate issues are lost sight of as invective, power strategies, and generalized intolerance become paramount. Under these conditions it becomes virtually useless to speak of right and wrong parties except perhaps in some vague and distorted ideological sense.

The real threat to the conditions of trust, rationality, and pluralism essential to democracy is extremism, not radicalism. The two must be distinguished. A radical may or may not be an extremist, depending upon the political style, *not the ideas,* he adopts. Radicalism refers to insistence on basic policy changes. Extremism, on the other hand, implies rejection or destruction of accepted mechanisms and processes through which such policies are made. If the general distinction between radicalism and extremism is grasped, it is not difficult to see that political crisis is often created not only by extremists but also by advocates of an intolerant, suspicious "moderation" that mistakes every proposal for policy change as an intolerable threat. In short, the combination of radical extremists and rigid moderates is itself a substantial threat to a democratic system, quite apart from the activity of many radicals who, as good citizens, advocate basic change within the existing social framework.

Part One

Roots—Societal Contexts of Radical Politics

The search for the roots or antecedent conditions of radical politics has embraced a wide variety of theories. These theories derive from concern with such factors as culture, institutions, socialization patterns, reference groups, personality development, political values, and social stress.

The selections in Part One focus on three such explanatory frameworks—historico-intellectual background, identity crisis, and intergenerational conflict.

CONTRIBUTORS

Victor C. Ferkiss: Professor of government at Georgetown University. He is the author of *Technological Man, Africa's Search for Identity, Communism Today,* and numerous other articles and books on a variety of political and historical subjects.

Eric Hoffer: Formerly a San Francisco longshoreman, is the author of such well-known works as *The True Believer, The Temper of Our Times,* and *The Ordeal of Change.* He has served as a research professor at the University of California at Berkeley and has been the subject of magazine articles and several television programs.

Lewis S. Feuer: Professor of sociology at the University of Toronto. He is the author of *The Scientific Intellectual* and is well-known for his many studies of student radicalism. He recently published *The Conflict of Generations,* a study of the history and meaning of student dissidence during the past two centuries.

2
Radicalism in American History

Victor C. Ferkiss

The United States owes its national existence to a revolution. Yet, when it comes to politics and to ideas, Americans are not a revolutionary people. Even the war for independence was in a sense conservative, an attempt to restore a state of affairs disrupted by an innovating British regime. America has the world's oldest constitution. We cling not only to our ancient institutions, modifying them only slowly and then rarely in radical degree, but above all to the ideas, and especially the rhetoric, behind them—so much so that some observers contend there never has been any significant dissent from the American consensus.[1]

Yet political upheavals have occurred in America: the revolutions of Jefferson and Jackson, of the Square Deal, the New Freedom, and the New Deal—all within the framework of our constitutional system—and the struggle over slavery, decided by the Civil War. These challenges to the prevailing political framework were successful and were incorporated into the American consensus.

Nature of American Radicalism

America has also spawned radical movements which advocated ideas diverging so sharply from the accepted consensus that their ad-

SOURCE: Victor C. Ferkiss, "Political and Intellectual Origins of American Radicalism, Right and Left," *Annals of the American Academy of Political and Social Science,* November, 1962. Reprinted by permission of the author.

[1] Daniel J. Boorstin, *The Genius of American Politics* (Chicago: University of Chicago Press, 1953); Louis Hartz, *The Liberal Tradition in America: An Interpretation of American Political Thought since the Revolution* (New York: Harcourt, Brace, 1955).

herents were forced to challenge the constitutional structure itself. Although these did not succeed in destroying the constitutional framework, they did alter or seriously threaten to alter it.

In America, radical movements have arisen both on the left and on the right, in response to liberal ideals and to authoritarian ones. In this paper, "left" is understood to mean support of government intervention to promote economic equality; "right," to mean opposition to such intervention. By "liberal" is meant support for widening the acceptable range of deviance from community norms governing behavior and ideas; by "authoritarian," a desire to narrow this range. In general, the radical right is both rightist and authoritarian; the radical left, leftist and liberal.

Radical movements in America are conditioned by the fact that our politics are the result of clashes of interest rather than of ideas. Radicalism is the product of social, economic, or psychological drives which cannot or can only with great difficulty be fulfilled within the existing political framework. Radical movements seek social and political changes so drastic and basic that it is easy for their adherents to become convinced that their values cannot be implemented through established political institutions or in terms of traditional political ground rules.

Despite this basic difference between radical and other movements, all political movements in America, whether radical or traditional, left or right, tend to use the same political language. So strong is the hold of concepts such as limited government, democracy, constitutionalism, equality, free enterprise, and the like that all try to subsume their particular goals under the traditional political terminology. "Communism is twentieth-century Americanism," the Communist party once proclaimed, and the radical right denounces decisions of the Supreme Court as unconstitutional! What is distinctive about extremist movements in America, therefore, is not so much the express content of their ideas as their methods, the nature of their appeal to their followers, and their inability to accommodate their goals to those of the dominant consensus.

American Radical Development

Throughout the eighteenth and nineteenth centuries, America experienced a gradual growth in liberty and equality. Radical movements were mostly leftist or liberal; right-wing and authoritarian movements were mainly concerned with preserving the *status quo*.

But basic social changes were occurring under pressure of technological, economic, and demographic factors, which led to the emergence of reactionary movements seeking to reverse the new economic trends by political means. Both populism and progressivism were in a real sense reactionary in that they sought a return to an era when the independent farmer and small businessman were the dominant forces in American society. The antitrust policies of Theodore Roosevelt and later administrations were one response to this desire to turn back the clock.

Nineteenth-century radicalism

The nineteenth century witnessed a number of radical movements, some successful in that their aims were ultimately included in the majority consensus. It is easy to forget how revolutionary some of the tenets of Jacksonianism were, so swift and complete was the triumph of such principles as full political equality and equalization of the conditions of economic competition. The Abolitionists, though an extremist minority both in their attack on slavery and in their willingness to resort to civil disobedience, managed to join their cause to others in the Republican party and thus to achieve their major goal. Their adversaries, the principled believers in political, economic, and racial inequality, retired from the field until the era of Social Darwinism,[2] when the growth of industrial capitalism presented the nation with *de facto* inequalities of status and power which had to be rationalized, as did the American conviction that it was America's Manifest Destiny to dominate the peoples of Latin America and the Far East.

Socialism and populism

The majority acceptance of economic and political inequalities led to new movements of protest on the left, in particular socialism and populism, which differed fundamentally in their goals. The Populists wanted to restore the small capitalist world of Jacksonianism, where all were economic equals. Primarily West and Midwest farmers, the Populists sought to preserve their economic independence and vanishing middle-class world against the changes inherent in growing concentration of capital. Authoritarian in social outlook, the Populists regarded the forces making for change as a deliberate

---

[2] See Richard Hofstadter, *Social Darwinism in American Thought* (Boston: Beacon Press, 1955).

conspiracy of the few, with international overtones.[3] They sought to fight this conspiracy by increasing the amount of direct popular control over government. They attempted, with considerable success, to modify representative government by introducing such instruments of direct plebiscitary democracy as the initiative, referendum, and recall, and direct election of a wide variety of government officials.

The Socialists sought to raise the living standards of the worker as such through widespread government ownership and regulation of the economy. American socialism was non-Marxian and largely inspired by such ideals as the "co-operative commonwealth" espoused by Edward Bellamy and Henry Demarest Lloyd. Like populism, it was largely agrarian in base, but, because of its cosmopolitan urban wings, it was less authoritarian. Basically, the Socialists accepted the inevitability of economic concentration and, rather than trying to halt this process, sought instead to subject it to public supervision and control and to redistribute its profits more equitably.[4]

The activities of Theodore Roosevelt and Woodrow Wilson, the reforms promoted by the Progressives, and prosperity destroyed populism and socialism as major political forces. But sources of radicalism remained. Economic conditions were depressed in farming areas through the 1920s. Certain forms of labor—mining, forestry, migrant farm labor—which isolated workers from society made possible such movements as the Industrial Workers of the World (IWW). And foreign policy took on new importance as major ethnic groups, the German and Irish particularly, nursed resentments of America's break with its isolationist tradition in World War I.[5]

Isolationism

Roosevelt's New Deal attempted to merge the forces of dissent into a new dominant coalition and, for a time, succeeded. Concessions to organized labor weakened the potential appeal of the Communist and Socialist parties. Social security, unemployment insurance, and the Agricultural Adjustment Act weakened the neo-Populist, protofascist appeals of Huey Long, Father Coughlin, Dr.

---

[3] Richard Hofstadter, *The Age of Reform: From Bryan to F.D.R.* (New York: Alfred A. Knopf, 1955), pp. 60–93.
[4] See David A. Shannon, *The Socialist Party of America: A History* (New York: The Macmillan Company, 1955).
[5] See Selig Adler, *The Isolationist Impulse: Its Twentieth-Century Reaction* (New York: Collier Books, 1961); also Samuel Lubell, *The Future of American Politics* (New York: Harper, 1951).

Townsend, and Gerald L. K. Smith—although Democratic Chairman James A. Farley estimated that Long would receive five million votes as a third-party candidate in 1936.[6]

Although the New Deal could temporarily satisfy leftist economic pressures, it could not prevent the growth of radicalism in foreign affairs. Roosevelt's switch from isolationism to interventionism split . . . both left and right, but especially the former. The American Socialist party was torn asunder on the issue. Most heirs of populism and progressivism, partly for ethnic reasons, remained faithful to an isolationist nationalism. Alarmed by the rise of communism and by trends in the direction of the cosmopolitan values they associated with it, they rejected Roosevelt's foreign policy and formed alliances with segments of the business community—mostly in the Midwest—which opposed the New Deal on both economic and foreign-policy grounds. Roosevelt was forced to turn to the Eastern business and financial community and to the South for support. From this political reorientation arose an extremist opposition combining nationalist isolationism, anticommunism, and elements of fascism which has endured to this day and is the forebear of the contemporary radical right.[7]

The Republican nomination of Willkie in 1940 preserved the American consensus by foreclosing effective political debate on the issue of intervention. The isolationists formed the America First Committee, which fought intervention to the bitter end.[8] Their creed was: military strength at home; no intervention on behalf of the Allies, especially Soviet Russia, which they contended would be the war's real victor; and opposition to control of American policy by what they considered to be a coalition of Jews, Communists, and Eastern business and financial interests. Socially, they consisted of Midwestern and Western heirs of the Populists and Progressives, lower-class urban ethnic groups, particularly Catholics, and a sprinkling of businessmen.

---

[6] Donald R. McCoy, *Angry Voices: Left-of-Center Politics in the New Deal Era* (Lawrence: University of Kansas Press, 1958), p. 137. Long was assassinated in 1935.

[7] See Victor C. Ferkiss, "Populist Influences on American Fascism," *Western Political Quarterly*, Vol. 10, No. 2 (June, 1957), pp. 350–373; Paul S. Holbo, "Wheat or What? Populism and American Fascism," *Western Political Quarterly*, Vol. 14, No. 3 (September, 1961), pp. 727–736; Victor C. Ferkiss, "Populism: Myth, Reality, Current Danger," *Western Political Quarterly*, Vol. 14, No. 3 (September, 1961), pp. 737–740.

[8] Wayne S. Cole, *America First* (Madison: University of Wisconsin Press, 1953).

McCarthyism

Father Coughlin, Gerald L. K. Smith, and Huey Long, like the Populists, had combined leftist economics with nationalism, isolationism, respect for traditional social values, and antiliberal attitudes toward civil liberties. After the war, prosperity diverted popular interest from economic reform, but resentment of the Roosevelt-Truman foreign policy and fear and hatred of international communism continued to grow. At the same time, war and postwar taxes and controls, as well as the rise of Communist power, made additional upper-class converts to ultraright nationalism.

Senator Joseph McCarthy capitalized on this postwar dissatisfaction. His appeal uniquely united the divergent ethnic and social groups comprising the opposition to the dominant consensus. He himself was not a rightist economically; his voting record was, in fact, somewhat left of center on major issues of government economic intervention. He did not attack the power of labor unions nor the prevalence of farm subsidies as evidences of creeping socialism. He was able to gain the support of some wealthy businessmen without alienating those followers who retained antibusiness sentiments.[9]

For McCarthyism, the locus of Communist subversion was the old Eastern upper-class elite, the traditional enemy of the Populists and the upwardly mobile urban ethnic groups. His unifying appeal combined nationalism and a neo-isolationism which emphasized the domestic Communist threat and presupposed an activist role in world affairs, although a unilateral one. The doctrines of McCarthyism accounted for America's seeming impotence in world affairs, made victory theoretically cheap and easy, and served as a form of revenge for the anti-interventionists against those who led the nation into World War II and now were the groups supposedly most vulnerable to Communist subversion.

When the Senator died, McCarthyism was already in eclipse, largely as a result of his inability to turn his primarily Republican following against the leadership of their party. But the coalition he created survives in the contemporary radical right.

Right-Wing Radicalism Today

Right-wing radicalism today can more easily be described than theoretically analyzed. Though it includes economic tenets resembling

---

[9] On McCarthyism, see Daniel Bell (ed.), *The New American Right* (New York: Criterion Books, 1955).

those of ultra conservatism,[10] its *raison d'être,* anticommunism, stems from international tensions. Its ideas derive both from the traditional right and the traditional left. Its followers come from widely divergent social groups. Its unity is one of mood and psychology—of a sense of frustration which leads it to espouse a theory of history which causes it to question the efficacy of traditional constitutional processes, hence its extremism.

Like all American political movements, the radical right is a coalition both ideologically and sociologically. Its ideology is not always coherent—though more so than that of the major parties—and is not equally accepted by all its members. Like all political ideologies, it finds expression at various levels of sophistication, from learned tomes to movies and cheap pamphlets. It is able to derive intellectual sustenance from a wide variety of sources, as long as they do not directly contradict its value premises or are not systematically opposed to its picture of the world. The list of books approved by the John Birch Society, for example, includes works by such scholars as David Dallin, Charles Beard, C. C. Tansill, Karl Wittfogel, Christopher Dawson, and Michael Polanyi.[11] Organs of the radical right include the *National Review* (which, however, has attacked Birch Society founder Robert Welch),[12] *Human Events,* and the Birch Society's *American Opinion.*

Though the radical right has organizations, it is not a single organized political force. Like members of the dominant political parties, members of the radical right cannot be identified exclusively with any specific ethnic, economic, or social groups. But, just as most Jews and union members are Democrats and most brokers and Anglo-Saxon Protestants are Republicans, so the radical right has a sociological coherence resulting from and reflected in its ideology.

Sociological basis

Economically, its members are largely middle class; the Birch Society appeals primarily to the upper middle class,[13] and the Reverend

---

[10] On ultra conservatism, see Clinton Rossiter, *Conservatism in America* (New York: Vintage Books, 1962), pp. 166 ff.
[11] Richard Vahan, *The Truth About the John Birch Society* (New York: Macfadden Books, 1962), pp. 136–144.
[12] "The Question of Robert Welch," *National Review,* Vol. 12 (1962), pp. 83–88.
[13] See S. M. Lipset, "Coughlinites, McCarthyites, and Birchers: Radical Rightists of Three Decades," in Daniel Bell, *The Radical Right* (Garden City: Anchor Books), 1963.

Billy Hargis' Christian Crusade appeals to a lower—but rising—middle class.[14] In religion, members of the radical right tend to belong to lower-class Protestant churches, especially fundamentalist ones,[15] or to be Catholics.[16] Its supporters consist of groups which are well-off but not sufficiently well-off not to feel themselves threatened by welfare-state taxes and controls. They are often persons who have risen into the middle class from lower-class origins, and many come from the newer immigrant groups or from small-town backgrounds. Regionally, the radical right's greatest strength is in areas of new—and insecure—wealth such as Florida, southern California, and the Southwest, in the "Bible belt" of the lower Midwest, and in urban areas with large concentrations of Catholics, such as New York or Boston. Former Communists loom large in the leadership of the radical right, as do retired military men. Post–World War II refugees from central and eastern Europe are significant sources of support.

The radical right has special appeal for the elderly and for the post–New Deal generation. Members are likely to be Republicans, except in the South and among Catholics. In education, like the politically energized generally, they rank higher than the norm. "New money" is important in financing the movement. The radical right differs from the prewar isolationist alliance in that German influence is less prominent—Eisenhower a Communist, perhaps; Adenauer, never—and the South is much more so.

The radical right, although organized in groups like the Birch Society and the Christian Crusade, finds its principal mode of expression in such *ad hoc* forms as the Schwarz Crusade and various special-purpose front groups.

Ideology

What ideas hold the radical right together? How do they resemble and differ from other political ideas, particularly those of ultraconservatives? What are the sources of these ideas, how are they interrelated, and what is the nature of their appeal? Although the ideology of the radical right is not very highly developed or explicit

---

[14] On Hargis, see Harold E. Martin, "Doomsday Merchant on the Far, Far Right," *Saturday Evening Post,* Vol. 235, No. 17 (April 28, 1962), pp. 19–24.

[15] David Danzig, "The Radical Right and the Rise of the Fundamentalist Minority," *Commentary,* Vol. 33, No. 4 (April, 1962), pp. 291–298.

[16] Edward T. Gargan, "Radical Catholics of the Right," *Social Order,* Vol. 11 (November, 1961), pp. 409–419.

on many matters, an intellectually and politically meaningful pattern is, nevertheless, discernible.

Absoluteness of the Communist menace

The single most important tenet of right-wing radicalism is the absoluteness of the menace of communism and the struggle against it. It is not only an important or the most important thing in the world, it is the only thing. Everything that happens is a function of it—a nationalist revolution in Africa, government medical care for the aged, or less homework in schools—just as for Marx everything was epiphenomenal to the control of the means of production. The Communists are winning because they recognize the absoluteness of the struggle; the United States is losing because, save for the radical right, it does not.

There are intellectual, psychological, and historical bases for this belief. This is essentially the picture of the world offered by such commentators on international affairs as James Burnham and John T. Flynn. Psychological support is provided by the need to be constantly engaged in an all-out crusade against evil, a need fostered in America by some types of religious preaching.

The semihysterical approach to international affairs has an honorable history. The demands of Manifest Destiny and the great crusades to make the world safe for democracy and to spread the Four Freedoms are cases in point. The radical right, in order to protest the policy of containment, invokes Lincoln's dictum that we cannot live half slave and half free. And it is easy for the leaders of the radical right, especially those who are former Communists, to transmute the crusading zeal of communism into their crusade against communism.

Conspiracy theory of history

Closely related to belief in the absolute importance of the fight against communism is the view of history as a conscious conspiracy. The conspiracy theory of history is a concomitant of all totalitarian movements. It explains why what is so obviously good does not prevail. For those who reject the existence of contingency, complexity, and confusion in the world, and the glacial nature of most social and political change, the only possible explanation is that those in high places are either stupid or evil or both.

For this idea, too, support is found in American tradition. The Populists believed their economic woes due to a cabal of British and

American bankers, aristocrats, and Jews who wished to steal their land and subvert the traditions of the American people. The Nye Committee—chaired by a neo-Populist and fascist fellow traveler and counseled by Alger Hiss—helped popularize the conspiracy theory of history by its revelations of the role of banking and the munitions industries in promoting American entry into World War I. Demi-Marxist historians have long regaled the public with tales of conspiratorial collusion between business and the State Department in strengthening Franco, seeking Middle East oil rights, and the like. Isolationist leaders blamed our entry in World War II on a conspiracy of bankers, Jews, Communists, and New Dealers. McCarthy assailed the same groups—minus the Jews—as responsible for loss of China and other Communist triumphs. As scholars have noted, Alger Hiss—Harvard-educated, Anglo-Saxon, and upper class—was the perfect target for McCarthy's neopopulism.[17] Today's radical right also sees the real menace as traitors among the elite.

Creeping communism

Related to the notion of history as conspiracy is the downgrading of the international importance of communism and concentration on the dangers of domestic subversion. This is a relic of traditional isolationism, the belief that America could never be successfully menaced from without. But, beginning with World War II, neo-isolationism modified this dogma to read that America, with adequate military defenses, could never be successfully menaced from without; isolationism and militarism went hand in hand. Today, however, the radical right de-emphasizes military as well as foreign-aid expenditures. It holds that the Communists are basically weak and that what makes them strong is our failure to use the strength we possess—a concomitant of our failure to recognize the absoluteness of the struggle. Get rid of the traitors, spies, and do-gooders in our midst, and we will triumph over communism with a minimum of effort and expense. This theory not only explains why the effort we have expended fighting communism has not yet eliminated the menace, it also promises a successful end to the struggle at the same time that harassing taxes and controls, justified as cold-war necessities, are reduced or eliminated.

This theory leads to and is bolstered by a subassumption, namely, that "creeping communism" is taking over through governmental en-

---

[17] Richard Hofstadter, "The Pseudo-Conservative Revolt," in Bell, *op. cit.*, p. 55.

croachment in the economic sphere and through Communist-motivated subversion of our national social and cultural life.

The United States will become Communist—our grandchildren will live under socialism, as Khrushchev boasted—because the United States will gradually be transformed—whether under foreign direction or not is not always clear—through governmental action into a state identical to the Soviet Union. This creeping communism, as represented by governmental intervention in the economy, the income tax, social insurance, and the like, will continue to the point where it will be too late to turn back, and we shall awaken to find not only a socialized economy but slave labor camps, official atheism, an end to free elections, and all the other concomitants of the dictatorship of the proletariat.

Intellectually, this theory stems from adherence to the values of nineteenth-century *laissez-faire* liberalism, the belief in free enterprise, and a limited state. The neoclassical economists Friedrich Hayek and Ludwig von Mises and their American followers are the prime intellectual exponents of these ideas, but their political force derives from the popularizations of such men as Clarence Manion, Frank Chodorov, Felix Morley, and Henry Hazlitt, who combine *laissez-faire* economics with attacks on any and all widening of central government powers. States' rights and local government are extolled, and Congress is exalted over the executive.

Laissez-faire values are held to be under a peculiar assault by stealth. Supposedly, a kind of continuum exists between *laissez faire* and communism, so that any movement away from the former is necessarily toward the latter, an obvious projection of the old right-wing Republican plaint about creeping socialism.

Appeal of the radical right

To what groups do such theories have a special appeal? They appeal to members of the so-called old middle classes, small businessmen, and professionals, who find their independence and status threatened by the rise of big business, big labor, and big government. Today, the radical right displaces the fears of these people from business to the socially more acceptable enemies, government and labor. Such theories also appeal to the members of rising ethnic and social groups who struggled to achieve occupations which, in the past, would have guaranteed secure middle-class status, only to find that these occupations no longer provide the relatively high economic and social position they once did—inevitably so, since this rise has been facilitated by a general inflation in the social-status system. But their frustration leads them to seek more sinister explanations.

Among the lower middle class, skilled and white-collar workers are dismayed to find that rising salaries do not mean an equivalent gain in standards of living, and they blame not the monetary inflation which made the higher salaries possible but political corruption and welfare and foreign-aid handouts paid for in higher taxes. The newly wealthy, especially those who made their money in such industries as oil, where rapid economic advancement is still possible, are dismayed to find that government does not give them the freedom it gave the wealthy of the nineteenth century and that old wealth may not accept them socially. All these groups have achieved what should be success according to the rules of old-style capitalism, and they are distressed to find it does not mean what they had hoped. So they blame a conspiracy for changing the rules.

Communism in the social fabric

The same social groups which accept the theory of creeping communism in the economy also tend to extend the concept to the whole of American life. They look upon the period of *laissez faire* not only as an ideal era in which government kept hands off the economy but as one in which traditional mores were maintained by community pressures, backed if necessary by government action. They see the decline of *laissez faire* associated in time with religious decline, increase in crime, weakening of traditional family and sexual norms, and substitution of one-worldism for patriotism. Because these two sets of events are sequentially associated, they are assumed to be causally related. The same factors which lead to government paternalism and economic interference must be those leading to the failure of government to maintain moral standards. Indeed, it is the blows against individualism and self-reliance, epitomized in socializing tendencies in the economy, which lead to a loss of a sense of individual worth and responsibility and hence to crime, moral deviance, and loss of patriotism, just as it is a lessened sense of individualism that makes possible further government inroads into the economy.

This belief has various origins. The city slicker, with his low moral standards, has always been associated in the rural Populist mind with the economic enemy, Wall Street. It is from the great cities, especially the Eastern cosmopolitan centers, that political support for socialism and moral degeneracy alike have come, as well as agitation for intervention in Europe's wars. The same organizations and social groups which favor the welfare state are also seen to support free speech for Communists, an end to censorship of indecent literature, coddling of criminals, and progressive education.

Practical consequences

The theory of creeping communism has obvious practical consequences. The followers of the radical right are not mad enough to see Soviet spies everywhere, but, if advocacy of social welfare measures is objectively part of a world conspiracy against freedom, the enemy *is* literally everywhere. If the threat is universal and absolute, then all anti-Communist measures are justified. Secrecy, infiltration, and calumny—established Communist methods—must be used against them; because their agents are everywhere—in universities, on school boards, in Congress—then the methods can be used anywhere. Here lies the special bite of ultraright extremism. It is an organized attempt to pervert the democratic process, based on a dialectical view of history which apes [the dialectics (dialecticism?) of] its enemies by converting all visible particulars into aspects of an underlying world struggle. The ultraright and the Communists are tactically united in their assault on the American consensus.

Racialism

This, then, is the ideological syndrome of the radical right: belief in a world in which communism is winning because of the treachery or ignorance of American leadership—winning in foreign affairs and transforming the very shape of our society itself.

One noteworthy element is missing: racialism. Traditionally, American right-wing movements have opposed racial equality, regarding darker races as inferior. Nineteenth-century populism, the protofascism of the 1930s, and isolationism were all anti-Semitic, even if not anti-Negro. But, beginning with McCarthy, the racial theme was dropped. McCarthy's followers were, if anything, more tolerant of race differences than the norm.[18] The Birch Society is anti–anti-Semitic and anti–anti-Negro, and its members are apparently little if any more prejudiced than others of their socioeconomic and educational level.[19] Whether the less upper-class elements moving into the radical right will maintain this pattern is another question. Hargis has already had to fight racist tendencies in his movement.[20]

---

[18] Lipset, *op. cit.*
[19] *Ibid.*
[20] Martin, *op. cit.*, p. 22.

This lack of racial bias has been attributed by one observer to trans-tolerance[21]—a tendency, when united in a common life or death cause, to regard comrades from a different background with special favor. After all, the real enemy is the upper-class elite which currently dominates the crucial sectors of American life.

Use of Direct Mass Action

The radical right is united, we have said, by a mood. It is extremist because if what it says is true—if even Eisenhower might be a secret Communist, if the Supreme Court is dominated by a pro-Communist chief justice, and if anyone, no matter how well-intentioned, can be an unwitting agent of communism—then normal constitutional means are obviously not enough to save the country. So, in practice, the radical right is forced to oppose constitutional safeguards. But this leads to a contradiction in theory. Populism followed in the Jacksonian egalitarian tradition. It, therefore, advocated increased popular participation in government. Coughlin, Long, and McCarthy could easily continue in this tradition, for they sought a mass following among those classes with little direct control over the major social, economic, and political institutions of American society.

But men such as Welch attack democracy on theoretical grounds and make much of the semantic quibble that the United States is a republic, not a democracy. Yet those constitutional institutions which are farthest removed from popular pressure in most respects— the Executive and the Court—are in the hands of the enemy, as are the universities and the press. So, despite their elitist beliefs, the leaders of the radical right are forced to adopt the Populist tradition of direct mass action—national indignation conventions, mass meetings, fronts, letter-writing campaigns, petitions, and so on. Their view of history as the conspiracy of a highly placed few forces them to take the road of direct popular democracy and to spurn that of representative democracy and constitutionalism.

Future of the Radical Right

What is the future of the radical right? This depends primarily on the course of world events. The ideas of the radical right can only be disproved by victory over communism under the leadership of representatives of the present dominant American consensus. Reverses like Cuba strengthen the radicals; defeats for communism

---

[21] Peter Viereck, "The Revolt against the Elite," in Bell, *op. cit.*, pp. 99 ff.

at least if they are perceived as such by the public, weaken them by dampening the anxieties on which they feed. Should the United States undergo a major recession which the radical right could attribute to government action and hence to Communist influence, the movement might grow rapidly. Economically disadvantaged groups might be attracted by their explanation of events and mobilized against a government of "socialist meddlers," thus seriously endangering constitutional government.

In part, the future of right-wing radicalism depends on the future of left-wing radicalism. Despite the existence of deep veins of poverty in our affluent society,[22] there is currently no substantial radical movement based on economic grievances. The issues which are stimulating new enthusiasms and organizations are civil rights, civil liberties, and peace through nuclear disarmament.[23] The growing dissatisfaction of Negroes with the pace of integration,[24] disapproval of the Un-American Activities Committee, and the growth of nuclear pacifism have led to such extralegal direct action as sit-ins, Freedom Rides, picketing, and sail-ins. Though nonviolent, these are expressions of a belief in the right of the individual or group to refuse to conform to decisions reached by democratic political processes, statements of despair of convincing a majority of the people of the justice and overriding importance of their cause or of convincing them in time. The radical left, like the radical right, is so certain of the supreme importance of its goals that it is ready to seek them outside the traditional constitutional framework.

It is impossible to predict what effect left- and right-wing radicalism will have on one another. They may cancel each other out, enabling a middle-of-the-road consensus to continue to dominate the political process. Or they may feed upon each other, confirming one another's worst fears for the future, and ultimately create a situation in which a stable consensus no longer dominates our political life. That the radicalism of either right or left will soon disappear is unlikely. They are attempts, however unpalatable to most Americans,

---

[22] See Michael Harrington, *The Other America* (New York: The Macmillan Company, 1962).
[23] See the symposium "The Young Radicals," *Dissent,* Vol. 9 (Spring, 1962), pp. 127–163.
[24] One special form of racial protest is the anti-integrationist Black Muslim movement. This may become the most significant radical group in America but has not been discussed in the paper because of its separatist rejection of the very context which gives the other movements their meaning, that is, American society itself.

to deal with objective problems—the world-wide Communist assault on democracy and the grave danger of nuclear holocaust. As long as these problems remain unsolved, they will continue to elicit extremist responses.

3

Faith of the Fanatic

Eric Hoffer

1

It is a truism that many who join a rising revolutionary movement are attracted by the prospect of sudden and spectacular change in their conditions of life. A revolutionary movement is a conspicuous instrument of change.

Not so obvious is the fact that religious and nationalist movements too can be vehicles of change. Some kind of widespread enthusiasm or excitement is apparently needed for the realization of vast and rapid change, and it does not seem to matter whether the exhilaration is derived from an expectation of untold riches or is generated by an active mass movement. In this country the spectacular changes since the Civil War were enacted in an atmosphere charged with the enthusiasm born of fabulous opportunities for self-advancement. Where self-advancement cannot, or is not allowed to, serve as a driving force, other sources of enthusiasm have to be found if momentous changes, such as the awakening and renovation of a stagnant society or radical reforms in the character and pattern of life of a community, are to be realized and perpetuated. Religious, revolutionary, and nationalist movements are such generating plants of general enthusiasm.

In the past, religious movements were the conspicuous vehicles of change. The conservatism of a religion—its orthodoxy—is the inert coagulum of a once highly reactive sap. A rising religious movement is all change and experiment—open to new views and techniques from all quarters. Islam when it emerged was an organizing and

SOURCE: From pp. 3-11, 12-13, 16-17 in *The True Believer* by Eric Hoffer. Copyright 1951 by Eric Hoffer. Reprinted by permission of Harper & Row, Publishers.

modernizing medium. Christianity was a civilizing and modernizing influence among the savage tribes of Europe. The Crusades and the Reformation both were crucial factors in shaking the Western world from the stagnation of the Middle Ages.

In modern times, the mass movements involved in the realization of vast and rapid change are revolutionary and nationalist—singly or in combination. Peter the Great was probably the equal, in dedication, power, and ruthlessness, of many of the most successful revolutionary or nationalist leaders. Yet he failed in his chief purpose, which was to turn Russia into a Western nation. And the reason he failed was that he did not infuse the Russian masses with some soul-stirring enthusiasm. He either did not think it necessary or did not know how to make of his purpose a holy cause. It is not strange that the Bolshevik revolutionaries who wiped out the last of the czars and Romanovs should have a sense of kinship with Peter—a czar and a Romanov. For his purpose is now theirs, and they hope to succeed where he failed. The Bolshevik revolution may figure in history as much an attempt to modernize a sixth of the world's surface as an attempt to build a Communist economy.

The fact that both the French and the Russian revolutions turned into nationalist movements seems to indicate that in modern times nationalism is the most copious and durable source of mass enthusiasm, and that nationalist fervor must be tapped if the drastic changes projected and initiated by revolutionary enthusiasm are to be consummated. One wonders whether the difficulties encountered by the present Labor government in Britain are not partly due to the fact that the attempt to change the economy of the country and the way of life of forty-nine million people has been initiated in an atmosphere singularly free from fervor, exaltation, and wild hope. The revulsion from the ugly patterns developed by most contemporary mass movements has kept the civilized and decent leaders of the Labor party shy of revolutionary enthusiasm. The possibility still remains that events might force them to make use of some mild form of chauvinism so that in Britain too "the socialization of the nation [might have] as its natural corollary the nationalization of socialism."

The phenomenal modernization of Japan would probably not have been possible without the revivalist spirit of Japanese nationalism. It is perhaps also true that the rapid modernization of some European countries (Germany in particular) was facilitated to some extent by the upsurge and thorough diffusion of nationalist fervor. Judged by present indications, the renascence of Asia will be brought about through the instrumentality of nationalist movements rather than by other mediums. It was the rise of a genuine nationalist movement which enabled Kemal Atatürk to modernize Turkey almost overnight. In Egypt, untouched by a mass movement, modernization is slow and faltering, though its rulers, from the day of Mehmed Ali, have welcomed Western ideas, and its contacts with the West have been many and intimate. Zionism is an instrument for the renovation of a backward country and the transformation of shopkeepers and brain workers into farmers, laborers, and soldiers. Had Chiang Kai-shek known how to set in motion a genuine mass movement, or at least sustain the nationalist enthusiasm kindled by the Japanese invasion, he might have been acting now as the renovator of China. Since he did not know how, he was easily shoved aside by the masters of the art of "religiofication"—the art of turning practical purposes into holy causes. It is not difficult to see why America and Britain (or any Western democracy) could not play a direct and leading role in arousing the Asiatic countries from their backwardness and stagnation: the democracies are neither inclined nor perhaps able to kindle a revivalist spirit in Asia's millions. The contribution of the Western democracies to the awakening of the East has been indirect and certainly unintended. They have kindled an enthusiasm of resentment against the West, and it is this anti-Western fervor which is at present rousing the Orient from its stagnation of centuries.

Though the desire for change is not infrequently a superficial motive, it is yet worth finding out whether a probing of this desire might not shed some light on the inner working of mass movements. We shall inquire therefore into the nature of the desire for change.

2

There is in us a tendency to locate the shaping forces of our existence outside ourselves. Success and failure are unavoidably related in our minds with the state of things around us. Hence it is that people with a sense of fulfillment think it a good world and would like to conserve it as it is, while the frustrated favor radical change. The tendency to look for all causes outside ourselves persists even when it is clear that our state of being is the product of personal qualities such as ability, character, appearance, health, and so on. "If anything ail a man," says Thoreau, "so that he does not perform his functions, if he have a pain in his bowels even . . . he forthwith sets about reforming—the world."

It is understandable that those who fail should incline to blame the world for their failure. The remarkable thing is that the successful, too, however much they pride themselves on their foresight, fortitude, thrift, and other "sterling qualities," are at bottom convinced that their success is the result of a fortuitous combination of circumstances. The self-confidence of even the consistently successful is never absolute. They are never sure that they know all the ingredients which go into the making of their success. The outside world seems to them a precariously balanced mechanism, and so long as it ticks in their favor they are afraid to tinker with it. Thus the resistance to change and the ardent desire for it spring from the same conviction, and the one can be as vehement as the other.

3

Discontent by itself does not invariably create a desire for change. Other factors have to be present before discontent turns into disaffection. One of these is a sense of power.

Those who are awed by their surroundings do not think of change, no matter how miserable their condition. When our mode of life is so precarious as to make it patent that we cannot control the circumstances of our existence, we tend to stick to the proven and the familiar. We counteract a deep feeling of insecurity by making of our existence a fixed routine. We hereby acquire the illusion that we have tamed the unpredictable. Fisherfolk, nomads, and farmers who have to contend with the willful elements, the creative worker who depends on inspiration, the savage awed by his surroundings—they all fear change. They face the world as they would an all-powerful jury. The abjectly poor, too, stand in awe of the world around them and are not hospitable to change. It is a dangerous life we live when hunger and cold are at our heels. There is thus a conservatism of the destitute as profound as the conservatism of the privileged, and the former is as much a factor in the perpetuation of a social order as the latter.

The men who rush into undertakings of vast change usually feel they are in possession of some irresistible power. The generation that made the French Revolution had an extravagant conception of the omnipotence of man's reason and the boundless range of his intelligence. Never, says de Tocqueville, had humanity been prouder of itself nor had it ever so much faith in its own omnipotence. And joined with this exaggerated self-confidence was a universal thirst for change which came unbidden to every mind. Lenin and the Bolsheviks who plunged recklessly into the chaos of the creation of a new world had blind faith in the omnipotence of Marxist doctrine. The Nazis had nothing as potent as that doctrine, but they had faith in an infallible leader and also faith in a new technique. For it is doubtful whether National Socialism would have made such rapid progress if it had not been for the electrifying conviction that the new techniques of blitzkrieg and propaganda made Germany irresistible.

Even the sober desire for progress is sustained by faith—faith in the intrinsic goodness of human nature and in the omnipotence of science. It is a defiant and blasphemous faith, not unlike that held by the men who set out to build "a city and a tower, whose top may reach unto heaven" and who believed that "nothing will be restrained from them, which they have imagined to do."

4

Offhand one would expect that the mere possession of power would automatically result in a cocky attitude toward the world and a receptivity to change. But it is not always so. The powerful can be as timid as the weak. What seems to count more than possession of instruments of power is faith in the future. Where power is not joined with faith in the future, it is used mainly to ward off the new and preserve the status quo. On the other hand, extravagant hope, even when not backed by actual power, is likely to generate a most reckless daring. For the hopeful can draw strength from the most ridiculous sources of power—a slogan, a word, a button. No faith is potent unless it is also faith in the future, unless it has a millennial component. So, too, an effective doctrine: as well as being a source of power, it must also claim to be a key to the book of the future.

Those who would transform a nation or the world cannot do so by breeding and captaining discontent or by demonstrating the reasonableness and desirability of the intended changes or by coercing people into a new way of life. They must know how to kindle and fan an extravagant hope. It matters not whether it be hope of a heavenly kingdom, of heaven on earth, of plunder and untold riches, of fabulous achievement or world dominion. If the Communists win Europe and a large part of the world, it will not be because they know how to stir up discontent or how to infect people with hatred, but because they know how to preach hope.

5

Thus the differences between the conservative and the radical seem to spring mainly from their attitude toward the future. Fear of the future causes us to lean against and cling to the present, while faith in the future renders us receptive to change. Both the rich and the poor, the strong and the weak—they who have achieved much or little—can be afraid of the future. When the present seems so perfect that the most we can expect is its even continuation in the future, change can only mean deterioration. Hence men of outstanding achievement and those who live full, happy lives usually set their faces against drastic innovation. The conservatism of invalids and people past middle age stems, too, from fear of the future. They are on the lookout for signs of decay, and feel that any change is more likely to be for the worse than for the better. The abjectly poor also are without faith in the future. The future seems to them a booby trap buried on the road ahead. One must step gingerly. To change things is to ask for trouble.

As for the hopeful: it does not seem to make any difference who it is that is seized with a wild hope—whether it be an enthusiastic intellectual, a land-hungry farmer, a get-rich-quick speculator, a sober merchant or industrialist, a plain workingman, or a noble lord—they all proceed recklessly with the present, wreck it if necessary, and create a new world. There can thus be revolutions by the privileged as well as by the underprivileged. The movement of enclosure in sixteenth- and seventeenth-century England was a revolution by the rich. The woolen industry rose to high prosperity, and grazing became more profitable than cropping. The landowners drove off their tenants, enclosed the commons, and wrought profound changes in the social and economic texture of the country. "The lords and nobles were upsetting the social order, breaking down ancient law and custom, sometimes by means of violence, often by pressure and intimidation." Another English revolution by the rich occurred at the end of the eighteenth and the beginning of the nineteenth century. It was the Industrial Revolution. The breathtaking potentialities of mechanization set the minds of manufacturers and merchants on fire. They began a revolution "as extreme and radical as ever inflamed the minds of sectarians," and in a relatively short time these respectable, God-fearing citizens changed the face of England beyond recognition.

When hopes and dreams are loose in the streets, it is well for the timid to lock doors, shutter windows, and lie low until the wrath has passed. For there is often a monstrous incongruity between the hopes, however noble and tender, and the action which follows them.

It is as if ivied maidens and garlanded youths were to herald the four horsemen of the apocalypse.

6

For men to plunge headlong into an undertaking of vast change, they must be intensely discontented yet not destitute, and they must have the feeling that by the possession of some potent doctrine, infallible leader, or some new technique they have access to a source of irresistible power. They must also have an extravagant conception of the prospects and potentialities of the future. Finally, they must be wholly ignorant of the difficulties involved in their vast undertaking. Experience is a handicap. The men who started the French Revolution were wholly without political experience. The same is true of the Bolsheviks, Nazis, and the revolutionaries in Asia. The experienced man of affairs is a latecomer. He enters the movement when it is already a going concern. It is perhaps the Englishman's political experience that keeps him shy of mass movements.

7

There is a fundamental difference between the appeal of a mass movement and the appeal of a practical organization. The practical organization offers opportunities for self-advancement, and its appeal is mainly to self-interest. On the other hand, a mass movement, particularly in its active, revivalist phase, appeals not to those intent on bolstering and advancing a cherished self, but to those who crave to be rid of an unwanted self. A mass movement attracts and holds a following not because it can satisfy the desire for self-advancement, but because it can satisfy the passion for self-renunciation.

People who see their lives as irremediably spoiled cannot find a worth-while purpose in self-advancement. The prospect of an individual career cannot stir them to a mighty effort, nor can it evoke in them faith and a single-minded dedication. They look on self-interest as on something tainted and evil, something unclean and unlucky. Anything undertaken under the auspices of the self seems to them foredoomed. Nothing that has its roots and reasons in the self can be good and noble. Their innermost craving is for a new life—a rebirth—or, failing this, a chance to acquire new elements of pride, confidence, hope, a sense of purpose and worth by an identification with a holy cause. An active mass movement offers them opportunities for both. If they join the movement as full converts, they are reborn to a new life in its close-knit collective body, or if attracted as sympathizers they find elements of pride, confidence, and purpose by identifying themselves with the efforts, achievements, and prospects of the movement.

To the frustrated a mass movement offers substitutes either for the whole self or for the elements which make life bearable and which they cannot evoke out of their individual resources.

* * *

When people are ripe for a mass movement, they are usually ripe for any effective movement, and not solely for one with a particular doctrine or program. In pre-Hitlerian Germany it was often a toss-up whether a restless youth would join the Communists or the Nazis. In the overcrowded pale of czarist Russia the simmering Jewish population was ripe both for revolution and Zionism. In the same family, one member would join the revolutionaries and the other the Zionists. Dr. Chaim Weizmann quotes a saying of his mother in those days: "Whatever happens, I shall be well off. If Shemuel [the revolutionary son] is right, we shall all be happy in Russia; and if Chaim [the Zionist] is right, than I shall go to live in Palestine."

This receptivity to all movements does not always cease even after the potential true believer has become the ardent convert of a specific movement. Where mass movements are in violent competition with each other, there are not infrequent instances of converts—even the most zealous—shifting their allegiance from one to the other. A Saul turning into Paul is neither a rarity nor a miracle. In our day, each proselytizing mass movement seems to regard the zealous adherents of its antagonist as its own potential converts. Hitler looked on the German Communists as potential National Socialists: "The *petit burgeosis* Social-Democrat and the trade-union boss will never make a National Socialist, but the Communist always will." Captain Röhm boasted that he could turn the reddest Communist into a glowing nationalist in four weeks. On the other hand, Karl Radek looked on the Nazi Brown Shirts (S.A.) as a reserve for future Communist recruits.

4

The Conflict of Generations

Lewis S. Feuer

* * *

The conflict of generations is a universal theme in history; it is founded on the most primordial facts of human nature, and it is a driving force of history, perhaps even more ultimate than that of class struggle. Yet its intensity fluctuates. Under fortunate circumstances, it may be resolved within a generational equilibrium. Under less happy circumstances, it becomes bitter, unyielding, angry, violent; this is what takes place when the elder generation, through some presumable historical failure, has become de-authoritized in the eyes of the young.

Every student movement is the outcome of a de-authoritization of the elder generation. This process can take place in small colleges as well as impersonal universities, in industrialized countries as well as underdeveloped ones, in socialist as well as capitalist ones.

Thus student movements have emerged in small, provincial German universities, in urban Russian institutions, and in Chinese schools of all varieties. They have flourished alike among the children of aristocrats and the middle classes, but less so among the sons of the working class. Student activists in different historical circumstances have tended to come from the most diverse fields of study: they were young theologians in the Germany of 1817, they were enthusiasts for natural science in Russia in 1874, they were social scientists in Asia and Africa in our time. Certain subjects in different historical circumstances were the ones in which generational conflict could define

SOURCE: Lewis S. Feuer, *The Conflict of Generations,* copyright 1969 by Lewis S. Feuer (New York: Basic Books, Inc., 1969). Reprinted by permission of the publisher.

itself most clearly. Thomas Hobbes in the middle of the seventeenth century felt that the study of the classics in the universities was undermining the political order because students were "furnished with arguments for liberty out of the works of Aristotle, Plato, Cicero, Seneca, and out of the histories of Rome and Greece, for their disputation against the necessary power of their sovereigns." Therefore he despaired "of any lasting peace among ourselves" until the universities desisted from teaching subversive subjects or ideas, and presumably occupied themselves with natural science and materialistic philosophy such as his own.

Student movements have been the chief expression of generational conflict in modern history. As intellectual elites of the younger generation, they have had their special ethic of redemption, self-sacrifice, and identification. They have attained the greatest heights of idealistic emotion even as they have been enthralled by compulsions to destruction.

These student movements are more than an episode in the "modernization" of developing nations, for they can affect advanced industrial societies as well as traditional or transitional ones. They arise wherever social and historical circumstances combine to cause a crisis in loss of generational confidence, which impels the young to resentment and uprising. Student movements have arisen in recent years in "underdeveloped countries" because generational disequilibrium is likely to arise in traditional societies which are sustaining the impact of advanced ideas. At the same time, student movements are likely to arise in advanced industrial, prosperous societies precisely because such societies do not afford environments with real, objective tasks, material challenges to youthful, aggressive energies. America in the nineteenth century was changing rapidly; it was neither in a class nor an economic equilibrium; it was, however, in a generational equilibrium. Rapid social change in and of itself does not necessarily involve student unrest.

We have tried to unravel the nature of political idealism, the complex of emotions of love, destruction, self-sacrifice, and nihilism on which it is founded. The unconscious ingredient of generational revolt in the students' idealism has tended to shape decisively their political expression. We have tried to bring to consciousness what otherwise are unconscious processes of history. That has been the whole purpose in our use of the psycho-historical method—to help defeat the cunning of history which has so often misused the idealistic emotions. With a melancholy uniformity, the historical record shows plainly how time and again the students' most idealistic movement has converted itself into a blind, irrational power hostile to liberal democratic values. Yet we refuse to accept a sociological determinism which would make this pattern into the fatality of all student idealism. Our working hypothesis is that knowledge can contribute to wisdom. When students perceive the historical defeat which has dogged their youthful hubris, they may perhaps be the more enabled to cope with irrational demonry; they may then make their political idealism into an even nobler historical force.

For student movements have thus far been too largely an example of what we might call *projective politics,* in the sense that they have been largely dominated by unconscious drives; the will to revolt against the de-authoritized father has evolved in to a variety of patterns of political action. This hegemony of the unconscious has differentiated student movements from the more familiar ones of class and interest groups. The latter are usually conscious of their psychological sources and aims, whether they be material economic interests or enhanced prestige and power. Student movements, on the other hand, manifest a deep resistance to the psychological analysis of their emotional mainspring; they wish to keep unconscious the origins of their generational revolt. A politics of the unconscious carries with it untold dangers for the future of civilization. We have seen the students Karl Sand and Gavrilo Princip adding their irrational vector to deflect the peaceful evolution of a liberal Europe; we have seen the Russian students helping to stifle the first possibilities of a liberal constitution; we have seen the American student movement in its blind alley of the Oxford Pledge and its later pro-Soviet immolation. All these were fruits of the politics of the unconscious. It is only by persisting in the understanding of these unconscious determinants that we can hope to see a higher wisdom in human affairs.

Guilt feelings fused with altruistic emotions have led students to seek a "back to the people" identification. In Joseph Conrad's novel, the guilt-tormented Lord Jim could conquer his guilt only by merging his self in the most romantic dedication to an alien, impoverished, exploited people. The aged ex-revolutionist Stein saw Jim's salvation rendered possible only by his immersing himself in the "destructive element"; thereby, guilt was assuaged. And since it is guilt which assails the sense of one's existence with the reproaches of one's conscience, it is by the conquest of guilt in a higher self-sacrifice that one recovers the conviction of one's existence. In a sense, every student seeking to merge himself with peasant, proletarian, the Negro, the poor, the alien race has had something of the Lord Jim psychology. His guilt is that of his generational revolt, his would-be parricide. He can conquer this guilt only with the demonstration that he is selfless and by winning the comforting maternal love of the oppressed; they bring him the assurance of his needed place in the universe. To reduce this determinism of unconscious guilt has been one purpose of this study. For only thus can we isolate and counteract the ingredient of self-destruction.

When generational struggle grows most intense, it gives rise to generational theories of truth. Protagorean relativism is translated into generational terms; only youth, uncorrupted, is held to perceive the truth, and the generation becomes the measure of all things. This generational relativism in the sixties is the counterpart of the class relativism which flourished in the thirties; where once it was said that only the proletariat had an instinctive grasp of sociological truth, now it is said that only those under thirty, or twenty-five, or twenty, are thus privileged. It would be pointless to repeat the philosophical criticisms of relativist ideology. This generational doctrine is an ideology insofar as it expresses a "false consciousness"; it issues from unconscious motives of generational uprising, projects its youthful longings onto the nature of the cosmos, sociological reality, and sociological knowledge, but represses precisely those facts of self-destruction and self-defeat which we have documented. Moreover, the majority of studentries have usually been at odds with the student activists, whose emotional compulsions to generational revolt they do not share. The engineering and working-class students, who so often have been immune to the revolt-ardor of middle-class humanistic students, stand as dissenters to the doctrine of generational privilege. They have held more fast their sense of reality, whereas the literary-minded have seen reality through a mist of fantasy and wish fulfillment.

The reactionary is also a generational relativist, for he believes that the old have a privileged perspective upon reality, that only the old have learned in experience the recalcitrance of facts to human desire. But the philosophical truth is that no generation has a privileged access to reality; each has its projective unconscious, its inner resentments, its repressions and exaggerations. Each generation will have to learn to look at itself with the same sincerity it demands of the other. The alternative is generational conflict, with its searing, sick emotions, and an unconscious which is a subterranean house of hatred.

The substance of history is psychological—the way human beings have felt, thought, and acted in varying circumstances—and the concept of generational struggle which we have used is a psychological one. There are those who see the dangers of "reductionism" in our psycho-historical method; they feel that the genesis of student movements in generational conflict has no bearing on the validity of their programs, goals, objectives. Of what import, they ask, is the psychology of student movements so long as they work for freedom, for liberating workers and peasants and colored races, for university reform and the end of alienation? To such critics we reply that the psychological origin of student movements puts its impress on their choice of both political means and underlying ends. Wherever a set of alternative possible routes toward achieving a given end presents itself, a student movement will usually tend to choose the one which involves a higher measure of violence or humiliation directed against the older generation. The latent aim of generational revolt never surrenders its paramountcy to the avowed patent aims. The assassination of an archduke, for instance, may be justified by an appeal to nationalistic ideals which are said to have a sanctity overriding all other consequences; actually the sacred cause, the nationalistic ideal, becomes too easily a pseudo-end, a rationalization, a "cause" which affords the chance to express in a more socially admired way one's desire to murder an authority figure.

When all our analysis is done, however, what endures is the promise and hope of a purified idealism. I recall one evening in 1963 when I met with a secret circle of Russian students at Moscow University. There were twelve or thirteen of them drawn from various fields but moved by a common aspiration toward freedom. Among them were young physicists, philosophers, economists, students of languages. Their teachers had been apologists for the Stalinist repression, and the students were groping for truthful ideas, for an honest philosophy rather than an official ideology. Clandestine papers and books circulated among them—a copy of Boris Pasternak's *Dr. Zhivago,* of George Orwell's *1984;* reprints of Western articles on Soviet literature; a revelation of the fate of the poet Osip Mandelstamm. The social system had failed to "socialize" them, had failed to stifle their longing for freedom. The elder generation was de-authoritized in their eyes for its pusillanimous involvement in the "cult of personality." Here on a cold March night in a Moscow academic office I was encountering what gave hope to the future of the Soviet Union. The conflict of generations, disenthralled of its demonry, becomes a drama of sustenance and renewal which remains the historical bearer of humanity's highest hopes.

Part Two

Sources — The Radical Right

A good deal of the recent literature by and about the radical right is issue oriented, dealing with particular problems such as student loyalty, trade relations, sex education, taxation, and the party system, to name a very few.

The purpose of the next set of readings is to portray the generalized ideological mood and apprehensions experienced by the contemporary right through writings of a characteristic group of public spokesmen and leaders.

CONTRIBUTORS

Robert Welch: Founder and head of The John Birch Society. He is a leading ultraconservative. He is best known for *The Life of John Birch, The Blue Book of The John Birch Society,* and *The Politician,* which are devoted to portrayal of and remedies for Communist subversion of most aspects of American life and culture.

Billy James Hargis: An ordained minister and founder and director of the Christian Crusade, a fundamentalist, anti-Communist organization. His crusading activities encompass radio and television appearances, newspaper columns, and many religious and political publications.

G. Edward Griffin: A past president of the American Bar Association and Honorary Life President of the International Bar Association. He is the author of *The Fearful Master,* an exposé of Communist activities in the United Nations, and *The Great Prison Break,* a critical study of the United States Supreme Court.

Fred Schwarz: Gave up a successful medical practice in Australia and migrated to the United States where he founded and is president of the Christian Anti-Communism Crusade. He travels and speaks widely. His organization sponsors antisubversive seminars throughout the country. He is the author of many articles and pamphlets.

Revilo P. Oliver: Professor of classics at the University of Illinois, is a militant spokesman for the ultraconservative position. During World War II he performed special research duties. Aside from several professional studies, he has written many articles for a variety of conservative publications on such themes as internal subversion, foreign policy, and domestic American politics.

5

Democracy Is a Fraud

Robert Welch

A republican form of government or of organization has many attractions and advantages, under certain favorable conditions. But under less happy circumstances it lends itself too readily to infiltration, distortion, and disruption. And democracy, of course, in government or organization, as the Greeks and Romans both found out, and as I believe every man in this room clearly recognizes—democracy is merely a deceptive phrase, a weapon of demagoguery, and a perennial fraud.[1]

For withstanding the stresses and strains of internal differences and external animosities, throughout changing political climates over long periods of time; for the building of morale and loyalty and a feeling of unified purpose and closely knit strength; for effective functioning in periods of crisis and a permanence of high dedication throughout more peaceful decades; for these and many other reasons The John Birch Society will operate under completely authoritative control at all levels. The fear of tyrannical oppression of individuals, and other arguments against the authoritative structure in the form of governments, have little bearing on the case of a voluntary association, where the authoritative power can be exercised and enforced only by persuasion. And what little validity they do have is outweighed by the advantages of firm and positive direction of the Society's energies. Especially for the near future, and for the fight against Communism which is the first great task of the Society, it is imperative

---

SOURCE: Robert Welch, *Blue Book of The John Birch Society,* 1961, passim. Reprinted by permission of The John Birch Society and Robert Welch, the copyright owner. Note: footnotes to this article begin on p. 299.

that all the strength we can muster be subject to smoothly functioning direction from the top. As I have said before, no collection of debating societies is ever going to stop the Communist conspiracy from taking us over, and I have no intention of adding another frustrated group to their number. We mean business every step of the way. The men who join The John Birch Society during the next few months or few years are going to be doing so primarily because they believe in me and what I am doing and are willing to accept my leadership anyway. And we are going to use that loyalty, like every other resource, to the fullest possible advantage that we can. Whenever and wherever, either through infiltration by the enemy or honest differences of opinion, that loyalty ceases to be sufficient to keep some fragment in line, we are not going to be in the position of having the Society's work weakened by raging debates. We are not going to have factions developing on the two-sides-to-every-question theme.[2]

Those members who cease to feel the necessary degree of loyalty can either resign or will be put out before they build up any splintering following of their own inside the Society. As I have said, we mean business every step of the way. We can allow for differences of opinion. We shall need and welcome advice. And we expect to use the normal measure of diplomacy always called for in dealing with human beings. But whenever differences of opinion become translated into a lack of loyal support, we shall have short cuts for eliminating both without going through any congress of so-called democratic processes. *Otherwise, Communist infiltrators could bog us down in interminable disagreements, schisms, and feuds before we ever became seriously effective.*[3]

The purpose of The John Birch Society, as officially stated, will be to promote less government, more responsibility, and a better world. The purpose, as unofficially described and discussed among ourselves will be exactly the same thing. Our short-range purpose, our long-range purpose, and our lasting purpose, is to promote less government, more responsibility, and a better world. That says it all. It is, I think, simple, understandable, and all-inclusive as to the goals for which we should strive.

Far from founding a religion, we are merely urging Protestants, Catholics, Jews, or Moslems to be better Christians, better Jews, or better Moslems, in accordance with the deepest and most humanitarian promptings of their own religious beliefs. And we are simply trying to draw a circle of faith in God's power and purpose, and of man's relationship to both, which is broad and inclusive enough to take each man's specific faith into that circle without violation. Yet the evangelical fervor, with which we expect our members to fight the forces of evil and work for a better world, makes certain principles with regard to religious groups apply to ourselves.

We are not beginning any revolution, nor even a counter-revolution, in any technical sense; because, while we are opposing a conspiracy, we are not ourselves making use of conspiratorial methods. Yet our determination to overthrow an entrenched tyranny is the very stuff out of which revolutions are made.

The net result of these reflections is that we are not a copy of any movement of the past. We are unique. We are ourselves. We are something new, as befits a moving force for a new age. We believe in profiting by all human experience, but we shall make our own amalgam of the organizational metals forged by that experience with the mercury of our own purpose. Without donning sackcloth and ashes we shall try to inspire saintly men to join our efforts to make this a better world; and without building barricades in the streets we shall still try to rally rational men to our efforts to preserve the best of the world we already have.

It is the imminence and horror of this danger which drives me to so desperate a course as to offer myself as a personal leader in this fight, and to ask you to follow that leadership. It is not because I want so frightening a responsibility. And it is certainly not because I think that you gentlemen, as good friends of mine as most of you are, recognize any such qualities of leadership in me as would make me a happy choice for the role. It's just that I don't know where you, or all of us, are going to find anybody else to undertake the job. And because I know in my own mind, beyond all doubt or question, that without dynamic *personal* leadership around which the split and frustrated and confused forces on our side can be rallied, rapidly and firmly, we do not have a chance of stopping the Communists before they have taken over our country. It is not that you would choose me, or that I would even choose me, against other possibilities. It is simply that, under the pressure of time and the exigencies of our need, you have no other choice, and neither do I.

Let me repeat just one thing that I said to you yesterday morning. There are in the satellite countries today thousands of men, just like you and me, who only ten years ago could regularly meet in such groups as I propose. Not only that, but they could go out openly, with and before larger groups, to try to spread the alarm and to stop the Communists from taking over their countries. These men now say to each other, but largely to themselves: "If I had only known. If I had only recognized and believed the danger, and the horror of Communist rule, in time. There is nothing I would not have given, to save my freedom, my family, my country, if I had only recognized the urgency and the desperate need. Now it is all too late, and any sacrifice, even of life itself, would be entirely in vain."

We do not have to be too late, and we do not have to lose the fight. Communism has its weaknesses, and the Communist conspiracy has its vulnerable points. We have many layers of strength not yet rotted by all of the infiltration and political sabotage to which we have been subjected. Our danger is both immense and imminent; but it is not beyond the possibility of being overcome by the resistance that is still available. All we must find and build and use, to win, is sufficient understanding. Let's create that understanding and build that resistance, with everything mortal men can put into the effort—while there still is time.

Then, while we are destroying and after we have destroyed the Communist tyranny, let's drive on towards our higher goals of more permanent accomplishment; towards an era of less government and more responsibility, in which we can create a better world.

6

The Rise of Soviet America

Billy James Hargis

America is in the midst of World War III. This is the most terrible war in the history of this Republic because it is a war we may lose. Liberal leadership such as we have had the last 30 years, can only bankrupt America and make us vulnerable for a communist attack within. We desperately need leadership that recognizes in communism the total lie. You can't do business with the communists; you can't trust a communist. America should quit trying.

The United States, against the advice and pleadings of its patriotic, conservative and Christian people, recognized the Soviet Union in 1933. At that time the communists promised to (a) settle all outstanding debts between the two countries, (b) develop mutual trade, (c) *end* Communist propaganda against our Constitution, and (d) refuse support of the Communists in America seeking to destroy our country.

Not one of these promises has been kept.

In gaining control over one-fourth of the world's nations, one-third of the earth's surface, and nearly one-half of all the world's peoples, the Communists promised to help people live better. They promised "peace," "democracy," and a "glorious destiny."

In not one instance have they delivered any of these things.

The USSR in less than 50 years has set a world's record of breaking pacts, promises, pledges and agreements. The Soviet Union and its Communist empire exists and thrives on lies—lies which are so sincere that they have the ring of truth. From such the Psalmist cried

---

SOURCE: Reprinted from "Communism: The Total Lie" by Dr. Billy James Hargis, Founder-Director, Christian Crusade, Chapter I of thirteen chapters.

in ancient times, "Deliver my soul, Oh Lord, from lying lips, and from a deceitful tongue." And Isaiah quoted the Lord, "Judgment also will I lay to the line, and righteousness to the plummet: and the hail shall sweep away the refuge of lies, and the waters shall overflow the hiding place, and your covenant with death shall be disannulled, and your agreement with hell shall not stand; when the overflowing scourge shall pass through, then ye shall be trodden down by it."

The entire world, taking refuge in lies, and trusting in covenants with death and hell, is being trodden down by the overflowing scourge of Communism, which surely is one of the indisputable signs of the ending of the times. "This know also," wrote Paul, "that in the last days, perilous times shall come. For men shall be lovers of their own selves, covetous, boasters, proud, blasphemers, unthankful, unholy, without natural affection, truce breakers, false accusers, incontinent, fierce, despisers of those that are good, traitors, heady, highminded, lovers of pleasures more than lovers of God."

Communists, who deny God, prove the truth of God by their lies, their trucebreaking, their false accusations, and by their treason.

From the beginning, Communists have been liars. Karl Marx and Frederich [sic] Engels, in their satanic *Communist Manifesto,* completely reversed the order of truth and untruth, declaring the basic truths established by man throughout the ages to be untrue, and every untruth established to be truth. To Marx and Engels, who were moved by the unholy spirit to write the gospel of Satan, the soul of truth was a lie. Only the constitution of the USSR, which "guarantees" basic human freedoms, rivals the *Communist Manifesto* of Marx and Engels as the greatest documentary mockery in history.

Lenin, the chief interpreter and apostle of Communism, and the first Communist dictator of Russia, declared, "Promises are like pie crusts—made to be broken." Lenin's body lies in a glass-enclosed case in Red Square in Moscow, meant to be preserved forever as the ideal of manhood, superior even to Jesus Christ. Yet one of the first acts of Lenin, upon seizing power in Russia, and after crushing all resistance, was to repudiate the just debts of his captive nation. Lenin repudiated everything honorable during his lifetime.

In forty-five years of expansion from Russia in 1917 to one-fourth of all the nations, one-third of all the land area, and nearly one-half of all the people upon earth, the Communists have entered into hundreds of agreements, and have broken practically all of them. They are grand champion international liars—but more to be marvelled at than that is the eagerness with which betrayed nations continue to invite more worthless agreements. Among the nations most eager for more agreements with the Communists is the United States of America, *in spite of the fact that the majority of the major agreements entered into to-date have been broken by the Communists.* America continues to ignore the warning of Admiral Stump that "No agreement with a Communist country is worth a scrap of paper."

In the 25 years prior to 1958, the United States held 3,400 meetings with the Communists—including Teheran, Yalta, Potsdam, Panmunjon [sic], and Geneva. More than 106,000,000 words were spoken. Out of these meetings came the 52 major agreements, 50 of which have already been broken by the Communists, and countless minor agreements, most of which have been broken by the Communists. Between 1955 and 1958, the United States met 73 times at Geneva with the Chinese Communists to negotiate the release of 450 American prisoners.

The result—absolutely nothing accomplished, not even an admission by the Communists that they held any American prisoners. Not one American serviceman has ever been accounted for or released— yet throughout America, even from American pulpits, is raised a hue and cry "recognize Red China," "admit Red China to the United Nations!" Still America continues to seek more and more worthless agreements with the Communists.

Petting a rattlesnake never has been known to change its nature or neutralize the poison in its fangs. Communism is an international boa constrictor, whose coils are choking the world, including that portion of the world which feeds it and pets it.

The only thing ever gained from Communist nations is the certainty of broken promises. By their Manifesto, they are pledged to lie, and pledged to break their pledges. To the Communist, lies, broken promises, repudiated debts, betrayals, insincere treaties, unkept pledges and agreements, and assurances of peaceful coexistence are "honorable" strategies of war. There is no hope of any Communist, or any Communist nation, ever keeping a promise. Every nation not controlled by the Communists is an enemy, and overtures of "friendship" are but necessary tactics to lull the enemy to sleep so that it can be strangled. The whole fabric of Communist lies is a necessary phase of the whole fabric of Communist strategy, complimenting [sic] infiltration, subversion, perversion, treason and the like. These are preludes of military conquest and use of force. These are "softening-up" tactics.

Acceptance of Communist lies as truth is the prelude to inevitable national disaster. America has accepted 52 major Communist agreements as truth, yet still refuses to recognize Russia as an enemy after 50 of those agreements have been violated. Surely disaster is about to fall upon America for honoring dishonor. The Communists are winning acceptance and prestige at the highest level—the summit—in spite of a 45 year record of lies and treachery unprecedented in all the nations in the past 2,000 years of history. Hundreds of thousands of pages are required to record the violations by the Soviet Union of literally hundreds of infamous agreements.

The Constitution of the Soviet Union after which the charter of the United Nations was apparently modelled, is a monumental lie. The Soviet Constitution, which was written by Stalin and is called Stalin's constitution, guarantees freedom of the press, freedom of religion, freedom of speech and freedom of assembly. Why the Communists want a constitution guaranteeing basic freedoms when no freedom whatsoever is permitted is one of the mysteries of the ages. There is no freedom of any kind in the Soviet Union, whether guaranteed by the constitution or not, and whether declared to be or not. Communists want Americans to believe that the people of Russia are free, and they have succeeded alarmingly in having even this lie believed in America by taking gullible Americans on guided tours through the unholy land and sending them back to give false reports to the American people. Among them are many clergymen in high places.

We now live in a world of lies, and our only salvation is to learn how to protect ourselves in such an evil atmosphere. If the Communist strategy continues to be successful, the time will soon come when American citizens actually will believe that all the crimes of Soviet aggressions actually were caused by the United States. American citizens will come to believe its own nation to be an "aggressor" nation, its own patriots as "warmongers," and will welcome with open arms the coils of the hideous boa constrictor.

The USSR calls itself a "union" of "republics," which is part of the total lie. The word "union" implies a voluntary union, such as the joining together of the 50 states in the American republic. Force and terror accomplished the "union." The word "republics" implies that the USSR has a government somewhat like that of the United States, which is actually a republic. Although there is absolutely no resemblance between the republic which is America and the "republics" which are said to exist within the so-called Soviet "Union," yet there are voices throughout the land praising Russia, glorifying the Soviet Union, and declaring that America lags far behind the USSR in all phases of progress and development. America is asked to confess its error, admit its inferiority, and become a "Soviet" America, which the ex-head of the Communist Party of the United States said must be.

Why must it be? Why a Soviet America?

Article 125 of the Soviet Constitution, which guarantees freedom of press and freedom of speech, also guarantees freedom of street processions and demonstrations. Yet Soviet troops have shot down demonstrators in city after city, country after country after country, and millions of citizens have been arrested, murdered, or sent to slave-labor camps for the exercise of even minimum citizenship privileges. Communism, as Louis Budenz has proven, exists entirely on slave labor, a regimented press, the terror system and the repression of all opposition. There is no such thing as freedom in Russia or in any Communist-controlled nation.

Article 124 of the Soviet Constitution guarantees freedom of religion, yet religion instruction is even forbidden; any church services still permitted in Russia, or Communist controlled nations, are merely false fronts and decoys to deceive the Christian nations into believing the monstrous lie that Antichrist Communism can still honor Christ by permitting worship of Him. There is no freedom of religion in Russia and the only religion in Russia recognized by the state is inhumanity to man. Any worship which exists is entirely underground. Communism hates Christ and must try to destroy faith and worship of Christ because Christ is truth. Communism, which is lie, cannot allow the freedom of truth. Although Communism seeks the abolishment of all religion, Christianity is crushed more fiendishly than all religions because only Christianity claims a Saviour who is the Truth and who also is the destroyer of the works of Satan.

The Communist system, disguised in its embryo stages as socialism, social reforms, liberalism, progressivism, and even as "liberty," is, on the contrary, a total lie. Neither Communism nor socialism, which are actually one and the same thing insofar as ultimate aim is concerned—neither of these two devilish systems has ever worked. They cannot be made to work. If Communism, or socialism, appears to anyone to be a working system, it is only because it exists on the backs of the people and has received strength through the financial and material aid of the free world, particularly from the United States of America. America alone has practically sustained the world's worst system of government in much of the world by aiding it with the surplus of its resources and with the excessive taxes taken from the American people under the false guise of strengthening the democracies against Communism.

Although Communism has been sufficiently exposed for all the civilized world to see, as Congressman Francis Walter says; and is public knowledge, as the late Whittaker Chambers said; yet Communist leaders and their admirers within America have convinced many influential American leaders and frightened many of the American people into believing that America's hope for peace and security lies only in negotiating and coexisting, only in entering into more agreements with them, and only in aiding them financially and materially. The entire civilized world knows, and it is public knowledge, that when Communism succeeds in engulfing the entire world, the result will be hell on earth. Like beasts of prey, the Communists will kill, torture, enslave, rape, destroy, exhaust and consume until the dark ages of antiquity will appear heavenly by comparison.

Communism once was called the Big Lie. Why is it no longer called the Big Lie? How is it that the strategists, who are so adept at creating words like "McCarthyism," "warmonger," and "reactionary," have managed to black out use of the effective anti-Communist expression, "Big Lie?" Communism not only is the Big Lie, it is TOTAL LIE. Communists are grand champion international total liars.

Herbert Aptheker, editor of the Communist journal *Political Affairs,* which relays Kremlin orders to American Communist strategists, wrote in April, 1959, "The U. S. government falsifies the nature of the World War II agreements because she has failed to abide by them." In the same issue, in comparing the position of the United States with that of Russia, Aptheker wrote, ". . . the government of the Soviet Union is right, and the government of the United States is wrong."

There are many strange voices like that of Aptheker in America today, calling the deceitful Soviet Union truthful, and the United States dishonorable. These voices are being echoed by multitudes of other voices, equally strange, and a confused host of Americans is being led to the left, into "liberal," "progressive," and "social" paths which are strands in the web of Communist strategy. Instead of running the rascals out, we invite them in, and shush the voices of opposition lest any of our enemies, within or without, be offended.

Is it no offense to America to be guided into slavery?

The present ruler of the Soviet Union and World Communism,

Nikita Khrushchev, whom America honored not so long ago by inviting him to free American soil, said in March, 1959, at the Leipzig Fair: "You should not take too seriously the treaties made with the imperialists. Lenin, too, signed a peace treaty after World War I that remained valid only so long as it proved necessary." Previously, Khrushchev said, "I will say now we will never go against the program of Lenin and will follow it in the future. We are not now going to reject what we have created." Soviet Russia, seat of World Communism, is committed to such utter perversion as advocated by Lenin and sworn to by Khrushchev—and includes violation of pledged word.

It is apparent upon examination that Communism cannot be of human origin, for human beings are of themselves incapable of total corruption. Only Satan could inspire in human beings complete dedication to utter folly, unspeakable horrors, and total untruth. Only Satan can be the inspiration for Communism, for Communism is total lie, and Communists are total liars. They are of their father the devil, who was a liar from the beginning, and the father of lies, as scripture declares. The *Bible* also reveals that in the last days evil men would "wax worse and worse, deceiving and being deceived." Never has there been as much deceit in the world as today. Never have there been more evil men, nor men more evil than today. Never have more people been deceived than are deceived throughout the entire world today, including throughout the length and breadth of America.

Added to those who have allowed themselves to be deceived by the poisonous doctrine of Communism are millions of American citizens who have become unwitting dupes in the Communist conspiracy to destroy America and enslave the world. America's only hope is in an awakening by those millions of Americans who are loyal, patriotic Christian men and women, and in those millions taking immediate and characteristic forthright action.

Premier Imre Nagy of Hungary and his defense minister, General Pal Maleter, accepted a written "guarantee" by the Communists that they would receive "safe conduct" during negotiation about the revolt of Hungarian citizens against Soviet tyranny. The written "guarantee" said they could go free. When they stepped out on that promise to meet with the Communists and negotiate with them, they were arrested and hanged.

Not only do the Communists consider their word as nothing, to the Communist, human life is nothing.

Their deceit is so devious that in Russia the word for "bread" in the Russian language is carried in large letters on trucks used to haul prisoners to slave-labor camps. John Noble, after nine and one-half years of imprisonment by the Communists, even though he was a free American citizen, was held for six months after the American government learned indisputably that he was being held and the Russians could no longer lie about it successfully. His captors held him six months after his release was arranged, transferred him to a place where he was treated with politeness, cordiality and respect. He was given the best food obtainable and new clothes to wear. When John Noble, a slave for nine and one-half years, finally was turned back to his native country and given the freedom he had prayed for during his many years of extreme cruelty and torturous treatment, it appeared that he had been well cared for all those years.

The Communists did all they could to erase the physical signs of their brutality upon the body of John Noble, and they did all they could to brainwash him so that he would not reveal the truth to the American people, but John Noble was not deceived. In two books, *I Was A Slave In Russia* and *I Found God In Soviet Russia,* John Noble exposed the Communists for what they are—total liars, grand champion liars, who have created the most brutal slavery in world history, and who are bringing hell to the earth. Voices like that of John Noble, however, do not receive the same respectful attention of the great American press as do the voices of treason and deceit, and so America continues to negotiate, coexist, and seek more agreements with the grand champion international liars of all time.

The deadly danger for the United States which is drawing nearer and nearer to reality is that "ultimate error" of entering into some binding agreement with the Kremlin which the Communists can use to deal the death blow while violating the "binding agreement" itself. Nothing can bind the Soviet Union. Nothing can bind a Communist or a Communist nation to a pledge, promise or agreement. Nothing. Absolutely nothing. America has been placed in great jeopardy because of the lie of Communism and agreements already made with Communism. The American people have been lied to, misguided and misled. They have been deceived and duped, from within as well as from without, into honoring lies and liars.

The American people must be given the truth, and they must take personal responsibility for the truth. The American people must awaken to what has already happened throughout the world and what has already happened inside America itself. The American people must take a hard look at what is going on, and at those who are running to and fro about the land leading the nation into the coils of Communism. The hope of America is in its common people where the Faith of Our Fathers still is strong.

As the great emancipator Abraham Lincoln has said, "I have faith in the common people. Tell the people the truth and the Nation will be saved."

The Communist liar and murderer Stalin was one of the original creators of the United Nations, yet the Soviet Union to-date has violated 37 of 39 agreements made with that international agency. Stalin was one of history's most wicked men, and he was one of history's champion liars. Lenin was a greater liar than Stalin, but the greatest liars of all were the authors of the gospel of Satan, Karl Marx and Frederich [sic] Engels. Yet, Marxist youth groups are being formed throughout America. Khrushchev, whose official title includes the glowing tribute, "Hero of the Soviet Socialist Republics," is today's grand champion liar.

Lenin said that Communists support Socialists only so far as "the hangman's rope supports the convict." Although Socialism and Communism are identical in purpose, Communism can support it only as "the hangman's rope supports the convict." Can the free world expect a better support from Communism, when freedom and Communism are direct opposites? Can the free world expect of Khrushchev any kind of support other than that of a "hangman's rope," when Khrushchev is the modern Lenin? If the free world recognizes Red China, will the murderous and treacherous Mao Tse-tung support it in any other way than as "the hangman's rope?"

The chains of almost one billion enslaved people throughout the world cry loudly, "No!"

"The hangman's rope which supports the convict" is far kinder than is Communism, and the convict is a paragon of virtue compared to the Communist. Communists hold "free" elections in their slave states, but when they announce the results to a waiting world the vote is always just barely under 100 percent in favor of unopposed Communist candidates. Communists take extreme pains to conceal truth, and to create the appearance of truth around their lies.

In spite of the terroristic purges of Stalin, in spite of the universal enslavement of captive nations, in spite of hundreds upon hundreds of broken pledges, does a free world still continue to base its hope for the future in coexistence, cooperation, mutual aid, and further agreements with the grand champion international liars of all times? Does America lead the world in such folly? Have not the American people learned the lessons of Cuba, Tibet, Laos, India, Indonesia, Korea, China, Russia, Poland, Lithuania, Latvia, Estonia and other nations? Do not the people of America remember that President Edouard Benes of Czechoslovakia trusted the Communists and entered into agreements of friendship with them? Himself trustworthy and reasonable, he sought to deal with the Communists as any honorable man wants to deal with his fellowman. Because his own word was good and the word of his nation was good, he believed the word of Russia was good. He entered into coexistence, cooperation and mutual aid with Russia—and thus led himself and his nation to disaster.

America and other nations still free have had the unparalleled advantage of learning the lessons of a host of unfortunate countries—and should profit by those lessons. Yet America, major hope of the free world, is disappointing the free world and destroying the hope of the enslaved world by consorting with the Communist hierarchy, seeking and entering into additional worthless agreements with them, and taking every possible step which will strengthen, rather than weaken, the strangling grip which Communism, thus aided, already has upon the nation.

Do Christian Americans think they can pray better in behalf of their nation from slave-labor camps?

Do American patriots think it will be soon enough to fight for their country when the enemy launches a two-ocean military invasion?

Do the American people take refuge in lies and hide themselves in falsehoods?

7

Danger from the Supreme Court

G. Edward Griffin

Oyez, Oyez, Oyez!
All persons having business before the Honorable, the Supreme Court of the United States are admonished to draw near and give their attention, for the Court is not sitting. God save the United States and this Honorable Court.

With these words, strangely reminiscent of a distant and almost forgotten heritage, nine men in long black robes emerge from behind a velvet curtain and take their seats. The gavel falls and the Supreme Court, the second highest Court in the land, is in session.

Yes, the *second* highest. Beyond this Court, beyond the marble facade and the traditional formality, the American people watch and listen. The Court is their creation. Indirectly, it derives its just powers from the consent of the governed. And the governed are becoming restless. For years, the people have been content with the work of their creation. Not that every act or decree has been exactly to their liking, for there have been many occasions when the servant has displeased and annoyed the master. But, for the most part, the people have been content, secure in the belief that the end result was as good as could be expected from any human institution.

The mood is changing. Crime runs rampant in the streets. Subversives, openly dedicated to the destruction of our nation, operate in our midst with complete freedom and impunity. Government has grown to gigantic proportions and is now directing the most

SOURCE: G. Edward Griffin, *The Great Prison Break* (Belmont, Mass.: Western Island, 1968), pp. 173–178. Reprinted by permission of the publisher.

67

minute details of daily existence. The people are beginning to question who is now master and who is servant. All across the nation, there is an awakening, a renewed interest in vital questions previously ignored or left to the professional politicians. The *Court of Public Opinion, the highest Court of the land,* is being called into session. And it is to that Court that this author's brief is submitted.

Ladies and Gentlemen of the Jury: At the very beginning of this Court session, it was pointed out that this presentation originally was intended to comprise just the first of a three-part study of the Supreme Court's role in encouraging the three deadly "C's" of our time: Crime, Communism, and Collectivism. Since, at this point, only one-third of the total canvas has been covered, it is necessary to sketch in at least the broad outline of the remaining parts so that the portion that *is* complete can be viewed in better perspective. A grasp of the total picture also is essential if we are to come to a realistic understanding of what can be done to reverse the trend and undo the damage. It is pointless to expose Court malfeasance without resolve to correct it, and it is equally futile to resolve to correct it without a sound and workable plan. Fortunately, one does not have to look any further than the Constitution, itself, to discover both the plan and the rationale.

Article II, Section 4, of the Constitution of the United States provides that civil officers, including justices of the Supreme Court, "shall be removed from office on impeachment for, and conviction of, Treason, Bribery, or other High Crimes and Misdemeanors." Certainly, there is nothing in the public record to justify the charges of treason or bribery. But what about "High Crimes and Misdemeanors?" What does that mean? Unfortunately, the Constitution itself does not define the phrase. That does not imply, however, that the words have no meaning, or that they are beyond our understanding.

As members of the jury, in this highest court, the Court of Public Opinion, you are asked to consider the evidence that justices of the Supreme Court, through the decisions in which they have concurred, have committed at least three *High Crimes and Misdemeanors.* Without questioning their personal motives, it becomes evident from the record that:

1. They have undermined the forces of law and order.
2. They have given aid and comfort to the enemy.
3. They have destroyed the vital checks and balances of our Constitutional republic.

The evidence submitted in this presentation has been restricted solely to the Supreme Court's undermining of law and order. Briefs for the remaining charges must await another session of this Court. But they are not really necessary in order for you, the jury, to take immediate action on the first count, which is serious enough by itself. As a matter of fact, the consequences of any *one* of these three acts pose a grave danger to the survival of our nation and our way of life. Clearly, if these traversties [travesties] do not constitute *High Crimes and Misdemeanors,* then nothing ever could!

In summary, Ladies and Gentlemen of the Jury, returning to the singular charge of the Court's attack against the forces of law and order, I submit that the evidence presented in this case is more than sufficient to suggest certain unpleasant but inescapable conclusions. In the interest of clarity and perspective, let us now move away from the finite details of endless specific decisions and summarize these conclusions in straightforward terms.

1. The modern Supreme Court has hindered the impartial administration of justice by denying juries full access to material evidence pertaining to the one question they are duty-bound to resolve—*the vital question of guilt.*

2. The modern Supreme Court has thrown a protective shield around unquestionably guilty criminals—particularly murderers and rapists—by preventing juries from learning that these criminals had *voluntarily confessed to their crimes.*

3. The modern Supreme Court has caused the release from prison of an untold number of dangerous convicts brought about by *a search for technical error* in original lower court proceedings.

4. The modern Supreme Court has set the pace for a national trend of unrealistic judicial leniency which has resulted in reduced sentences, parole or total release of hardened criminals who return time and again *to repeat their crimes of passion and violence.*

5. The modern Supreme Court officially has *sanctioned massive lawlessness, anarchy and revolution* masquerading as "civil disobedience."

6. The modern Supreme Court has *stymied the States and Municipalities in any effective control of pornography* which, like narcotics, is directly related to and partly responsible for the rising crime rate in America.

7. The modern Supreme Court has *prohibited the free exercise of religion* for believers, and *has established Agnosticism as the official*

religious doctrine of the United States, thus undermining one of the most vital pillars supporting our system of law and order.

In order to see the judicial forest a little better, let us take yet another step away from the trees and restate our conclusions in even more compact form.

1. *The modern Supreme Court, through its rather imaginative construction of the Fourteenth Amendment, has instituted itself as the nation's final arbiter and grand umpire over all matters pertaining to crime prevention and law enforcement; thus denying to the State and local government the freedom and flexibility to act in these areas as originally granted to them by the Tenth Amendment.*

2. *The modern Supreme Court has abused this self-proclaimed monopoly by using it in such a way that the rights of criminals have been given considerably more weight on the scales of justice than the corresponding rights of victims, both actual and potential.*

3. *The modern Supreme Court has struck a potential fatal blow to the religious and moral foundations of our American system—foundations which, in the final analysis, are even more important to the maintenance of an orderly society than all the written statutes against crime.*

In other words, Ladies and Gentlemen of the Jury, if you will permit one final condensation of this summary, it can be said without fear of exaggeration: *justices of the modern Supreme Court, through the decisions in which they have concurred, have undermined the forces of law and order.*

Does this qualify as a "high crime?" If it does not, then words have no meaning.

Does this High Crime truly justify removal from office through the process of impeachment? If it does not, then Article II, Section 4 of the Constitution was written in jest.

Are there easier or less controversial ways to bring about reform at the Supreme Court? If there are, they all require additional laws or amendments to the Constitution, most of which, in due course, would themselves become subject to review or "interpretation" by the same justices who created the need for Court reform in the first place. One thing is certain, no justice is going to declare his own impeachment to be unconstitutional. Besides, we now need fewer laws, not more.

Can the impeachment process succeed in bringing about the necessary reform at the Supreme Court? If it cannot, then such reform is impossible, and our Republic faces continued decay and an ultimate return to barbarism.

Do we dare publicly call for impeachment? Here is the only question that yet remains unanswered. While there is a rising tide of indignation over the Court's actions, still, many Americans are reluctant jurists in this Highest Court of the Land. They prefer to grumble and complain, but recoil from voting to check the power granted for life to those nine men in Washington. To jurists in this category, it must be pointed out that the rules of this Court are such that everyone must vote. *Silence automatically is registered as a vote of acquittal.* The only way for our vote to be recorded otherwise is for us personally to be willing to stand up and to be counted!

As a final reminder, Ladies and Gentlemen of the Jury, it is important for you to recognize that you are far more than mere spectators in this Court. In a very real sense, you yourself are the plaintiff. You see, this is your case! The law and order being undermined is the law and order in front of your house. And the very life, liberty and property at stake is none but yours.

8

Communists Can Be Trusted

Fred Schwarz

The thesis of this book is very simple. It is that Communists are Communists. I intend to show that they are exactly what they say they are; they believe what they say they believe; their objective is the objective they have repeatedly proclaimed to all the world; their organization is the organization they have described in minute detail; and their moral code is the one they have announced without shame. Once we accept the fact that Communists are Communists, and understand the laws of their thought and conduct, all the mystery disappears, and we are confronted with a movement which is frightening in its superb organization, strategic mobility, and universal program, but which is perfectly understandable and almost mathematically predictable.

In the battle against Communism, there is no substitute for accurate, specific knowledge. Ignorance is evil and paralytic. The best intentions allied with the most sincere motives are ineffective and futile if they are divorced from adequate knowledge. Consider a mother who has a small daughter to whom she is devoted. For this daughter she is determined to do all that a mother may do. She feeds her a well-balanced diet to build a healthy body; she provides the finest education to develop her mind; she cares for her spiritual well-being, and gives her a lovely home. In the environment of this young girl, there are men who specialize in gaining the confidence of little girls by giving them candy and enticing them into automobiles

SOURCE: Fred Schwarz, *You Can Trust the Communists (To Be Communists)* (Englewood Cliffs, N.J.: Prentice-Hall, 1962). Reprinted by permission of the author.

to molest them. If the mother neglects to give her child the specific information to meet such a situation, she will fail in her duty, and all her loving care will count for nothing when the crisis comes. There is no substitute for specific knowledge.

It is the purpose of this book to give that knowledge. Some of it is a little technical. Some of it may seem a long way from the everyday needs and activities of life. Nonetheless, the information contained in it is essential to survival.

The statement is frequently heard: "You cannot trust the Communists!" This is incorrect; you can trust the Communists.

They are extremely trustworthy. You can trust a cancer cell to obey the laws of its lawless growth. You can trust an armed bank robber to take the money and try to escape. Similarly, you can trust the Communists to act in accordance with the laws of their being.

When people operate according to clearly defined principles, they are both trustworthy and predictable. While we continue to believe that the Communists think, feel and believe as we do, the Communist movement is, as Winston Churchill described it, "a riddle wrapped in an enigma." The movements of the heavenly bodies appeared mysterious and unpredictable till Copernicus discovered the governing laws. When we understand the philosophy of Communism, the unifying purpose concealed in their frequently chaotic and contradictory conduct is revealed.

Marxism-Leninism

Nikita Khrushchev said: "Anyone who thinks we have forsaken Marxism-Leninism deceives himself. That won't happen till shrimps learn to whistle." We can trust the Communists to practice Marxism-Leninism.

What is Marxism-Leninism? Stripped to its barest essentials, Marxism is the doctrine of the universality of class warfare, and Leninism is the doctrine of the historic role of the Communist Party to consummate the universal class war in world Communist victory. The basic doctrine of Marxism-Leninism is that a state of war exists and that the Communist Party has been created to win this war. The war was originally discovered, not declared, by Karl Marx. It is between two classes of society which he called the proletariat and the bourgeoisie. The bourgeoisie is the class of property ownership, the class that owns the means of production. The proletariat he defined as the class of wage labor. Between these two classes, Marx claimed to discover a state of war. The bourgeoisie desires profit; the proletariat desires high wages. If wages go up, profits come down. If profits go up, wages come down. Thus there is a fundamental conflict between these two classes. This conflict Marx called the class war.

Marx taught that the bourgeoisie is the established class in Capitalist society. It has created the State as an instrument to oppress and exploit the proletariat. In reaction the proletariat creates the Communist Party to wage war against the State. Thus the class war manifests itself as war between the Communist Party and the State. With the progress of history, the Communist Party has come to power in Russia, China, and Eastern Europe. The bourgeoisie remains in power in America and her associated allies. Thus the class war has transferred itself from the national to the international plane. The fundamental doctrine of Marxism, therefore, is that Russia and America are at war; that China and America are at war—not that they could be at war; not that they might be at war; not that they will be at war; but that they are at war. This war is historically declared; it is universal; it encompasses every aspect of society; in it there can be no vestige of truce. The Communists did not choose it; they simply recognized it. Their duty is to prosecute the war to total and complete victory.

The weapons of this warfare are not merely the classical weapons of guns, tanks, bombs, and aircraft. The weapons are universal. Education is a weapon; language is a weapon; trade is a weapon; diplomacy is a weapon; religion is a weapon; cultural interchange is a weapon. The Communists view every act and judge every situation as part of the class war. When the Bolshoi Ballet performs in the United States, that is an action in the class war; when a group of American clergymen visits Russia, that is an action in the class war; when the Soviet participates in negotiations for "peace," they fight a battle in the class war. Their participation in the United Nations is part of this warfare. The basic Communist doctrine is: "We are at war!" This is the frame of reference within which every action and thought must be assessed and judged.

It does not take two to make a fight. An idea in the mind of one is enough. Let me illustrate. During the war against Japan, I was a doctor in the Brisbane General Hospital. Brisbane, capital city of the state of Queensland in north-eastern Australia, was the headquarters of General MacArthur and the American troops for the advance to the Philippines and Japan. Into the hospital, there came one day a man who told me that he had put his finger down his throat to make himself vomit because the Americans were going to poison him. I looked at him in some astonishment.

"How do you know they are going to poison you?" I asked.

"I saw them watching me as I was having my dinner."

"Why are they going to poison you?"

"I don't know."

I sought for an explanation of his attitude. "Has your wife been running around with the Americans?"

That was the only time he showed any emotion. He became quite indignant and said, "Oh, no, nothing like that!"

"They are not going to poison you."

"Yes they are."

"I know they're not."

"I know they are."

He was not angry. He was not yelling, shouting, or screaming. He did not have piercing, staring, penetrating eyes. He had none of the external characteristics of insanity. He looked perfectly normal. Nonetheless, I diagnosed him as a mental case and sent him down to the mental ward. However, he was not a bad case. His wife came in and took him home.

Some days later, an American officer went into a public rest room in Queen Street, Brisbane, and was shot dead with a sawed-off shot gun. His assailant ran away. The police, assuming that the criminal was a man like unto themselves, thinking as they thought, and moved by their motives, investigated without success. They considered the normal motives for murder—robbery, jealousy, revenge, alcoholic fury—but they could not find one clue.

A week later in a suburb of Brisbane, another American officer was killed by the same sawed-off shot gun. This time they caught the assailant. It was the man whom I had treated at the hospital.

He had been working on a baker's delivery van, going from house to house delivering bread to the housewives, handling the money, giving the change, playing with the children. Apparently he was quite normal. But deep down in his conscious and unconscious mind, he believed a lie. He knew the Americans were going to kill him. He wished they were not so determined but he knew they were. A man must protect himself. He took a shot gun, sawed off the barrel, sawed off the stock, and carried it around with him for self-protection. He walked into the rest room. He saw the American officer. He knew his life was in danger. He pulled out the gun, shot the officer dead, and ran for his life. A week later he repeated the same process. He was taken, convicted of criminal insanity, and sentenced to an asylum for the insane.

It did not take two to make a quarrel. An idea in the mind of one was enough. Those American officers had never seen the man in their lives. Towards him they had no attitude except goodwill. But he believed that they were bent on his destruction. Suddenly a gun flashed and a man died. It does not take two to make a quarrel. An idea in the mind of one is enough.

The Communists believe that they are at war with us. This conviction will never be changed in the slightest degree by any action of the Free World. If, tomorrow, the leaders of the Free Nations were to accede to every demand made by the Communist leaders, if they were to neutralize every Strategic Air Command base, if they were to grant the demands on Germany, if they were to neutralize Formosa, if they were to recognize Red China and admit it to the United Nations, if the United States were to withdraw every serviceman and weapon within the borders of continental United States, the Communists would merely believe they had won massive victories in the class war. A step towards our final conquest and destruction would have been taken. We must either recognize this and defend against it, or ignore it and be destroyed. We have no other choice.

Peace

Since the Communists are at war, they naturally desire peace. Wherever you find a Communist, you find an advocate of peace. "Peace" is one of the golden words of their vocabulary. They have "peace" movements of every kind; they have peace campaigns, peace prizes, peace conferences, peace processions. Every Communist is a devotee of peace.

Most people, watching the military preparations of the Communists, noting the enormous percentage of their budget devoted to military objectives, observing their ruthless, brutal repression of any attempt by their captive nations to secure freedom, classify the Communists as blatant hypocrites. This is far from the truth. The Communists are not hypocrites. They are sincerely and genuinely dedicated to peace. If you gave a mature Communist a lie detector test and asked him if he desired peace with all his heart, he would pass with flying colors. They live for peace; they long for peace; they would willingly die for peace.

What is this peace which they desire? During the war against Japan, most Americans undoubtedly wanted peace. Peace was the thought that comforted mothers whose sons were in danger on distant battlefields; peace was the word which sustained wives, lonely and anxious without their husbands; peace was the goal that motivated servicemen who knew the boredom, the loneliness, and the danger of war. Had they been asked to define peace, they would doubtless have described it as the termination of hostilities in the defeat of the enemy by the Allies. Not under any circumstances would victory by Japan have been termed peace. To the American people, peace meant only one thing—American victory. The Communists believe they are at war. They desire "peace" with all their hearts. But to them, peace is that golden consummation when the progressive force of Communism totally overwhelms American imperialism and climaxes in Communist world conquest. By definition, "peace" is Communist world conquest.

Since this is true, any action that advances Communist conquest is a "peaceful" action. When the armies of the Communist Chinese emcompass the Tibetans, robbing them of their land and food, stimulating them to frantic, hopeless revolt, and then massacring them, they are consummating peace. When Khrushchev ordered Russian tanks into Budapest to fire into the apartment buildings, reducing them to rubble, entombing man, woman, and child in his heart he had a song of peace.

The Communists use the word "peace" in their own sense with total sincerity. We interpret it in our sense. We are the victims, not of their hypocrisy, but of our own ignorance.

The Communists are not hypocrites. They suffer from paranoic delusions of an intense sincerity. They are so enmeshed in the delusions of Marxism-Leninism that they are beyond the scope of rational argument and conviction. All observed phenomena are interpreted within the framework of their preconceived conclusions. If they were hypocrites, it would be much easier to deal with them. You can make a bargain with a hypocrite; you can scare a hypocrite. When you are dealing with paranoics of highly organized delusional patterns, your sole recourse is to acknowledge and understand these patterns and take appropriate measures to protect yourself against the conduct which results from the delusions.

Truth

The Communists invariably tell the "truth," but it is the Marxist-Leninist "truth." Those who believe that the Communists will lie in the interests of Communism are mistaken. In fact, it is not possible for a Communist to lie in the interests of Communism. By definition, if a statement is in the interests of Communism, it is the truth.

Jesting Pilate asked the question: "What is truth?" Christians believe that God is Truth. Truth is a quality of God Himself. An absolute God created an absolute Truth. Truth is. The Communists affirm that this is nonsense. There is no God; there are no absolutes; everything is relative; Truth itself is a relative of the class struggle. Lenin said: "The Communist Party is the mind, the conscience, and the morals of our epoch. Proletarian morality is determined by the exigencies of the class struggle." Truth is a weapon of the class war, and any statement that advances Communist conquest is "true." We can trust the Communists always to say that which will advance Communist conquest. We can trust them always to tell the Marxist-Leninist "truth."

Millions of dollars are being spent on the production of beautiful literature telling this "truth." The truth, according to their literature, is simple: Where Communism comes to power, everyone is happy, prosperous, and free; America on the other hand, is the vilest, most evil, most degenerate nation the world has ever seen.

An excellent example of the Marxist-Leninist truth is contained in a beautiful, photographic magazine published in English by the Communists in North Korea. Most of the magazine is given over to the portrayal of the radiant happiness and glorious prosperity of North Korea under Communism. Towards the end, however, they present the picture of America. On a page entitled "Massacre Committed by American Brutes," there are six photographs of bodies taken from a mass grave lying side by side upon the ground. Their relatives weep over them. Underneath, is the following text:

> Mankind remembers the shocking atrocities the Hitlerites perpetrated in the concentration camps in Majdanek and Oswiecim. [Auschwitz].
>
> Recently another case of atrocities by the American murderers which exceeds in its cruelty the atrocities by the Hitlerites was discovered in Korea.
>
> In a shaft of the Rakyun Mine, Jangyun County, South Hwanghai Province, some 800 dead bodies were discovered.
>
> During their temporary occupation of Jangyun County during the Korean War, the American murderers rounded up miners of the Rakyun Mine and the peasants in the nearby villages and put them through severe torture. Then the American devils

kicked the tortured miners and peasants into the shaft 100 meters deep.

In the shaft corpses were piled up on top of one another, and the torn pieces of the bodies bore bullet holes and scars made by the bayonets. Many mothers had their babies tied on their backs. The shaft presented a most gruesome scene.

Honest-minded people can not but hate and condemn the American Imperialist murderers whose lust for blood knows no end.

Funeral services for the murdered took place in the Rakyun mine in the midst of children's crying for their lost fathers, old women wailing over their dead sons. The people's enmity and curses upon the American devils rent the air. 'Avenge us of the American imperialists!' This was the cry of the 800 murdered.

But even at the moment in South Korea, the American murderers are slaughtering our brothers and sisters. This we can not tolerate.

American cannibals get out of Korea immediately.[1]

This is the Marxist-Leninist truth. The objective truth is, of course, quite different. When the Communists retreated in North Korea, they took with them all the able-bodied personnel to serve as laborers. Those who could not stand the rigors of the northward journey—old men and women, pregnant women, very young children and babies—they massacred and buried in a mass grave if they belonged to the untrustworthy social classes. The advancing American troops time and again found mass graves filled with the bodies of those murdered by the Communists. The Communists merely disinterred one of their own mass graves, and, with moral indignation, indicted America for it before the conscience of the world. Their moral indignation was real, not simulated. This is almost incomprehensible.

Hitler worked on the principle: Tell a lie, make it big, repeat it often, and the majority of the people will believe you. The Communists have further developed this concept. Any lie that advances Communist conquest is, by definition, not a lie but the Marxist-Leninist truth. The maturity of a Communist can be judged by the extent to which he can divorce himself from the evidence of his senses and totally identify himself with the verdict of the Communist Party.

---

[1] *Korea,* Vol. 25, 1958 (Pyongyang, Democratic People's Republic of Korea: Foreign Languages Publishing House).

When confronted with a choice between the evidence of his eyes and the verdict of the Communist Party, the mature Communist will believe with such conviction what the Party has said that, were he given a lie detector test, he would pass it with flying colors. He would experience all the emotions associated with truth when he thought of the decision of the Party.

We are astounded when we see evidence of this. An American plane was shot down over Soviet Armenia. The American forces recorded the conversation of the Russian pilots as they shot down the plane. When Mikoyan, visiting America, was confronted with the evidence, he was not confounded in the least. He did not believe it. It was not true. He was a Communist, a Marxist-Leninist. The Communist Party had said that it did not happen, and the verdict of the Party is the Marxist-Leninist truth.

All Communists do not attain this maturity. Many of them would possibly feel a slight element of doubt in such a situation. Final maturity is attained with the ability to identify one's emotions completely with the verdict of the Party.

Communist scientists finally derive their "truth" from the verdict of the Communist Party. Laboratory experimentation is secondary and must be interpreted in accordance with the policy outlined by the Party.

In the late 1940's there arose in Russia a great debate in the realm of Biology. It concerned the question of transmissibility to offspring of characteristics acquired during the life of the parent. Most reputable biologists teach that such characteristics cannot be transmitted.

The Communists attribute this theory to Mendel and Morgan and call it Mendel-Morgan genetics. A Russian biologist, Michurin, developed a theory at variance with this. His theory was advocated by a plant breeder called Lysenko.

The biological section of the Russian Academy of Sciences met to discuss this issue. The Foreign Languages Press of Moscow published a full report of the conference under the title, "Proceedings of the Academy of Science on the Teaching of Academician Lysenko." The verbatim speeches of the leading Russian scientists were published. Many of these, on the basis of their long laboratory experience, contended that the Michurin-Lysenko school was in error. As scientists, they detailed the evidence on which they based their conclusions.

The issue was resolved very simply. Near the end of the report there is a chapter entitled, "Concluding Remarks of Academician L.

D. Lysenko." He reports: "Comrades, the question is asked in a note handed to me: 'Has the Central Committee of the Party adopted any position with regard to your report?' I wish to state that the Central Committee of the Communist Party has read my report and has approved it." (*Prolonged ovation. Great applause. All rise.*)

A strange sequence ensues. The leading Russian scientists who had opposed the Lysenko position on the basis of their laboratory experience, had a crisis revelation during the night. The following day, they asked permission to make statements. When permission was granted, they rose and indicated that the error of their way had now been revealed to them. They repented of their former service to imperialist biology and dedicated themselves to true proletarian biology.

The cynic may say: "That is easy to understand. They were scared. They knew what would happen to them if they did not agree with the Party line." However, the question goes deeper than that. They were scientists and they were Communists. They were Communists first and scientists second. As Communists they believed the Communist Party to be "the mind of our epoch," the fountain of all "truth." The verdict of the Party must take precedence over the experience of the senses, even in the scientific experiment.

It may be argued that this situation no longer exists, that things have changed. Russian scientists do not all agree with Lysenko now.

The question at issue is not the rightness or wrongness of the Lysenko theories, but the right of the Communist Party to determine scientific truth by edict. That situation has not changed. Russian scientists may have changed their views, but only because they have been permitted to do so by the Party. "Truth" remains the exclusive province of the party.

Righteousness

The Communists demand and develop characters of "righteousness," that is, Marxist-Leninist righteousness. In the book, *How to Be a Good Communist,* Liu Shao-chi, President of Communist China and brilliant theoretical writer says:

> But if sacrifice has to be made for the Party, for class and national liberation, that is, for the emancipation of mankind, for social evolution and for the interests of the greatest majority of mankind embracing countless millions of people, countless Communist Party members will face death with equanimity and make any sacrifice without the slightest hesitation. To the ma-

jority of Communist Party members, it will be accepted as a matter of course "to lay down one's life for a noble cause" or "to die for righteousness," if necessary.[2]

What is this righteousness for which they are ready to die? Righteousness is conduct which will advance Communist world conquest. According to this definition, Joseph Stalin was the very personification of Marxist-Leninist righteousness. The many who believe that Khrushchev attacked and condemned Stalin missed the point of his speech entirely. Khrushchev did two things: He described Stalin, and he condemned him. His description depicted a man so vile that most folk took it for condemnation. What he said, in effect, was this: Stalin was a murderer; he was not a reluctant murderer, but an enthusiastic murderer. He enjoyed murder. He got a thrill out of the torture of his own friends. When the Jewish doctors were arrested and accused of poisoning Zdanov, Stalin called in the man responsible for examining them and indicated the type of torture to be given each one. He gave three fundamental rules for getting confessions: "Beat, beat, and beat again." He said: "If you don't get a confession by this date, we will shorten you by a head!"

Khrushchev indicated that Stalin was a stark, raving madman. "When you went in to see him in the morning, he would look at you and say, 'What have you been up to? You have a shifty look in your eye today.' You never knew whether you would leave as his friend or under armed guard to be shot." He presents a picture of a murderer of limitless appetite, a picture of megalomaniacal, sadistic madness. But he concludes by saying: "Don't misunderstand me. Stalin was a good man. He was a Marxist-Leninist. He did these things as a Marxist-Leninist." No higher praise could have been given by Khrushchev.

How could he justify both description and designation? Let us project ourselves into the stream of history, and look at Stalin in historic perspective. Stalin assumed power when the Communists were a beleaguered garrison and he brought them to the verge of world conquest. It was Stalin who set up their educational program which today is graduating three times as many engineers and scientists as the American program. It was Stalin who became the patron of scientific research. It was Stalin who established their submarine and

---

[2] Liu Shao-chi, *How to Be a Good Communist* (Peking: Foreign Languages Press), pp. 55–6.

missile programs which have caused the shadow of impeding [impending] death to fall over the life of every person in the Free World. It was Stalin who organized the conquest of China. It was Stalin who deceived American and Free World statesmen. Stalin brought Communism to the very verge of world conquest. A few generations hence, when Communism has conquered the world, and regenerate mankind lives in perfect happiness and complete abundance, the name of Stalin, who did so much to bring this to pass, will be honored and revered. His personal idiosyncrasies will be ignored and forgotten. Dead men do not complain. Who worries about last year's fallen leaves? Stalin is the superb exemplar of Marxist-Leninist righteousness.

Love

We can trust the Communists to manifest pure, Marxist-Leninist "love." One of the best pictures of Marxist-Leninist "love" was revealed in the boast made by Klementi Voroshilov, now president of Russia, to William C. Bullitt, America's first ambassador to the Soviet Union. At a banquet in Russia in 1934, Voroshilov told Bullitt that in 1919 he persuaded eleven thousand Czarist officers at Kiev to surrender by promising them that, if they surrendered, they, their wives and their families would be permitted to return to their homes. When they surrendered, he executed the eleven thousand officers and all male children, and sent the wives and daughters into the brothels for the use of the Russian army. He mentioned in passing that the treatment they received in the brothels was such that none of them lived for more than three months.[3]

Voroshilov was merely acting in obedience to the dictates of Marxist-Leninist "love." Believing as he believed, he acted in a truthful, righteous, and loving manner. There he stood, one of history's anointed, entrusted with the destiny of world conquest and human regeneration. There stood a group of male and female animals which he could utilize selfishly by keeping his promise to them and making himself feel good in the bourgeois sense, or which he could utilize for the ultimate regeneration and happiness of all mankind by destroying them. His duty lay clearly before him. As a Communist he had no choice. He was nothing; these people were nothing; the

---

[3] William C. Bullitt, "A Talk with Voroshilov," printed in *The Great Pretense*, prepared and released by the Committee on Un-American Activities, U.S. House of Representatives, Washington, D.C., May 19, 1956, pp. 18–19.

will of history was everything. He saw his duty clear. To the executioners went all the males, and to the brothels went all the females. The Red Army was strengthened, world conquest came a day nearer, human regeneration a little closer, and Voroshilov had a conscience as clear as spring water, and a sense of duty nobly done. He was comforted by an acute awareness of the fulfillment of Marxist-Leninist "love."

Communists believe they have a destiny. Their destiny is to create a new world and regenerate mankind. To do this they must conquer the world, shatter the Capitalist system, and, by Communist dictatorship, establish the regenerative environment of Socialism. This new environment will rear the young to perfection.

An inescapable step of their scientific program for the regeneration of mankind is the elimination of the residual diseased social classes following world conquest. A few years ago, the American Communist Party would openly acknowledge that, having conquered this country, they would need to put to death one third of the American people. This is not punishment; it is Social Science. It is not cruelty; it is "love." It is as though the surgeon took the scalpel in a loving fashion to cut away the gangrenous tissue so that the new and perfect might come to maturity.

Communism is applied godless materialism. St. Paul writes:

> Because that, when they knew God, they glorified him not as God, neither were thankful; but became vain in their imaginations, and their foolish heart was darkened. Professing themselves to be wise, they became fools, and changed the glory of the uncorruptible God into an image made like to corruptible man, and to birds, and fourfooted beasts, and creeping things. Wherefore God also gave them up to uncleanness through the lusts of their own hearts, to dishonour their own bodies between themselves: who changed the truth of God into a lie, and worshipped and served the creature more than the Creator, who is blessed for ever.[4]

Emerging from its lair of godless materialism, dressed in garments of science, Communism seduces the young and utilizes their perverted religious enthusiasm to conquer the world. Building on the doctrines of godless materialism, Communism has completely reversed the meaning of our basic moral terms. When we, in our ignorance of this fact, insist on interpreting their phraseology as if they believed

---

[4] Romans 1:21–25.

the Christian philosophy from which we have derived our basic concepts, we aid and abet them in their program for our conquest and destruction. Once it is known what the Communists believe, there is no difficulty in understanding, interpreting, and predicting their conduct. On the foundation of knowledge, and on that foundation alone, may an edifice of survival be built.

9

Who Killed John F. Kennedy?

Revilo P. Oliver

* * *

Why was Kennedy murdered by the young Bolshevik? With a little imagination, it is easy to excogitate numerous explanations that are not absolutely impossible. For example: (a) Oswald was a "madman" who acted all alone just to get his name in the papers; (b) Oswald was a poor shot who was really trying to kill Governor Connally or Mrs. Kennedy and hit the President by mistake; (c) the person killed was not Kennedy but a double, and the real Kennedy is now a guest aboard a "flying saucer" on which he is heroically negotiating with Martians or Saturnians to Save the World. With a little time and a fairly wide reading in romantic fiction, anyone can think of sixty or seventy fantasies as good or better than those that I have mentioned.

On the evidence, however, and with consideration of human probabilities, there are only three explanations that are not preposterous, viz.:

1. That Kennedy was executed by the Communist Conspiracy because he was planning to turn American. For this comforting hypothesis there is no evidence now known. Ever since January, 1961, some hopeful Americans have maintained that Jack was a conservative at heart, that he deliberately packed his administration with Schlesingers, Rostows, and Yarmolinskys so that these would bring our nation so near to disaster that even the stupidest "Liberal," not in the employ of the Conspiracy, could not overlook the obvious, and that when an unmistakable crisis at last made it politically feasible, Ken-

SOURCE: Revilo P. Oliver, "Marxmanship in Dallas," *American Opinion*, February, 1964, pp. 18–24. Published by permission of The John Birch Society.

nedy would carry out a sudden and dramatic *volte-face,* sweep the scum out of Washington, and rally the forces of the great majority of loyal and patriotic Americans.

I wish I could believe that. It is true that the late Senator McCarthy praised young Kennedy, but although the Senator was a great American whose memory we must all revere, he was not preternaturally gifted: He could have been either deceived by a smooth-talking hypocrite (as have been greater men than he in the past) or mistaken in his estimate of a person who, although then sincere in his allegiance to what then seemed to be the winning side, later thought it expedient to change sides. It is also true that Kennedy said some fine things in speeches delivered just before his death, but those statements did not significantly differ from the pro-American flourishes normally used as seasoning in the boob-bait manufactured by Salinger's technicians during the past three years.

If Kennedy did entertain laudable designs, he cannot have kept them entirely *in petto;* he must have disclosed them to a few persons, perhaps including his father, in whom he had confidence. And if he did, the time for those persons to give evidence is now, while there is still a chance to clear the reputation of the deceased.

2. That the assassination was the result of one of the rifts that not infrequently occur within the management of the Communist Conspiracy, whose satraps sometimes liquidate one another without defecting from the Conspiracy, just as Persian satraps, such as Tissaphernes and Pharnabazus, made war on one another without revolting or intending to revolt against the King of Kings.

Now it was generally suspected for some time before the assassination that Khrushchev and Kennedy were planning to stage another show to bamboozle the American suckers just before the [next] election. . . . According to this plan, a fake "revolt" against Castro would be enacted by the Communist second team, which has long been kept in reserve for such an eventuality. (Cf. *American Opinion,* March, 1962, p. 33.) The "democratic revolution" was to be headed by a Communist agent who differed from Fidel only in being less hairy and less well known to Americans, so that the *New York Times,* the State Department, the Central Intelligence Agency, and our other domestic enemies could swear once again that the vicious criminal was an "agrarian reformer," an "anti-Communist," and the "George Washington of Cuba." (It is confidently believed in conspiratorial circles that the dumb brutes in the United States will never learn—until it is much too late.)

What is not certain is the script for the third act of the comedy. Most (but not all) informed observers believe that this performance in Cuba was to accomplish two things: (a) the re-election of Kennedy and most of his stooges in Congress, which would, of course, be impossible without some seasonably contrived and major "crisis"; and (b) the endlessly repeated and trite device of making the tax-paying serfs in the United States, who have financed every important Communist conquest since 1917, work to provision and fortify another conquest under the pretext that by so doing they in some mysterious way "fight Communism."

Now, if those observers are correct in their projections, the scenario called for the "success" of the "democratic revolution." And that would involve, if the play was to be convincing, the liquidation of Fidel and a few of his more notorious accomplices. And that, as is well known to everyone who has made even the slightest study of Communism, would be merely commonplace and normal.

The rabid rats of Bolshevism devour one another—and no one knows that better than the rats themselves. Almost all of the Conspiracy's most famous murders—Trotsky, Zinoviev (Apfelbaum), Kirov (Kostrikov), Kamenev (Rosenfeld), Yezhov, Beria, and a hundred others, possibly including Stalin—were murdered by their insatiably blood-thirsty confederates. Indeed, it is a general rule that only accident or disease can save a Communist "leader" from assassination or execution by other Communists as soon as his usefulness to the Conspiracy is ended or his liquidation will provide an opportunity for useful propaganda.

Cornered rats will fight for their lives. Castro, of course, knew of the planned "revolution," and if the dénouement was correctly foreseen by American observers, he also knew that, whatever solemn pledges may have been given him by his superiors, he would not survive. It is possible, therefore, that Fidel arranged the assassination of Jack in the hope of averting, or at least postponing, his own. Now that Oswald is silenced and superiors who gave him his orders are unidentified, it may never be possible completely to disprove that hypothesis, although there are a number of considerations that weigh against it.

We should note, also, that a few American observers believed that the Communist scenario had a different third act. According to their forecast, the Communist second team was to stage an indecisive "revolt" against the first team. Jack, pretending to carry out after four years the pledge that he made to get himself elected, would commit the United States to support the second team. At the scheduled moment on the eve of elections Nick would "intervene" and yell about a "nuclear holocaust," thus producing a "crisis" which would call for a "bipartisan" cancellation of the election. The gang in the Pentagon, hypocritically wringing its greasy hands, would claim that we were even weaker than its concerted sabotage of our defenses had in fact made us by that time. That would suffice to set craven "intellectuals" and neurotic females to running through our streets howling for "peace" and the "United Nations." After much tension, a great "statesmanlike solution" would be found: surrender of our sovereignty and weapons to an "international" body, with the Russians agreeing to do likewise. Then the savages in the "international police force" would move in, and the glorious and long-awaited butchery of the American boobs would get under way.

Those who make this prognosis support it by pointing out that the Conspiracy has already fallen far behind its schedule for the United States, and that the slow but ever increasing awakening of the American people from their hypnotic lethargy makes it necessary for the Conspiracy to adopt drastic and precipitate measures now, if it is not to fail utterly. If those observers are right, then interference by Castro is excluded, for the plan itself would guarantee his safety until the United States had been abolished.

3. That the Conspiracy ordered the assassination as part of systematic preparation for a domestic take-over. If so, the plan, of course, was to place the blame on the "right-wing extremists" (if I may use the Bolsheviks' code-word for informed and loyal Americans), and we may be sure that a whole train of "clues" had been carefully planted to lead or point in that direction as soon as Oswald was safe in Mexico. These preparations were rendered useless when Oswald was, through some mischance, arrested—probably in consequence of some slip-up of which we as yet know nothing. He may, for example, have missed connections with some agent of the Conspiracy who was to transport him to the airport, and it may be significant that, when observed on the street, he was walking directly toward the apartment of the Jakob Rubenstein (alias Jack Ruby) who later silenced him.

Two objections to this explanation are commonly raised, but neither is cogent.

The first is the assumption that, if the International Conspiracy had planned the assassination, there would have been no slip-up. That is absurd. The degenerates are not Supermen. Their agents make blunders all the time—blunders that could destroy whole segments of the apparatus, if the Conspiracy did not have so many criminals planted in communications and politics to cover up the blunders and to paralyze the normal reactions of a healthy society. It would take pages even to list the mistakes that the Conspiracy's agents, including their branch manager, Castro, have made in the course of the Cuban operation. For that matter, a potentially serious and quite unnecessary mistake was made when the Communist Party's *official* publication, *The Worker,* yelled for the appointment of Earl Warren to "investigate" the assassination *before* the appointment was made —or at least, before the appointment was disclosed to the public. Nothing was gained by that mistake in timing, which serves only to give away the whole show.

The second argument is that the Conspiracy could not have wanted to eliminate Kennedy, who was doing so much for it. But that is a miscalculation. For one thing, the job was not being done on schedule. A few measures had been forced through Congress, but not, for example, what is called "Civil Rights," a very vital part of the vermin's preparations for the final take-over. Virtually nothing was done to speed up national bankruptcy and the total economic collapse that is doubtless scheduled to accompany the subjugation of the American people. The Congress was, on the whole, the most American Congress that we have had for many years, and it blocked the measures most cunningly designed to destroy the nation. It was not the fault of any one man, to be sure, but the record for 1963 was, for all practical purposes, a stalemate. Our "Liberals," always impatient for open dictatorship and terrorism, were beginning to feel frustrated; some of them were screeching in our more prominent daily, weekly, and monthly liepapers about the "standpatism" of Congress and hinting that that nasty relic of the Constitution must be abolished in the interests of "effective democracy." Others were beginning to lose confidence.

That is what the Conspiracy cannot afford. It is already sadly behind schedule. Of course, its secret plans, like the identity of its master strategists, are undisclosed, but at the end of 1958 some competent observers, after the most careful and painstaking study of all available indications, concluded that 1963 was the year scheduled for the effective capture of the United States. And those analysts—without exception, so far as I know—still believe that they were right; they believe that the Communist schedule was retarded and partly disrupted by the awakening of the American people and their growing awareness of the Communist Conspiracy and its designs. It is known from past operations that the Conspiracy's plans always call for constantly *accelerated* subversion in the final phase of a conquest, and so even a stalemate is, from the standpoint of our enemies, an alarming tactical failure. They cannot afford many more without suffering total defeat.

The Conspiracy, we must remember, does not have the resilience of a nation at war, which, unless thoroughly rotted, can rely on the powerful cohesive force of patriotism. To be sure, a frenzied hatred of mankind and human civilization is an even more powerful cohesive force among the born Bolsheviks who direct and manage the Conspiracy, and it has been able to excite race hatred among certain "minorities" and so acquire some fanatical shock-troops; but for a very large part of the work of subversion it must rely on low-grade criminals, opportunistic collaborators, and stupid employees. And its power of discipline over those groups largely depends on their complete confidence that the Conspiracy's triumph is inevitable.

Careful observers were aware of the feeling of crisis in conspiratorial circles before the assassination. In June of 1963, an experienced American military man made a careful analysis of the situation at that time, and in his highly confidential report concluded, on the basis of indications in Communist and crypto-Communist sources, that the Conspiracy's schedule called for a major incident to create national shock *before Thanksgiving*. Taylor Caldwell, who combines feminine sensitivity with artistic perception, sensed in the tone of Communist and "Liberal" publications a direction that made the assassination of Kennedy "very probable"—and she said so in an explicit warning published on October 31 and written about a week earlier. Other observers, who saw that Communist plans called for some sensational act of violence in the United States naturally considered the assassination of Kennedy (possibly in a crash of his airplane so arranged as to show unmistakable sabotage) as one of the expedients that the Conspiracy might adopt, although they did not, so far as I know, regard it as the *most* likely at the present juncture.

But, aside from the Conspiracy's obvious need for some drastic means of checking the growth of American patriotism, there is the consideration that Kennedy was rapidly becoming a political liability. Despite the best efforts of the lie-machines, it was clear that his popularity was diminishing so rapidly that some observers doubted whether even the most cunningly contrived and timed "crisis" could procure his re-election. His conduct was exciting ever increasing disgust even among the credulous; and what was worse, the vast cesspool in Washington was beginning to leak badly.

The bandits of the New Frontier, of whom Billie Sol Estes was but a puny specimen, had operated a little too openly. It had not been possible entirely to conceal the theft of wheat worth $32 million in a single raid or the probable "disappearance" of another $109 million in the same way. It had not been possible completely to suppress the TFX scandal, which would incense the entire nation if it were really exposed; it had not been possible to prevent the public from finding out *something* about little Bobby Baker; and a hundred other boils of corruption (including, it is rumored, some murders thus far successfully disguised as "accidental deaths") are ready to burst at the slightest pressure. Only the most desperate exertions, involving the *personal* intervention of two of the most prominent members of the Administration, have kept the lid—precariously and temporarily—on the modernized badger game that is operated (at the taxpayers' expense and partly on government property) to entrap and subject to blackmail members of Congress not responsive to bribery and other routine pressures from the Administration. There are rumors that an even more filthy scandal, involving both sadistic sexual perversions and the use of governmental powers for the importation and distribution of hallucinatory narcotics, is simmering dangerously near to the surface. I am told that documentary evidence of secret shipments of secret munitions of war to the Soviet by the Administration in treasonable defiance of law is available in a place in which it is secure from both burglary and bribery. Even so minor a matter as the recent exposure of "scientists" in the employ of the Department of Health, Education and Welfare as having forged spectrographic data for use in a smear-job on an American physician disquieted some theretofore complacent and somnolent citizens. For aught I know to the contrary, the assassination of Kennedy may have been necessary as the *only* means of avoiding, or even long deferring, national scandal so flagrant as to shock the whole of our brainwashed and hypnotized populace back to sanity.

In summary, then, there is not a single indication that the Conspiracy did not plan and carry out the assassination of Kennedy. On the other hand, there is evidence which very strongly suggests that it did.

First of all, there is the suspicious celerity with which the broadcasting agency sardonically called Voice of America, Tass in Moscow, Earl Warren, and many publicists and politicians noted for their services to the Conspiracy in the past, began to screech that the murder was the work of "right-wing extremists" almost as soon as the shot was fired. One is justified in asking whether the leaders of this chorus went into action as soon as they received news *that they were expecting.* Or, if they did not know the precise moment, were they not prepared in advance for news of that kind? Is it conceivable that the same story would have occurred independently to so many different persons, however intense their hatred of the American people, or that they would have dared to announce *as fact* a malicious conjecture, if they had no assurance that their statements would be confirmed by "evidence" to be discovered subsequently? Not even the most addle-pated emulator of Sherlock Holmes would pretend to identify a murderer without a single clue. But the screechers went much farther than that: What they said was the precise *opposite* of what was suggested by the first indications available (the arrest of a Negro, reported on the radio while the Presidential automobile was starting for the hospital)—an indication which, although it later proved to be wrong, no prudent person could have disregarded at the time, unless he had assurance, from some source that he trusted, that contrary indications would soon be produced.

Persons whose business it is to tamper with the news are naturally accustomed to lying, but even they do not lightly take the risk of being caught promptly in a particularly improbable and offensive lie. The case of Earl Warren is even more puzzling. No one would suspect him of concern for truth, but surely the Chief Justice of the Supreme Court must be shrewd enough not to make allegations without some reason to believe that he will be able to produce some shreds of "evidence" to support them.

It seems that preparations had been made for rioting and murder throughout the country. Americans known to be opponents of the Conspiracy, including General Walker, prominent members of The John Birch Society, and leaders of other conservative organizations, began to receive threats of death by telephone from creatures who somehow knew that Kennedy was dead *before* he reached the hospital. In many communities, mobs composed of the dregs of humanity and openly proposing to burn the homes and murder the families of known conservatives, began to form in the evening, as though in obedience to orders that had not been countermanded to all sectors. I do not suggest that the local vermin were entrusted with a foreknowledge of precisely what was to happen in Dallas, but it seems very likely that they had been prepared to respond to a signal and told what to do when the signal came.

10

To the Negroes of America

Robert Welch

Wake up, my misguided friends!

They really do think you are stupid. And some of you seem determined to prove that *they* are right.

Enough of you, in fact, to make all of you run a terrible risk. For *they* are making some of you believe their vicious lies. And *they* are thus leading all of you straight into the gates of this hell on earth which *they* have planned.

Stop a minute, my fellow citizens of the greatest country on earth. Indeed, stop twenty minutes to consider some of the plain facts to which *they* are making you close your eyes. There are now about twenty million of you on American soil. You first became masters of your own fate, as four and one-half million penniless former slaves, only a hundred years ago. Let's take a look together at what you have been able to accomplish in *only three generations*.

We must gather our facts out of a vast confusion of statistics. So we cannot guarantee precise accuracy. We have done our homework properly, however. The figures used are as honest and dependable as we could arrive at from the sources available. Besides, we are simply trying to tell a story. And it is a true story, whether all of the details are exact to the third decimal place or not. We think it is an amazing and a happy story. Also, it is a story of which both you, and your country as a whole, can be very proud.

Suppose you think of yourselves, for the minute—*and purely for statistical purposes*—almost as if you were a separate nation. And

---

SOURCE: Robert Welch, *To the Negroes of America.* Copyright 1967 by Robert Welch. Repristed by permission of the author.

let's call this imaginary nation *Our Negro Population*. Then let's compare it, on both material and spiritual levels, with all of the other 120 nations on earth outside of the United States. In doing so, please keep constantly in mind the population of some of these other countries, such as the following: Great Britain, 52 million; France, 49 million; Soviet Russia, 230 million; Japan, 98 million; India, 472 million. And you have only twenty million, to compete with these numbers in possessions and accomplishments.

Let's look first at the simplest and easiest of the measures of material progress. *Our Negro Population* stands fifth, for instance, among all of these other nations of the world (regardless of size) in the ownership of automobiles. Or, to put it another way, you—the twenty million Negroes of America—own more than twice as many automobiles as Albania, Bulgaria, Czechoslovakia, East Germany, Hungary, Poland, Yugoslavia, and all of Soviet Russia combined.

In the census year of 1960, *Our Negro Population* would have ranked tenth among the other nations of the world in radio sets owned, and sixth in the ownership of television sets. As to households with bathrooms, percentage-wise *Our Negro Population* is seventh among these 120 nations. Also, almost exactly fifty percent of the Negro households in the United States have washing machines. And since there are not enough of these very useful contraptions in most other countries for there to be any satisfactory statistics about them, we strongly suspect that *Our Negro Population* would rank very near the top on this list for the whole world.

Some of the more basic figures are hard to nail down. We cannot give you the value, for instance, of all the goods and services produced by *Our Negro Population*. For there is no way to determine what part of our "gross national product" is turned out by Negroes. We are unable to arrive at anything more than a careful estimate of the total wealth of *Our Negro Population,* but believe it would stand somewhere between tenth and twentieth on that worldwide list. With regard to average income per person, *Our Negro Population* stands somewhere around fifth among all of the other nations. There are some published tables which show that the total money income of *Our Negro Population* stands about tenth in this list, regardless of the size of all the other nations. And there is a final indicator, in this area of material standards, about which we *can* be more precise. It is that between 35% and 38% of all Negro households in America own the homes in which they live. And we believe *that* to be a very high figure for any people in any country in the world.

But let's get away from material things, and glance at some spiritual needs. The comparisons should certainly please you. Some years ago, for instance, a British paper discovered and published the fact that a larger percentage of American Negroes get college educations than the percentage of Englishmen. This surprised many people—including the English! But the actual facts are much more amazing. For they show that *Our Negro Population* has nearly twice as many students in colleges as all of Great Britain with its fifty-two million people. And approximately the same ratio holds when we deal with the annual crop of *college graduates* instead of merely the number of students enrolled.

The climax of this comparison comes, however, when we look at these percentages throughout the world. In 1960 the 711,618 college students in Japan came to about 72/100th of one percent of the population. The 937,442 college students in India equalled 21/100ths of one percent. We'll not go through the list. And frankly we do not know how reliable the statistics are for such countries as India or Soviet Russia—or until we come to Western Europe. But for both France and Western Germany the college students constitute about one-half of one percent of the population. Please note, therefore, that the 232,278 American Negroes enrolled in all American colleges in 1963 amounted to over 1.1% of *Our Negro Population*. So we make a rather astounding discovery. It is that, outside of the United States as a whole, *the American Negroes have the highest percentage of their number attending college of any people in the world.*

Finally, in this statistical workout, let's look at another truly amazing comparison. The United States has more Protestant churches, by a huge margin, than any other country. Great Britain (or the United Kingdom, by which we mean England, Scotland, Wales, and Northern Ireland) comes second. But *Our Negro Population* alone runs neck and neck with Great Britain, and just ahead of it—both having about fifty-five thousand Protestant churches. Now Great Britain is predominantly Protestant. So are the twenty million American Negroes. Yet they have slightly more churches for their dominant religion than does Great Britain with its fifty-two million inhabitants. And again, in this category, *Our Negro Population* leads all the countries of the world except the United States as a whole.

All of this is a noble achievement, my friends. It has taken toil and frugality and ambition and patience on the part of countless thousands of Negroes themselves. It has taken the good will and the helping hand of the white people among whom you have lived. And above all it has taken a glorious combination of freedom and opportunity. These have been provided by the American system in greater measure during the last hundred years than anywhere else on earth at any time in human history.

For—note carefully—what we are talking about is how far you American Negroes have climbed, starting from scratch only a hundred years ago; not just in comparison with the Negro people elsewhere, but in comparison with the *total* population of the most advanced countries of the globe. And nowhere else but in the United States of America could you possibly have made this progress in *only three generations*.

Yet some of you are beginning to listen to rabble-rousing pro-Communist criminals who want you to rise up and play a leading role in destroying this whole great American system! Don't listen, my friends. These Communists and their dupes are simply trying to *use* you. They want you to help them to create the bitterness and turmoil and anarchy which they need. For out of the resulting chaos *they* hope to bring forth and impose on all of us together the brutal tyranny of their Communist rule.

These criminal conspirators try to foment dissatisfaction among you by comparing your lot with that of the American whites. But the white people of the United States have had well over three hundred years in which to acquire property and education and stability. You have had only one hundred. So what the Communists are really saying is that these white people should have *given* you outright enough of *their* possessions to make yours equal with their own. But you do not believe in such Communist nonsense any more than we do. Would you like to have a Communist one-world government take *your* automobiles and *your* radio sets and *your* savings accounts and divide them among the people who have none—in Nigeria, or India, or Red China. It is exactly what *they* plan, my friends, and are trying to get you to advocate in theory.

This Communist policy of "sharing the wealth" always leads in practice to an equal distribution of *poverty for all*. There is not a Communist nation on earth which can even feed itself properly. In most of them, right now, about one-third of the people are being kept above a starvation diet by wheat and other grain from "capitalistic" nations like the United States and Canada. Do you want to be *used* to bring about that same condition of *equality* and *poverty* in our country, and all over the earth?

Actually, what the white people of America have done is far better than "sharing their wealth" with you. They have given you the opportunity to earn, create, and acquire wealth of your own. Already your property and education and spiritual endowment place *Our Negro Population* among the top five nations of the world, by almost any combination of valid measurements. And this is *oppression?!* Do not let them make fools of you, my fellow Americans, as they have done to so many millions elsewhere to serve their criminal purposes.

The Communists are trying to make you hate the *present* white people of America because their ancestors held your ancestors as slaves. Stop and think, my friends. Slavery was practiced everywhere in the world in those days, on white people as well as black people. And it was the black chieftains of your own race in Africa who captured your forefathers and sold them into slavery. It was the white people of America who finally took the lead for the whole world in completely abolishing the curse of slavery. Of all of this the American Negroes were fully and gratefully aware until the Communists began to try to arouse bitterness among you with their vicious lies. Are you going to fall for such cruel and dangerous propaganda?

Of course there are agitators now trying to stir up the white people to hate *all* Negroes because of the riots being fomented by Negro trouble makers. This is all part of the Communist game. Many of us are doing all we can to offset and expose this cruel and cunning strategy. About a dozen years ago I wrote *A Letter To The South,* in which I pleaded with the good white people of our Dixie states not to blame the Negroes of their respective communities for all of the turmoil and crime which we could foresee was on the way, but to place this blame squarely where it belonged, on the shoulders of the Communists. The pamphlet has had wide distribution. And while it probably played only a very small part in the total development, your white neighbors in the South have, as a general rule, adopted this attitude. Now I plead with you, our Negro fellow citizens, to show equal wisdom, morality, patience, and common sense.

Shameless liars like M[artin] L[uther] King, foreign trouble-makers like Stokely Carmichael, perverted characters like Bayard Rustin, would-be commissars like Walter Reuther, and dozens of other agitators—white as well as black—are working ceaselessly to have you arise against your present "bondage" (!), and seek "freedom" (!), or "liberation" (!). Right on their face these slogans and expressions are all parts of a Communist *Big Lie,* of the kind that is used

To the Negroes of America 99

by Communists everywhere. They have no real relationship at all to your actual situation.

Look at the facts. You can exercise all the rights of citizenship to whatever extent you have the wish to do so. You can occupy *any* office in government, or in national organizations and associations, for which your ambition, your labor, and your political skill may qualify you. In fact, most of the white people in most of our country today bend over backwards to help to get Negroes promoted to higher jobs or positions just as fast as their qualifications will permit. And this is *"bondage,"* my friends? Don't let them make you sound ridiculous, or childish.

Unlike the people in most of the rest of the contemporary world, you are absolutely free to go where you please, work where you please, and spend your money where and how you please. Today even an Englishman cannot take but a very small amount of his own money out of his own country for a short vacation. You have no such restrictions on your movements, or your pleasures, or your ambitions of any kind. And yet this is a condition in which you must demand and fight for *"freedom"*? Don't be absurd, or let the criminal agitators make you so.

There are scores of Negro millionaires in the United States today who employ hundreds or even thousands of white people in their successful businesses. In fact, there are undoubtedly more Negro men than there are white women running really sizable business organizations in our country at the present time. And in both cases the limiting factors are simply individual ability and personal inclination. Yet this is *"slavery,"* from which you must fight to be *"free"*? Just how crazy, or gullible, do *they* think you are?

Most of the furor over your grievances has been created by the Communists. And as soon as any real grievance is overcome, *they* invent an artificial new one to take its place. But maybe you think there are still honest grievances and damaging discriminations which should be eliminated. And maybe there really are. Should you throw away the tremendous advance you were making and all of America was making in this respect before the Communists stirred up the storm?

Your greatest Negro magazine said truthfully some dozen years ago that the United States had made more progress in solving a difficult racial problem than any other nation on earth. Are you going to help our Communist enemies to sink a great ship, on the pretense that this is the only way of washing a few splotches off the deck? Or should you follow the counsel of my good friend, a Negro publisher named Al Smith? He carries in big type on the front page of every issue of his weekly newspaper this sage advice:

> In America Our First Job Is To Stop And Rout The Communists. Then All Other Problems, Including Racial Problems, Can Be Settled In Peace And Freedom.

About three years ago the Communists picked the small city of Americus, Georgia for destruction. It was to be "torn apart" and "torn down" by racial strife. For about three months of rising tensions and bitterness and turmoil (including vandalism and even murder), it was anybody's guess as to whether or not the agitators would make good on their threat.

During those three months the members of The John Birch Society, organizing other good citizens into committees to help them, appealed by every means possible to the residue of good will between the races; and constantly preached through every medium that "love not hate" was the Christian and the American way of life. And finally, when the climax came and passed, even representatives of the U.S. Department of Commerce stated publicly that it was these actives of The John Birch Society which had saved Americus from the horrible holocaust.

We, the good white people of America, do not want our cities to be burned, our country torn to pieces, and the ruins taken over by the Communists. We know that you, the Negro citizens of America, do not want this either. But you are being deceived and inflamed today by Communist lies, in the hope that you will actually help the Communist-led agitators to achieve those results.

Wake up, my friends. Stop listening to these voices of Satan, which preach the Communist theme of *hatred* as the very core of their strategy. Go to work to make all other good people of your race understand how they are being used as fools, and snared by Communist bait.

Wherever doubt exists, remember just one rule. It is the one we referred to above which saved Americus, and can still save all of America. It is a very simple rule: *Not hatred but love is the Christian and the American way of life.* And good will towards all men of all races is as much a part of the greatness of America as are its prosperity and its freedom.

This is our America. It is your country, and mine, and the last best hope of all mankind. Let's stand up and save it together, at whatever cost in labor, and sacrifice, and dedication.

Part Three

Sources—The New Left

The internal heterogeneity and ideological elusiveness of the new left movement is readily apparent in the writings of the next group of authors. Several of them probe the meaning of the new left in an introspective, philosophical spirit, while others address themselves to some of the specific political and historical events that lead them to the conclusion that American society is in a state of crisis. The tone of crisis orientation clearly reveals radical perceptions of the movement and revolutionary implications for the society of which it is a part.

CONTRIBUTORS

C. Wright Mills: Late professor of sociology at Columbia University, is the author of *White Collar, The Marxists, The New Collar,* and *Images of Man.* Frequently read by new left intellectuals, his more controversial works include *The Power Elite, The Causes of World War Three,* and *Listen Yankee.*

Mark Rudd: A leader of the revolutionary Weatherman faction of Students for a Democratic Society. A former student at Columbia, he was at one time the leader of its SDS chapter and played a central role in the 1968 campus turmoil at that institution.

James Forman: Gained initial prominence as president of the board of directors of the Student Nonviolent Coordinating Committee. More recently, he has been a founder and principal spokesman of the National Black Economic Development Conference. His militant demands for financial reparations from American churches as partial payment for the past slavery and oppression of black Americans have stirred considerable controversy.

Huey Newton: A cofounder and Minister of Defense of the Black Panther Party. A militant voice in the black power movement, he has delivered many speeches and written a variety of articles on the political psychology and future of black–white race relations.

Carl Oglesby: A former president of Students for a Democratic Society. As a leading spokesman for the new left movement, he has made numerous public appearances on college campuses and has published a variety of commentaries on radical politics and American society. He is coauthor of *Containment and Change*.

Herbert Marcuse: Is professor of philosophy at the University of California at San Diego. He has taught previously at Columbia, Harvard, and Yale. Many members of the new left movement in the United States have been influenced by his writings, for example *Reason and Revolution, Eros and Civilization, Essay on Liberation,* and *One-Dimensional Man*.

11

To the British Left: The Need for Utopianism

C. Wright Mills

It is no exaggeration to say that since the end of World War II in Britain and the United States smug conservatives, tired liberals and disillusioned radicals have carried on a weary discourse in which issues are blurred and potential debate muted; the sickness of complacency has prevailed, the bipartisan banality flourished. There is no need—[. . .]—to explain again why all this has come about among "people in general" in the NATO countries; but it may be worthwhile to examine one style of cultural work that is in effect an intellectual celebration of apathy.

Many intellectual fashions, of course, do just that; they stand in the way of a release of the imagination—about the cold war, the Soviet bloc, the politics of peace, about any new beginnings at home and abroad. But the fashion I have in mind is the weariness of many NATO intellectuals with what they call "ideology," and their proclamation of "the end of ideology." So far as I know, this began in the mid-fifties, mainly in intellectual circles more or less associated with the Congress for Cultural Freedom and the magazine *Encounter*. Reports on the Milan Conference of 1955 heralded it; since then, many cultural gossips have taken it up as a posture and an unexamined slogan. Does it amount to anything?

Its common denominator is not liberalism as a political philosophy, but the liberal rhetoric, become formal and sophisticated and

---

SOURCE: C. W. Mills, "Letter to the New Left," *New Left Review*, September-October, 1960. Reprinted by permission of *New Left Review*, London.

used as an uncriticised weapon with which to attack Marxism. In the approved style, various of the elements of this rhetoric appear simply as snobbish assumptions. Its sophistication is one of tone rather than of ideas: in it, the *New Yorker* style of reportage has become politically triumphant. The disclosure of fact—set forth in a bright-faced or in a dead-pan manner—is the rule. The facts are duly weighed, carefully balanced, always hedged. Their power to outrage, their power truly to enlighten in a political way, their power to aid decision, even their power to clarify some situation—all that blunted or destroyed.

So reasoning collapses into reasonableness. By the more naive and snobbish celebrants of complacency, arguments and facts of a displeasing kind are simply ignored; by the more knowing, they are duly recognised, but they are neither connected with one another nor related to any general view. Acknowledged in a scattered way, they are never put together: to do so is to risk being called, curiously enough, "one-sided."

This refusal to relate isolated facts and fragmentary comment with the changing institutions of society makes it impossible to understand the structural realities which these facts might reveal; the longer-run trends of which they might be tokens. In brief, fact and idea are isolated, so the real questions are not even raised, analysis of the meanings of fact not even begun.

Practitioners of the no-more-ideology school do of course smuggle in general ideas under the guise of reportage, by intellectual gossip, and by their selection of the notions they handle. Ultimately, the end-of-ideology is based upon a disillusionment with any real commitment to socialism in any recognisable form. *That* is the only "ideology" that has really ended for these writers. But with its ending, *all* ideology, they think, has ended. *That* ideology they talk about; their own ideological assumptions, they do not.

Underneath this style of observation and comment there is the assumption that in the West there are no more real issues or even problems of great seriousness. The mixed economy plus the welfare state plus prosperity—that is the formula. US capitalism will continue to be workable; the welfare state will continue along the road to ever greater justice. In the meantime, things everywhere are very complex, let us not be careless, there are great risks ...

This posture—one of "false consciousness" if there ever was one —stands in the way, I think, of considering with any chances of success what may be happening in the world.

First and above all, it does rest upon a simple provincialism. If the phrase "the end of ideology" has any meaning at all, it pertains to self-selected circles of intellectuals in the richer countries. It is in fact merely their own self-image. The total population of these countries is a fraction of mankind; the period during which such a posture has been assumed is very short indeed. To speak in such terms of much of Latin-America, Africa, Asia, the Soviet block is merely ludicrous. Anyone who stands in front of audiences—intellectual or mass—in any of these places and talks in such terms will merely be shrugged off (if the audience is polite) or laughed at out loud (if the audience is more candid and knowledgeable). The end-of-ideology is a slogan of complacency, circulating among the prematurely middle-aged, centred in the present, and in the rich Western societies. In the final analysis, it also rests upon a disbelief in the shaping by men of their own futures—as history and as biography. It is a consensus of a few provincials about their own immediate and provincial position.

Second, the end-of-ideology is of course itself an ideology—a fragmentary one, to be sure, and perhaps more a mood. The end-of-ideology is in reality the ideology of an ending: the ending of political reflection itself as a public fact. It is a weary know-it-all justification—by tone of voice rather than by explicit argument—of the cultural and political default of the NATO intellectuals.

All this is just the sort of thing that I at least have always objected to, and do object to, in the "socialist realism" of the Soviet Union.

There too, criticism of milieux are of course permitted—but they are not to be connected with criticism of the structure itself: one may not question "the system." There are no "antagonistic contradictions."

There too, in novels and plays, criticisms of characters, even of party members, are permitted—but they must be displayed as "shocking exceptions": they must be seen as survivals from the old order, not as systematic products of the new.

There too, pessimism is permitted—but only episodically and only within the context of the big optimism: the tendency is to confuse any systematic or structural criticism with pessimism itself. So they admit criticism, first of this and then of that: but engulf them all by the long-run historical optimism about the system as a whole and the goals proclaimed by its leaders.

I neither want nor need to overstress the parallel, yet in a recent series of interviews in the Soviet Union concerning socialist realism I was very much struck by it. In Uzbekistan and Georgia as well as in

Russia, I kept writing notes to myself, at the end of recorded interviews: "This man talks in a style just like Arthur Schlesinger Jr." "Surely this fellow's the counterpart of Daniel Bell, except not so—what shall I say?—so gossipy; and certainly neither so petty nor so vulgar as the more envious status-climbers. Perhaps this is because here they are not thrown into such a competitive status-panic about the ancient and obfuscating British models of prestige." The would-be enders of ideology, I kept thinking, "Are they not the self-coordinated, or better the fashion-coordinated, socialist realists of the NATO world?" And: "Check this carefully with the files of *Encounter* and *The Reporter*." I have now done so; it's the same kind of . . . thing.

Certainly there are many differences—above all, the fact that socialist realism is part of an official line; the end-of-ideology is self-managed. But the differences one knows. It is more useful to stress the parallels—and the generic fact that both of these postures stand opposed to radical criticisms of their respective societies.

In the Soviet Union, only political authorities at the top—or securely on their way up there—can seriously tamper with structural questions and ideological lines. These authorities, of course, are much more likely to be intellectuals (in one or another sense of the word—say a man who actually writes his own speeches) than are American politicians. . . . Moreover, such Soviet authorities, since the death of Stalin, *have* begun to tamper quite seriously with structural questions and basic ideology—although for reasons peculiar to the tight and official joining of culture and politics in their set-up, they must try to disguise this fact.

The end-of-ideology is very largely a mechanical reaction—not a creative response—to the ideology of Stalinism. As such it takes from its opponent something of its inner quality. What does it all mean? That these people have become aware of the uselessness of Vulgar Marxism, but not yet aware of the uselessness of the liberal rhetoric.

But the most immediately important thing about the "end-of-ideology" is that it *is* merely a fashion, and fashions change. Already this one is on its way out. Even a few Diehard Anti-Stalinists are showing signs of a reappraisal of their own past views; some are even beginning to recognize publicly that Stalin himself no longer runs the Soviet party and state. They begin to see the poverty of their comfortable ideas as they come to confront Khrushchev's Russia.

We who have been consistently radical in the moral terms of our work throughout the postwar period are often amused nowadays that various writers—sensing another shift in fashion—begin to call upon intellectuals to work once more in ways that are politically explicit. But we shouldn't be merely amused—we ought to try to make their shift more than a fashion change.

The end-of-ideology is on the way out because it stands for the refusal to work out an explicit political philosophy. And alert men everywhere today do feel the need of such a philosophy. What we should do is to continue directly to confront this need. In doing so, it may be useful to keep in mind that to have a working political philosophy means to have a philosophy that enables you to work. And for that, at least four kinds of work are needed, each of them at once intellectual and political.

In these terms, think—for a moment longer—of the end-of-ideology:

1. It is a kindergarten fact that any political reflection that is of possible public significance is *ideological:* in its terms, policies, institutions, men of power are criticised or approved. In this respect, the end-of-ideology stands, negatively, for the attempt to withdraw oneself and one's work from political relevance; positively, it is an ideology of political complacency which seems the only way now open for many writers to acquiesce in or to justify the *status quo.*

2. So far as orienting *theories* of society and of history are concerned, the end-of-ideology stands for, and presumably stands upon, a fetishism of empiricism: more academically, upon a pretentious methodology used to state trivialities about unimportant social areas; more essayistically, upon a naive journalistic empiricism—which I have already characterised above—and upon a cultural gossip in which "answers" to the vital and pivotal issues are merely assumed. Thus political bias masquerades as epistemological excellence, and there are no orienting theories.

3. So far as the *historic agency of change* is concerned, the end-of-ideology stands upon the identification of such agencies with going institutions; perhaps upon their piecemeal reform, but never upon the search for agencies that might be used or that might themselves make for a structural change of society. The problem of agency is never posed as a problem to solve, as our problem. Instead there is talk of the need to be pragmatic, flexible, open. Surely all this has already been adequately dealt with: such a view makes sense politically only if the blind drift of human affairs is in general beneficent.

4. So far as political and human *ideals* are concerned, the end-of-

ideology stands for a denial of their relevance—except as abstract ikons. Merely to hold such ideals seriously is in this view "utopian."

But enough. Where do *we* stand on each of these four aspects of political philosophy? Various of us are of course at work on each of them, and all of us are generally aware of our needs in regard to each. As for the articulation of ideals: there I think [new left] magazines have done their best work so far. That is *your* meaning—is it not?—of the emphasis upon cultural affairs. As for ideological analysis, and the rhetoric with which to carry it out: I don't think any of us are nearly good enough, but that will come with further advance on the two fronts where we are weakest: theories of society, history, human nature; and the major problem—ideas about the historical agencies of structural change.

We have frequently been told by an assorted variety of dead-end people that the meanings of Left and of Right are now liquidated, by history and by reason. I think we should answer them in such way as this:

The Right, among other things, means—what you are doing, celebrating society as it is, a going concern. Left means, or ought to mean, just the opposite. It means: structural criticism and reportage and theories of society, which at some point or another are focussed politically as demands and programmes. These criticisms, demands, theories, programmes are guided morally by the humanist and secular ideals of Western civilization—above all, reason and freedom and justice. To be "Left" means to connect up cultural with political criticism, and both with demands and programmes. And it means all this inside *every* country of the world.

Only one more point of definition: absence of public issues there may well be, but this *is* not due to any absence of problems or of contradictions, antagonistic and otherwise. Impersonal and structural changes have not eliminated problems or issues. Their absence from many discussions—that *is* an ideological condition, regulated in the first place by whether or not intellectuals detect and state problems as potential *issues* for probable publics, and as *troubles* for a variety of individuals. One indispensable means of such work on these central tasks is what can only be described as ideological analysis. To be actively Left, among other things, is to carry on just such analysis.

To take seriously the problem of the need for a political orientation is not of course to seek for A Fanatical and Apocalyptic Vision, for An Infallible and Monolithic Lever of Change, for Dogmatic Ideology, for A Startling New Rhetoric, for Treacherous Abstractions—and all the other bogeymen of the dead-enders. These are of course "the extremes," the straw men, the red herrings, used by our political enemies as the polar opposite of where they think they stand.

They tell us, for example, that ordinary men can't always be political "heroes." Who said they could? But keep looking around you; and why not search out the conditions of such heroism as men do and might display? They tell us we are too "impatient," that our "pretentious" theories are not well enough grounded. That is true, but neither are they trivial; why don't they get to work, refuting or grounding them? They tell us we "don't really understand" Russia —and China—today. That is true; we don't; neither do they; we are studying it. They tell us we are "ominous" in our formulations. That is true: we do have enough imagination to be frightened—and we don't have to hide it: we are not afraid we'll panic. They tell us we "are grinding axes." Of course we are: we do have, among other points of view, morally grounded ones; and we are aware of them. They tell us, in their wisdom, we don't understand that The Struggle Is Without End. True: we want to change its form, its focus, its object.

We are frequently accused of being "utopian"—in our criticisms and in our proposals; and along with this, of basing our hopes for a New Left *politics* "merely on reason," or more concretely, upon the intelligentsia in its broadest sense.

There is truth in these charges. But must we not ask: what now is really meant by utopian? And: Is not our utopianism a major source of our strength? "Utopian" nowadays I think refers to any criticism or proposal that transcends the up-close milieux of a scatter of individuals: the milieux which men and women can understand directly and which they can reasonably hope directly to change. In this exact sense, our theoretical work is indeed utopian—in my own case, at least, deliberately so. What needs to be understood, and what needs to be changed, is not merely first this and then that detail of some institution or policy. If there is to be a politics of a New Left, what needs to be analysed is the *structure* of institutions, the *foundation* of policies. In this sense, both in its criticisms and in its proposals, our work is necessarily structural—and so, *for us,* just now—utopian.

Which brings us face to face with the most important issue of political reflection—and of political action—in our time: the problem of the historical agency of change, of the social and institutional means of structural change. There are several points about this problem I would like to put to you.

First, the historic agencies of change for liberals of the capitalist societies have been an array of voluntary associations, coming to a political climax in a parliamentary or congressional system. For socialists of almost all varieties, the historic agency has been the working class—and later the peasantry; also parties and unions variously composed of members of the working class or (to blur, for now, a great problem) of political parties acting in its name—"representing its interests."

I cannot avoid the view that in both cases, the historic agency (in the advanced capitalist countries) has either collapsed or become most ambiguous: so far as structural change is concerned, *these* don't seem to be at once available and effective as *our* agency any more. I know this is a debatable point among us, and among many others as well; I am by no means certain about it. But surely the fact of it—if it be that—ought not to be taken as an excuse for moaning and withdrawal (as it is by some of those who have become involved with the end-of-ideology); it ought not to be bypassed (as it is by many Soviet scholars and publicists, who in their reflections upon the course of advanced capitalist societies simply refuse to admit the political condition and attitudes of the working class).

Is anything more certain than that in 1970—indeed this time next year—our situation will be quite different, and—the chances are high —decisively so? But of course, that isn't saying much. The seeming collapse of our historic agencies of change ought to be taken as a problem, an issue, a trouble—in fact, as *the* political problem which *we* must turn into issue and trouble.

Second, is it not obvious that when we talk about the collapse of agencies of change, we cannot seriously mean that such agencies do not exist? On the contrary, the means of history-making—of decision and of the enforcement of decision—have never in world history been so enlarged and so available to such small circles of men on both sides of The Curtains as they now are. My own conception of the shape of power—the theory of the power elite—I feel no need to argue here. This theory has been fortunate in its critics, from the most diverse points of political view, and I have learned from several of these critics. But I have not seen, as of this date, any analysis of the idea that causes me to modify any of its essential features.

The point that is immediately relevant does seem obvious: what is utopian for us is not at all utopian for the presidium of the Central Committee in Moscow, or the higher circles of the Presidency in Washington, or—recent events make evident—for the men of SAC and CIA. The historic agencies of change that have collapsed are those which were at least thought to be open to *the left* inside the advanced Western nations: those who have wished for structural changes of these societies. Many things follow from this obvious fact; of many of them, I am sure, we are not yet adequately aware.

Third, what I do not quite understand about some New Left writers is why they cling so mightily to "the working class" of the advanced capitalist societies as *the* historic agency, or even as the most important agency, in the face of the really impressive historical evidence that now stands against this expectation.

Such a labour metaphysic, I think, is a legacy from Victorian Marxism that is now quite unrealistic.

It is an historically specific idea that has been turned into an a-historical and unspecific hope.

The social and historical conditions under which industrial workers tend to become a class-for-themselves, and a decisive political force, must be fully and precisely elaborated. There have been, there are, there will be such conditions; of course these conditions vary according to national social structure and the exact phase of their economic and political development. Of course we can't "write off the working class." But we must *study* all that, and freshly. Where labour exists as an agency, of course we must work with it, but we must not treat it as The Necessary Lever—as nice old Labour Gentlemen in your country and elsewhere tend to do.

Although I have not yet completed my own comparative studies of working classes, generally it would seem that only at certain (earlier) stages of industrialisation, and in a political context of autocracy, etc., do wage-workers tend to become a class-for-themselves, etc. The "etcs." mean that I can here merely raise the question.

It is with this problem of agency in mind that I have been studying, for several years now, the cultural apparatus, the intellectuals—as a possible, immediate, radical agency of change. For a long time, I was not much happier with this idea than were many of you; but it turns out now, in the spring of 1960, that it may be a very relevant idea indeed.

In the first place, is it not clear that if we try to be realistic in our utopianism—and that is no fruitless contradiction—a writer in our countries on the Left today *must* begin there? For that is what we are, that is where we stand.

In the second place, the problem of the intelligentsia is an extremely complicated set of problems on which rather little factual work has been done. In doing this work, we must—above all—not confuse the problems of the intellectuals of West Europe and North America with those of the Soviet Bloc or with those of the underdeveloped worlds. In each of the three major components of the world's social structure today, the character and the role of the intelligentsia [are] distinct and historically specific. Only by detailed comparative studies of them in all their human variety can we hope to understand any one of them.

In the third place, who is it that is getting fed up? Who is it that is getting disgusted with what Marx called "all the old crap"? Who is it that is thinking and acting in radical ways? All over the world—in the bloc, outside the bloc and in between—the answer's the same: it is the young intelligentsia.

I cannot resist copying out for you, with a few changes, some materials I've just prepared for a 1960 paperback edition of a book of mine on war:

"In the spring and early summer of 1960—more of the returns from the American decision and default are coming in. In Turkey, after student riots, a military junta takes over the state, of late run by Communist Container Menderes. In South Korea too, students and others knock over the corrupt American-puppet regime of Syngman Rhee. In Cuba, a genuinely left-wing revolution begins full-scale economic reorganisation—without the domination of US corporations. Average age of its leaders: about 30—and certainly a revolution without any Labour As Agency. On Taiwan, the eight million Taiwanese under the American-imposed dictatorship of Chiang Kai-shek, with his two million Chinese, grow increasingly restive. On Okinawa—a US military base—the people get their first chance since World War II ended to demonstrate against US seizure of their island: and some students take that chance, snake-dancing and chanting angrily to the visiting President: "Go home, go home—take away your missiles." (Don't worry, 12,000 US troops easily handled the generally grateful crowds; also the President was "spirited out the rear end of the United States compound"—and so by helicopter to the airport.) In Great Britain, from Aldermaston to London, young—but you were there. In Japan, weeks of student rioting succeed in rejecting the President's visit, jeopardise a new treaty with the USA, displace the big-business, pro-American Prime Minister, Kishi. And even in our own pleasant Southland, Negro and white students are—but let us keep that quiet: it really *is* disgraceful.

"That is by no means the complete list; that was yesterday; see today's newspaper. Tomorrow, in varying degree, the returns will be more evident. Will they be evident enough? They will have to be very obvious to attract real American attention: sweet complaints and the voice of reason—these are not enough. In the slum countries of the world today, what are they saying? The rich Americans, they pay attention only to violence—and to money. You don't care what they say, American? Good for you. Still, they may insist; things are no longer under the old control; you're not getting it straight, American: your country—it would seem—may well become the target of a world hatred the like of which the easy-going Americans have never dreamed. Neutralists and Pacifists and Unilateralists and that confusing variety of Leftists around the world—all those tens of millions of people, of course they are misguided, absolutely controlled by small conspiratorial groups of trouble-makers, under direct orders straight from Moscow and Peking. Diabolically omnipotent, it is *they* who create all this messy unrest. It is *they* who have given the tens of millions the absurd idea that they shouldn't want to remain, or to become, the seat of American nuclear bases—those gay little outposts of American civilisation. So now they don't want U-2's on their territory; so now they want to contract out of the American military machine; they want to be neutral among the crazy big antagonists. And they don't want their own societies to be militarised.

"But take heart, American: you won't have time to get really bored with your friends abroad: they won't be your friends much longer. You don't need *them;* it will all go away; don't let them confuse you."

Add to that: In the Soviet bloc, who is it that has been breaking out of apathy? It has been students and young professors and writers; it has been the young intelligentsia of Poland and Hungary, and of Russia too. Never mind that they've not won; never mind that there are other social and moral types among them. First of all, it has been these types. But the point is clear—isn't it?

That's why we've got to study these new generations of intellectuals around the world as real live agencies of historic change. Forget Victorian Marxism, except whenever you need it; and read Lenin again (be careful)—Rosa Luxemburg, too.

"But it's just some kind of moral upsurge, isn't it?" Correct. But under it: no apathy. Much of it is direct non-violent action, and it seems to be working, here and there. Now we must learn from their practice and work out with them new forms of action.

"But it's all so ambiguous. Turkey, for instance. Cuba, for instance." Of course it is; history-making is always ambiguous; wait a bit; in the meantime, *help* them to focus their moral upsurge in less ambiguous political ways; work out with them the ideologies, the strategies, the theories that will help them consolidate their efforts: new theories of structural changes of and by human societies in our epoch.

"But it's utopian, after all, isn't it?" No—not in the sense you mean. Whatever else it may be, it's not that: tell it to the students of Japan.

Isn't all this, isn't it something of what we are trying to mean by the phrase, "The New Left"? Let the old men ask sourly, "Out of Apathy—into what?" The Age of Complacency is ending. Let the old women complain wisely about "the end of ideology." We are beginning to move again.

12

Fascism and Imperialism

Mark Rudd

Increasingly, movements of the oppressed peoples of the world for national liberation—especially the struggles of the Vietnamese and of the black and brown nations within the United States—have been countered with more and more violent repression by the U.S. ruling class. This repression constitutes one part of what can only be described as all-out attacks on the oppressed peoples—sometimes reaching genocidal proportions, as in Vietnam and many black communities in the U.S. The burn-and-destroy tactics of the U.S. armed forces in Vietnam can only be compared to the fascist German genocide committed against the Jews and others during the Nazi era in Europe.

As the attacks on the imperialist system grow to more threatening proportions, the use of violence and terror by the ruling class grows. It is not, however, the case that new "right" or "conservative" elements seize power from the old, "liberal," "democratic," "normal" rulers: the terror merely represents a switch in tactics by our old acquaintances, the imperialist bourgeoisie.

"The development of fascism assume(s) different forms in different countries . . . This does not prevent fascism, when its position becomes particularly acute, from endeavoring to extend its basis and without altering its class nature, combining open terrorist dictatorship with a crude plan of parliamentarism." (Dimitroff, the United Front Against Fascism.) In this country the state apparatus for fascism already exists. Economic, military, and political power are already concentrated into the hands of a small, unified ruling class. To

SOURCE: Mark Rudd, "Fight Fascism: Bring the War Home," *New Left Notes,* July 23, 1969, pp. 1–2.

the extent that there are differences within this class, they are worked out in committee rooms in the Pentagon, not in the halls of Congress or on convention floors.

Certain appearances of bourgeois democracy remain: elections, Congress, jury trials, but these are a smokescreen, a swindle.

The Carrot and the Stick; the Hangman and the Priest

The bourgeois ruling class always has at its disposal two types of seemingly contradictory tactics: first is the tactic of deception, co-optation, and even reform. Schools and the media teach out-and-out lies about democracy, the American way, opportunity, and a thousand other myths which both reinforce confidence in and allegiance to the imperialist system, and also promote the specific mechanisms of control, such as the teaching of racist history which only divides workers further. Another part of the first tactic is the granting, up to a point, of certain reforms, such as social welfare, to make it look as if the system is capable of self-repair or even evolution ("peaceful progress").

The other tactic is the "hard" one, the stick which is used when the carrot fails to get Vietnamese, or blacks, or white mother-country workers to pull the imperialist cart. Beatings, burnings, rape, murder have always been used against black people (starting on the coasts of Africa) to force their enslavement. When AID money fails to create the "progress" (to hold back national liberation movements) the U.S. desires in Latin America, in go the Green Berets. When striking workers refuse to obey court orders (the law), troops or police have, throughout American history, been used against them. The violence of the ruling class is as American ("normal") as cherry pie or lying newspapers or "social security" you can't live on.

Imperialism is a system not just because it integrates mother country and colonies. Also, because it integrates the use of the two tactics simultaneously. Thus, every bourgeois society needs both teachers and cops. It also needs priests and hangmen. If one fails, they use the other.

So it is the same with broad tactics of the imperialist class against those who fight for freedom and for the destruction of that class. Nelson Rockefeller, "liberal" governor of New York, proposes minimum wages and also puts Martin Sostre, a black freedom fighter, behind bars for four years. Liberal Robert Kennedy shakes hands with residents of the black communities, sponsors "rehabilitation" programs, and also helps send troops to invade and blockade socialist

Cuba and later votes for appropriations to send troops to Vietnam, Chicago, and Watts. Even Hitler, while he killed millions, created the Volkswagen, the "People's Car."

To believe that different parts of the bourgeoisie, more liberal vs. more reactionary elements, represent the two tactics is tantamount to committing historical suicide. For while a "revolutionary" organization is out drumming up working-class support for Lyndon B. Johnson, the liberal peace candidate, against the right-wing, reactionary Barry Goldwater, Johnson is secretly planning the escalation of the war in Vietnam, more repression against black and brown people, and wage freezes and surtaxes for all workers. The choice of which tactic the ruling class will follow is not up to the whim of individuals or even whole parts of that class, no matter how slick and "liberal" the Eastern capitalists are. The use of fascist terror, of violent repression, occurs as a historical necessity, the necessity of a class protecting itself from destruction.

There will be debate, as between McCarthy and Humphrey, as to which tactic to follow at a given time (withdrawal from Vietnam with continued economic and political control vs. continued fascist military aggression), but revolutionaries should not enter into this debate; they should know that even the "progressive" bourgeoisie will turn on revolutionary peoples and the working class generally when the attack on imperialism grows strong enough. Ultimately, it is not the McCarthys who determine U.S. imperialist policy in Vietnam or in the black nation, but rather the oppressed peoples of the world, the people of Vietnam and of the black nation, who will be waging anti-imperialist war, and thus force the imperialists to lash back with armed force. With his back to the wall, the aggressor has only one last response—frenzied murder, jailings, bombings. The "soft" tactic must fail, so the "hard" tactic will be used. Better public relations by Kennedy-McCarthy cannot feed the starving people of the world. Thus, force is their only weapon.

There are two more characteristics to note about American fascism. One is that the fascist, terrorist tactics are no less legal than the soft, deceptive, reformist ones. Neither were Hitler's emergency laws illegal. Fascism, especially in America, inevitably takes a legal cover: currently the linking of the two concepts in the ruling class's battle cry, "law and order." Law always serves the interests of the class in power.

Besides fascism being legal, it can also be directed. It does not have to be "indiscriminate." For example, the black colony can come under attack, as has happened all over the country, while the white neighborhoods are not necessarily affected. It may be, however, that terror will come down in broad, indiscriminate forms in those places where the movement in the mother country has developed into a serious threat, as in Berkeley. This has happened in Vietnam and has contributed to the development of resistance among masses of non-peasant, non-proletarian Vietnamese. Fascism in America recently has been isolated to specific revolutionary and potentially revolutionary targets; this is especially true of terror used against the black and brown nations, which only rarely has spilled over into the white population.

This does not mean that the apparatus for fascism does not exist in the white mother country. Quite the opposite: counter-insurgency experience gained against the blacks has already sharpened the ability of the repressive forces of the state to deal with rebellion among students, youth, and workers in the mother country. But terror tactics have been used relatively sparingly, as at Columbia University in 1968, San Francisco State and Berkeley in '68 and '69, Richmond Oil Strike and other militant strikes; in almost all cases bourgeois civil liberties were reinstated after the rebellion. This is not at all the case in the black communities, where the police act as occupation troops both within and without the law, and where white racist courts hold black prisoners for impossible ransom on no legal grounds. The New York Panther 21 are each being held on $100,000 bail.

The development of a unified ruling class, with a unified machinery, means, among other things, that local pig forces have more political power in practice than the local mayor; a nation-wide pig apparatus co-ordinates counter-insurgency and intelligence efforts as well as repressive actions against the people; this is where military, political, and economic power come together in their one mailed fist. The apparatus for genocide exists; it is activated at will; it can be operated alongside elections or without elections, against black and brown people alone, or against all the people, discriminately or indiscriminately.

What Is to Be Done?

The fact that fascism does not yet exist within the white mother country does not in any way mitigate the job of all revolutionaries, white and black. Rather, it puts a special task on the white revolutionaries—to educate the white working class to understand that the black people within the United States, and the Third World peoples outside, are in the forefront of the struggle for the liberation of the entire working class, for the destruction of the imperialist class and its corrupt system; and it is they who face fascist genocide every day. This means we must build a mass anti-imperialist movement around many things—around the fascism aimed at the blacks and Vietnamese which exposes the weaknesses of the imperialist system; around the oppression of white mother-country youth and workers directly caused by the crisis in U.S. imperialism, on issues of the draft, the oppression of women, decaying imperialist schools, the surtax and increasing taxes, the decline in real wages, speed-up, unemployment, greater police control over youth, the ideological and cultural breakdown itself. It means explaining the discontent and hatred people feel toward the "opportunities" and institutions, and the lives which are open to them in America, in terms that bring people into the world-wide anti-imperialist struggle.

Fighting fascism does not in any way mean a cut-back in the political line, say, to fighting for civil liberties against fascist encroachments, or a cut-back in the tactics and militancy of the struggle. It does not mean sacrificing numbers for revolutionary consciousness. To do either would be opportunist and ineffectual in both the short and long runs. Since fascist terror is not spread out evenly or even indiscriminately at this stage, organizing around fascism means winning people to a full anti-imperialist position and raising the level of struggle in order to build a revolutionary fighting force capable of defeating fascism and imperialism; it means creating an understanding of the international nature of the proletarian revolution and of the socialist society to be built on the ruins of this horror.

Developing this internationalist consciousness will not be easy. There are no shortcuts, especially when a rich imperialist system has been able to provide "crumbs off the imperialist table," "white skin privileges," relative advantages of whites in the mother country over the colonized people that help maintain both in slavery. These privileges provide the material basis for racism and national chauvinism, and to say they are in the long run phony privileges is not to deny their reality; rather, job security, higher pay, access to better education, false attitudes of superiority have for the history of American labor (and the entire American people) been the stuff on which racist and pro-imperialist allegiance to the system is based. This is not to say that this false consciousness based on privilege will continue forever, that the working class is "bought off." Rather, it indicates how hard a job mother-country revolutionaries have—to build the working-class, anti-imperialist movement, and that the phenomenon we will have to relate to will be the erosion of privilege and the increased oppression of the people due to the attack on imperialism by the colonized nations. It will also mean we will have to hit out at attitudes and practices of white supremacy, male supremacy, and national chauvinism before a self-conscious anti-imperialist movement can be built. It means a long hard struggle, but one which the people of the world will eventually win.

Ultimately, there are two ways to fight repression. One is to give up, to do just what the bourgeoisie wants, to stop fighting. The other is to fight harder, re-raising the original anti-imperialist issues, gaining a larger and larger mass working-class base, running risks, suffering casualties, trying to defend yourself. A revolutionary, like anyone else, will not live forever. At this stage, he will win or die fighting for the people of the world. A revisionist, on the other hand, is a person who believes he can live forever, who wants a painless, riskless way to the revolution. (Most revisionists have already lived too long anyway.) At this point, our task is to build on as sound a basis as we can. It is to raise and re-raise issues of war, imperialism, racism, and the fascist attacks. We must raise the blacks and the Vietnamese as the vanguards of the revolution. It is to unite all so-called revolutionary organizations around defense of the victims of the fascist attacks, and to fight no less because we are of the white oppressor nation. Ours is to fight just as hard as those in the lead, those like Huey Newton who have taken the barrel end of the ruling class's bag of tricks. Ours is to show the example of whites from the mother country militantly fighting imperialism, militantly allying with the blacks and the other Third World people, deepening the fight against imperialism already under way in the belly of the monster. Ours is to bring the war home!

ALL POWER TO THE PEOPLE.

13

The Black Manifesto

James Forman

We the black people assembled in Detroit, Michigan for the National Black Economic Development Conference are fully aware that we have been forced to come together because racist white America has exploited our resources, our minds, our bodies, our labor. For centuries we have been forced to live as colonized people inside the United States, victimized by the most vicious, racist system in the world. We have helped to build the most industrial country in the world.

We are therefore demanding of the white Christian churches and Jewish synagogues which are part and parcel of the system of capitalism, that they begin to pay reparations to black people in this country. We are demanding $500,000,000 from the Christian white churches and the Jewish synagogues. This total comes to 15 dollars per nigger. This is a low estimate for we maintain there are probably more than 30,000,000 black people in this country. $15 a nigger is not a large sum of money and we know that the churches and synagogues have a tremendous wealth and its membership, white America, has profited and still exploits black people. We are also not unaware that the exploitation of colored peoples around the world is aided and abetted by the white Christian churches and synagogues. This demand for $500,000,000 is not an idle resolution or empty words. Fifteen dollars for every black brother and sister in the United States is only a beginning of the reparations due us as people who have been exploited and degraded, brutalized, killed and perse-

SOURCE: James Forman, speech delivered to the National Black Economic Development Conference, April 26, 1969.

cuted. Underneath all of this exploitation, the racism of this country has produced a psychological effect upon us that we are beginning to shake off. We are no longer afraid to demand our full rights as a people in this decadent society.

We are demanding $500,000,000 to be spent in the following ways:

1. We call for the establishment of a Southern land bank to help our brothers and sisters who have to leave their land because of racist pressure for people who want to establish cooperative farms, but who have no funds. We have seen too many farmers evicted from their homes because they have dared to defy the white racism of this country. We need money for land. We must fight for massive sums of money for this Southern Land Bank. We call for $200,000,000 to implement this program.

2. We call for the establishment of four major publishing and printing industries in the United States to be funded with ten million dollars each. These publishing houses are to be located in Detroit, Atlanta, Los Angeles and New York. They will help to generate capital for further cooperative investments in the black community, provide jobs and an alternative to the white-dominated and controlled printing field.

3. We call for the establishment of four of the most advanced scientific and futuristic audio-visual networks to be located in Detroit, Chicago, Cleveland and Washington, D.C. These TV networks will provide an alternative to the racist propaganda that fills the current television networks. Each of these TV networks will be funded by ten million dollars each.

4. We call for a research skills center which will provide research on the problems of black people. This center must be funded with no less than 30 million dollars.

5. We call for the establishment of a training center for the teaching of skills in community organization, photography, movie making, television making and repair, radio building and repair and all other skills needed in communication. This training center shall be funded with no less then ten million dollars.

6. We recognize the role of the National Welfare Rights Organization and we intend to work with them. We call for ten million dollars to assist in the organization of welfare recipients. We want to organize the welfare workers in this country so that they may de-

mand more money from the government and better administration of the welfare system of this country.

7. We call for $20,000,000 to establish a National Black Labor Strike and Defense Fund. This is necessary for the protection of black workers and their families who are fighting racist working conditions in this country.

8. We call for the establishment of the International Black Appeal (IBA). This International Black Appeal will be funded with no less than $20,000,000. The IBA is charged with producing more capital for the establishment of cooperative business in the United States and in Africa, our Motherland. The International Black Appeal is one of the most important demands that we are making for we know that it can generate and raise funds throughout the United States and help our African brothers. The IBA is charged with three functions and shall be headed by James Forman:

(a) Raising money for the program of the National Black Economic Development Conference
(b) The development of cooperatives in African countries and support of African Liberation movements.
(c) Establishment of a Black Anti-Defamation League which will protect our African image.

9. We call for the establishment of a Black University to be funded with $130,000,000 to be located in the South. Negotiations are presently under way with a Southern University.

10. We demand [allocation of] all unused funds in the planning budget to implement the demands of this conference.

In order to win our demands we are aware that we will have to have massive support, therefore:

(1) We call upon all black people throughout the United States to consider themselves as members of the National Black Economic Development Conference and to act in unity to help force the racist white Christian churches and Jewish synagogues to implement these demands.

(2) We call upon all the concerned black people across the country to contact black workers, black women, black students and the black unemployed, community groups, welfare organizations, teacher organizations, church leaders and organizations explaining how these

demands are vital to the black community of the U.S. Pressure by whatever means necessary should be applied to the white power structure of the racist white Christian churches and Jewish synagogues. All black people should act boldly in confronting our white oppressors and demanding this modest reparation of 15 dollars per black man.

(3) Delegates and members of the National Black Economic Development Conference are urged to call press conferences in the cities and to attempt to get as many black organizations as possible to support the demands of the conference. The quick use of the press in the local areas will heighten the tension and these demands must be attempted to be won in a short period of time, although we are prepared for protracted and long range struggle.

(4) We call for the total disruption of selected church sponsored agencies operating anywhere in the U.S. and the world. Black workers, black women, black students and the black unemployed are encouraged to seize the offices, telephones and printing apparatus of all church sponsored agencies and to hold these in trusteeship until our demands are met.

(5) We call upon all delegates and members of the National Black Economic Development Conference to stage sit-in demonstrations at selected black and white churches. This is not to be interpreted as a continuation of the sit-in movement of the early sixties, but we know that active confrontation inside white churches is possible and will strengthen the possibility of meeting our demands. Such confrontation can take the form of reading the Black Manifesto instead of a sermon or passing it out to church members. The principle of self-defense should be applied if attacked.

(6) On May 4, 1969 or a date thereafter, depending upon local conditions, we call upon black people to commence the disruption of the racist churches and synagogues throughout the United States.

(7) We call [for] . . . a central staff to coordinate the mandate of the conference and to reproduce and distribute in mass literature, leaflets, news items, press releases and other material.

(8) We call upon all delegates to find within the white community those forces which will work under the leadership of blacks to implement these demands by whatever means necessary. By taking such actions, white Americans will demonstrate concretely that they are willing to fight the white skin privilege and the white supremacy and racism which has forced us as black people to make these demands.

(9) We call upon all white Christians and Jews to practice patience, tolerance, understanding and nonviolence as they have encouraged, advised and demanded that we as black people should do throughout our entire enforced slavery in the United States. The true test of their faith and belief in the Cross and the words of the prophets will certainly be put to a test as we seek legitimate and extremely modest reparations for our role in developing the industrial base of the Western world through our slave labor. But we are no longer slaves, we are men and women, proud of our African heritage, determined to have our dignity.

(10) We are so proud of our African heritage and realize concretely that our struggle is not only to make revolution in the United States, but to protect our brothers and sisters in Africa and to help them rid themselves of racism, capitalism, and imperialism by whatever means necessary, including armed struggle. We are and must be willing to fight the defamation of our African image wherever it rears its ugly head. We are therefore charging the Steering Committee to create a Black Anti-Defamation League to be funded by money raised from the International Black Appeal.

(11) We fully recognize that revolution in the United States and Africa, our Motherland, is more than a one-dimensional operation. It will require the total integration of the political, economic, and military components and therefore, we call upon all our brothers and sisters who have acquired training and expertise in the fields of engineering, electronics research, community organization, physics, biology, chemistry, mathematics, medicine, military science and warfare to assist the National Black Economic Development Conference in the implementation of its program.

(12) To implement these demands we must have a fearless leadership. We must have a leadership which is willing to battle the church establishment to implement these demands. To win our demands we will have to declare war on the white Christian churches and synagogues and this means we may have to fight the total government structure of this country. Let no one here think that these demands will be met by our mere stating them. For the sake of the churches and synagogues, we hope that they have the wisdom to understand that these demands are modest and reasonable. But if the white Christians and Jews are not willing to meet our demands through peace and good will, then we declare war and are prepared to fight by whatever means necessary. We are, therefore, proposing the election of the following Steering Committee:

Lucious Walker	Ken Cockrel	Mike Hamlin
Renny Freeman	Chuck Wooten	Len Holt
Luke Tripp	Fannie Lou Hamer	Peter Bernard
Howard Fuller	Julian Bond	Michael Wright
James Forman	Mark Comfort	Muhammed Kenyatta
John Watson	Earl Allen	Mel Jackson
Dan Aldridge	Robert Browne	Howard Moore
John Williams	Vincent Harding	Harold Holmes

Brothers and sisters, we no longer are shuffling our feet and scratching our heads. We are tall, black and proud.

And we say to the white Christian churches and Jewish synagogues, to the government of this country and to all the white racist imperialists who compose it, there is only one thing left that you can do to further degrade black people and that is to kill us. But we have been dying too long for this country. We have died in every war. We are dying in Vietnam today, fighting the wrong enemy.

The new black man wants to live and to live means that we must not become static or merely believe in self-defense. We must boldly go out and attack the white Western world at its power centers. The white Christian churches are another form of government in this country and they are used by the government of this country to exploit the people of Latin America, Asia and Africa, but the day is soon coming to an end. Therefore, brothers and sisters, the demands we make upon the white Christian churches and the Jewish synagogues are small demands. They represent 15 dollars per black person in these United States. We can legitimately demand this from the church power structure. We must demand more from the United States Government.

But to win our demands from the church which is linked up with the United States Government, we must not forget that it will ultimately be by force and power that we will win.

We are not threatening the churches. We are saying that we know the churches came with the military might of the colonizers and have been sustained by the military might of the colonizers. Hence, if the churches in colonial territories were established by military might, we know deep within our hearts that we must be prepared to use force to get our demands. We are not saying that this is the road we want to take. It is not, but let us be very clear that we are not opposed to force and we are not opposed to violence. We were captured in Africa by violence. We were kept in bondage and political servitude and forced to work as slaves by the military machinery and the Christian church working hand in hand.

We recognize that in issuing this manifesto we must prepare for a long range educational campaign in all communities of this country, but we know that the Christian churches have contributed to our oppression in white America. We do not intend to abuse our black brothers and sisters in black churches who have uncritically accepted Christianity. We want them to understand how the racist white Christian church with its hypocritical declarations and doctrines of brotherhood has abused our trust and faith. An attack on the religious beliefs of black people is not our major objective, even though we know that we were not Christians when we were brought to this country, but that Christianity was used to help enslave us. Our objective in issuing this manifesto is to force the racist white Christian church to begin the payment of reparations which are due to all black people, not only by the Church but also by private business and the U.S. Government. We see this focus on the Christian church as an effort around which all black people can unite.

Our demands are negotiable, but they cannot be minimized, they can only be increased and the Church is asked to come up with larger sums of money than we are asking. Our slogans are:

ALL ROADS MUST LEAD TO REVOLUTION
UNITE WITH WHOMEVER YOU CAN UNITE
NEUTRALIZE WHEREVER POSSIBLE
FIGHT OUR ENEMIES RELENTLESSLY
VICTORY TO THE PEOPLE
LIFE AND GOOD HEALTH TO MANKIND
RESISTANCE TO DOMINATION BY THE WHITE CHRISTIAN CHURCHES
   AND THE JEWISH SYNAGOGUES
REVOLUTIONARY BLACK POWER
WE SHALL WIN WITHOUT A DOUBT

14

Succeeding at Revolution

Huey Newton

Most human behavior is learned behavior. Most things the human being learns are gained through an indirect relationship to the object. Humans do not act from instinct as lower animals do. Those things learned indirectly many times stimulate very effective responses to what might be later a direct experience. At this time the black masses are handling the resistance incorrectly. The brothers in East Oakland learned from Watts a means of resistance fighting by amassing the people in the streets, throwing bricks and molotov cocktails to destroy property and create disruption. The brothers and sisters in the streets were herded into a small area by the gestapo police and immediately contained by the brutal violence of the oppressor's storm troops. This manner of resistance is sporadic, short-lived, and costly in violence against the people. This method has been transmitted to all the ghettos of the black nation across the country. The first man who threw a molotov cocktail is not personally known by the masses, but yet the action was respected and followed by the people.

Party Must Provide Leadership

The vanguard party must provide leadership for the people. It must teach the correct strategic methods of prolonged resistance through literature and activities. If the activities of the party are respected by the people, the people will follow the example. This is the primary job of the party. This knowledge will probably be gained second-hand by the masses just as the above mentioned was gained

---

SOURCE: Huey Newton, "In Defense of Self Defense," *New Left Notes*, February 12, 1969. Reprinted by permission of the author.

indirectly. When the people learn that it is no longer advantageous for them to resist by going into the streets in large numbers, and when they see the advantage in the activities of the guerrilla warfare method, they will quickly follow this example.

But first, they must respect the party which is transmitting this message. When the vanguard group destroys the machinery of the oppressor by dealing with him in small groups of three and four, and then escapes the might of the oppressor, the masses will be overjoyed and will adhere to this correct strategy. When the masses hear that a gestapo policeman has been executed while sipping coffee at a counter, and the revolutionary executioners fled without being traced, the masses will see the validity of this type of approach to resistance. It is not necessary to organize thirty million Black people in primary groups of two's and three's, but it is important for the party to show the people how to go about revolution. During slavery, in which no vanguard party existed and forms of communication were severely restricted and insufficient, many slave revolts occurred.

There are basically three ways one can learn: through study, through observation, and through actual experience. The black community is basically composed of activists. The community learns through activity, either through observation of or through participation in the activity. To study and learn is good, but the actual experience is the best means of learning. The party must engage in activities that will teach the people. The black community is basically not a reading community. Therefore it is very significant that the vanguard group first be activists. Without this knowledge of the black community, one could not gain the fundamental knowledge of the black revolution in racist America.

The main function of the party is to awaken the people and to teach them the strategic method of resisting the power structure, which is prepared not only to combat the resistance of the people with massive brutality, but to totally annihilate the black community, the black population.

If it is learned by the power structure that black people have "x" amount of guns in their possession, this will not stimulate the power structure to prepare itself with guns, because it is already more than prepared.

The end result of this education will be positive for Black people in their resistance and negative for the power structure in its oppression, because the party always exemplifies revolutionary defiance. If the party is not going to make the people aware of the tools of liberation and the strategic method that is to be used, there will be no means by which the people will be mobilized properly.

Raise Consciousness of Masses

The relationship between the vanguard party and the masses is a secondary relationship. The relationship between the members of the vanguard party is a primary relationship. It is important that the members of the vanguard group maintain a face-to-face relationship with each other. This is important if the party machinery is to be effective. It is impossible to put together functional party machinery or programs without this direct relationship. The members of the vanguard group should be tested revolutionaries. This will minimize the danger of Uncle Tom informers and opportunists.

The main purpose of the vanguard group should be to raise the consciousness of the masses through educational programs and certain physical activities the party will participate in. The sleeping masses must be bombarded with the correct approach to struggle through the activities of the vanguard party. Therefore, the masses must know that the party exists. The party must use all means available to get this information across to the masses. If the masses do not have knowledge of the party, it will be impossible for the masses to follow the program of the party.

The vanguard party is never underground in the beginning of its existence, because this would limit its effectiveness and educational processes. How can you teach people if the people do not know and respect you? The party must exist above ground as long as the dog power structure will allow, and hopefully when the party is forced to go underground the message of the party will already have been put across to the people. The vanguard party's activities on the surface will necessarily be short-lived.

This is why it is so important that the party make a tremendous impact upon the people before it is driven into secrecy.

At this time, the people know the party exists, and they will seek out further information on the activities of this underground party.

Many would-be revolutionaries work under the fallacious illusion that the vanguard party is to be a secret organization that the power structure knows nothing about, and the masses know nothing about, except for occasional letters that come to their homes by night. Underground parties cannot distribute leaflets announcing an underground meeting. These are contradictions and inconsistencies of the so-called revolutionaries. The so-called revolutionaries are in fact afraid of the very danger that they are advocating for the people. These so-called revolutionaries want the people to say what they themselves are afraid to say, and the people to do what they themselves are afraid to do. This makes the so-called revolutionary a coward and a hypocrite.

If these impostors would investigate the history of revolution, they would see that the vanguard group always starts out above ground and is later driven underground by the aggressor. The Cuban Revolution exemplifies this fact; when Fidel Castro started to resist the butcher Batista and the American running dogs, he started by speaking on the campus of the University of Havana in public. He was later driven to the hills. His impact upon the dispossessed people of Cuba was very great and received with much respect. When he went into secrecy, Cuban people searched him out. People went to the hills to find him and his band of twelve. Castro handled the revolutionary struggle correctly. If the Chinese revolution is investigated, it will be seen that the Communist Party was quite on the surface so that they would be able to muster support from the masses. There are many areas one can read about to learn the correct approach, such as the revolution in Kenya, the Algerian Revolution, Fanon's *The Wretched of the Earth,* the Russian Revolution, the works of Chairman Mao Tse-tung, and a host of others.

On the Media and the Message

A revolutionary must realize that if he is sincere, death is imminent due to the fact that the things he is saying and doing are extremely dangerous. Without this realization, it is impossible to proceed as a revolutionary. The masses are constantly looking for a guide, a Messiah, to liberate them from the hands of the oppressor. The vanguard party must exemplify the characteristics of worthy leadership. Millions and millions of oppressed people might not know members of the vanguard party personally or directly, but they will gain through an indirect acquaintance the proper strategy for liberation via the mass media and the physical activities of the party. It is of prime importance that the vanguard party develop a political organ, such as a newspaper produced by the party, as well as employ strategically revolutionary art and destruction of the oppressor's machinery. For example, Watts. The economy and property of the oppressor was destroyed to such an extent that no matter how the oppressor tried to whitewash the activities of the black brothers, the real nature and the real cause of the activity was communicated to every black community. For further example, no matter how the oppressor tries to distort and confuse the message of Brother Stokely Carmichael, Black people all over the country understand it perfectly and welcome it.

The Black Panther Party for Self Defense teaches that in the final analysis, the amount of guns and defense weapons, such as hand grenades, bazookas, and other necessary equipment, will be supplied by taking these weapons from the power structure, as exemplified by the Viet Cong. Therefore, the greater the military preparation on the part of the oppressor, the greater is the availability of weapons for the black community. It is believed by some hypocrites that when the people are taught by the vanguard group to prepare for resistance, this only brings the man down on them with increasing violence and brutality; but the fact of the matter is that when the man becomes more oppressive, this only heightens the revolutionary fervor. The people never make revolution. The oppressors by their brutal actions cause the resistance by the people. The vanguard party only teaches the correct methods of resistance. So, if things can get worse for oppressed people, then they will feel no need for revolution or resistance. The complaint of the hypocrites that the Black Panther Party for Self Defense is exposing the people to deeper suffering is an incorrect observation. People have proved that they will not tolerate any more oppression by the racist dog police through their rebellions in the black communities across the country. The people are looking now for guidance to extend and strengthen their resistance struggle.

15

Free the People

Carl Oglesby

If wars fought for the acquisition of empire are politically the same as wars fought for the protection of empires already acquired, then there is no radical difference between the politics that takes the United States to Vietnam and the politics that took Spain to Mexico, England to North America, France to Africa, and the whole awesome armada of European powers together to old Asia.

From the time of the decay of the Islamic empire and the waning of the Middle Ages, from the onset of the great northern commercial Renaissance, the expansionary dynamic of Western commercial culture has been the root, the denominating constant, of modern history.

The grandeur of Western liberalism, its material abundance, the flourishing of its arts and sciences, its painful construction of constitutional democracy—these interconnected achievements have been financed by the sustained theft called imperialism.

America's frontier epic copied on a continental scale the larger, overarching story of the transoceanic imperialisms. Having filled the North American continent and gathered up and centralized its might, the United States unhesitatingly embarked upon its own course of empire-building, south to the Caribbean, east to the Philippines, to Japan and the mainland of Asia.

The same imperial plunder continues, Gargantuan now, justified as usual by some combination of the three traditional elements of orthodox imperialist ideology: keeping the peace, now called "Free

---

SOURCE: Reprinted with permission of The Macmillan Company from *Containment and Change* by Carl Oglesby and Richard Shaull. Copyright © Carl Oglesby and Richard Shaull, 1967.

World responsibility"; conquest of the wilderness, now called "developing the underdeveloped"; and defeating the Heathen (Pagan, Barbarian, Savage), a figure who is now brought up to date and secularized as the Red Menace—same as the redskin, this Red, except more ferocious, wilder, more resistant and cunning.

First issue revised: Instead of a choice between freedom and tyranny, Americans will have to make a choice between continuing the theft and breaking it off. If we decide to continue the theft, Vietnamese-type wars will be as typical of our worsening future as they have been of our lamentable past.

And if history is cumulative instead of repetitive, then there is a second issue to be revised, this one even more personal, more intimate for Americans than the first.

Toward the end of the nineteenth century, in his inaugural address at the University of Freiburg, Max Weber, one of the modern West's great social economists, made a rare prophecy:

> Together with the machine, the bureaucratic organization is engaged in building the houses of bondage of the future, in which perhaps man will one day be like peasants in the ancient Egyptian State, acquiescent and powerless, while a purely technical good—that is, rational official administration and provision—becomes the sole, final value, which sovereignly decides the direction of their affairs.

The drive for the "rationalization" of the state is not the product of one political philosophy or another. It springs, rather, from the development of techniques that make such a rationalization possible, from the consolidation around those techniques of professional, bureaucratized elitist groups whose special interest becomes the extension of the use of their techniques, and from the coordination of such groups within larger, corporated, institutional power structures. It does not much matter whether these power structures call themselves "public" or "private." They strive in either case to perpetuate themselves and to extend the social territory in which their influence is dominant.

Look again at Weber's prophecy. See if the system he predicts from a "capitalist" viewpoint is so very different from the one demanded by Thorstein Veblen from a "technocratic-socialist" viewpoint:

> [The] technological specialists whose constant supervision is indispensable to the due working of the industrial system con-

stitute the general staff of industry, whose work it is to control the strategy of production at large and to keep an oversight of the tactics of production in detail. . . . It is essential that that corps of technological specialists who by training, insight, and interest make up the general staff of industry must have a free hand in the disposal of its available resources, in materials, equipment, and man power, regardless of any national pretensions or any vested interests.

Or see if the same kind of cultural spirit does not animate the following passage from a recent *Fortune* polemic against antitrust.

As for conglomerate mergers, public policy ought to welcome them. The trend to conglomerates allows corporate capital or managerial skill to be applied in new markets that might otherwise languish for lack of these ingredients. . . . The real "social and moral" danger to this society is that we will continue to pursue our present line of economic development while keeping alive in antitrust policy a set of ideals, derived from the Bryan-Brandeis form of conservatism [*sic*], which denigrate the business system we have. . . . Every year the business system cries out more loudly for men of independence and character to take on the massive new burdens of decision making in an innovating society.

In the light of the foregoing quoted passages, reflect on the following from Charles Francis Adams' biography of his grandfather, John Quincy Adams.

Among the federalists . . . were to be found a large body of the patriots of the Revolution, almost all the general officers who survived the war, and a great number of the substantial citizens along the line of the seaboard towns and populous regions. . . . But these could never have succeeded in effecting the establishment of the Constitution [i.e., a strong central government] had they not received the active and steady cooperation of all that was left in America of attachment to the mother country, as well as of the moneyed interest, which ever points to strong government as surely as the needle to the pole.

The single pattern unfolds again and again from itself, the dimensions steadily enlarging, the forms retaining their identity. As in 1789, against the evident will of the American people, big business demanded and acquired a strong central government to protect it against the unruly states of the former Confederation, so in our time it demands a federal government for protection against the unruly states of the world. The scope of American commerce now being global, the scope of the federal government must also be global. Without the federal interventionary forces on continuous alert, American fruit interests could not plunder the "banana republics," and the Brazilian oligarchy could not fearlessly ignore the Brazilian people's most elemental economic and social needs. Imperialism is the national public concomitant of private commercial expansionism; big business makes big government, and multinational business globalizes it. And as business and government cooperate to rationalize and dominate the world political economy, chanting "peace, law, order" just as the old Romans did, so they cooperate to rationalize and dominate the domestic political economy. The ultimate demand is for nothing short of total order, total control—the total state of the total world. As clearly as we can now see that the Inquisition was only the Crusades turned inward, we should also be able to see that the totalitarian society is the logical interior of the imperialist state.

A totalitarian society need not be an outright police state. Whether or not it becomes one will depend on its traditions and on the character of the resistance which the people are able to conceive and express. There is a possibility that the total American state will more resemble Huxley's *Brave New World* than Orwell's *1984*. Small solace. But we can hardly forget that the impulse for police-statism has been with us at least from the time of the Alien and Sedition Act, the forerunner of our time's McCarran Act and the phenomenon of McCarthyism. If our society has for the most part resisted this impulse, that says neither that it has shown itself proof against it nor that it will continue to resist it in the future. Once the foundation of the total state is laid, whether or not that state is benevolently administered in the beginning, the probability of ultimate totalitarian malevolence exists.

What seems especially ominous about the current situation with America is that a number of interlocked forces seem bent on cooperatively stimulating the drive toward the totalizing of economic and political society.

First, the Vietnam crisis is unparalleled. By no means the first of its kind (Mexico, Cuba, the Philippines), it is still the first of its kind to be so protracted, to require so much American effort to achieve even an ambiguous standoff; the first to be fought under slogans so transparently hypocritical; the first which an entire world has watched close up in the intimacy of its living rooms; the first in which the reputation of the state has been unconditionally, repeatedly, and publicly laid on the line. At the crest of her relative power, modern America experiences for the first time a frustration that begins to seem impenetrable. This initiation to limits is infuriating and her composure shakes.

Second, the historical situation of this war may make it climactic, may mean that the culture will not be able easily to tolerate another of its kind. Who has a clear imagination of "victory" which is not also absurd? At best, the third administration from now may find itself in the possession of a corpse—a forecast which assumes, precariously, that succeeding administrations will maintain the obstinacy of the present one and that history will in other respects stand still. At the same time, "defeat" is also inconceivable without an immense upheaval in the American consciousness and conscience, two markedly unlikely events. Even a superbly skillful political maneuver probably could not represent a "compromise" as a "victory" (as with Korea); and on the terms by which the war has been explained to the American people, and given the suffering which no doubt still awaits them, nothing short of victory can sustain the present legitimacy of the state. If victory cannot be achieved and defeat cannot be dissembled, there is no resolution that will not in some way traumatize at least a large segment of the polity. In this case, the only escape for those whom power has made responsible lies in suppression of the terminal event, either by concealing or overriding it with a larger event (as war with China), or by forcibly expunging it from current history via the silencing of historical criticism.

Third, the economics of the war has the effect of raising to still greater power both the warfare generalists and those individual-interest groups which have most to gain from warfare expenditures. Relatedly, the war deepens and intensifies the economy's already advanced addiction to federal defense subsidies, which directly and through the multiplier effect may account for as much as a quarter of the nation's gross national product. Thus, at the very moment in which the economy stands in clearest "need" of war—or contrariwise, is least able to withstand the declaration of defense spending—power gathers in the hands of those whose special interests bias them toward greater bellicosity abroad and toward more direct forms of political suppression at home. Those who administer these interests, along with multinational corporatists generally, constitute the American political oligarchy, the prestigious, decision-making class; and their power has never been less subject to popular review or veto than it is now. Thus, if the classical decision between war and depression must again be made, it will once more be made by the group which has most to gain from war and most to lose from depression.

Finally, the agonies of the war intermesh psychologically with the agonies of urban decay and racial turbulence. There is a clear mechanical connection between the war and the problems of the American ghettos, the welfare state having been trimmed down to make room for the warfare state. More important still is the spiritual connection. Black America, whose political actions have a complex impact on poor-white America, is at the moment being driven toward total alienation from white power and total solidarity against a system whose hypocrisies have never before been so nakedly on view.

In sum, the uncommon military resistance and moral visibility of the emeny, the virtual impossibility of resolving the conflict within America's present political environment, the increasing influence of the militarists within the increasingly militarized political economy, and the coincident heightening of racial and class unrest all combine to stimulate the corporate society's inherent impulses toward totalitarian reaction. The problems that loom before us now are, after all, scarcely the sort that have tempted other authoritarians to experiment with democracy or tolerance or political freedom.

Moreover, the apparatus by which the society can be totalized exists and is in running order: The corporate state has effective control of key elements of the communications system, exclusive control of the primary ganglia of political and economic power, and access to a matured nationalist ideology pregnant with violence and capable of justifying any reasonably sophisticated or adroit authoritarian action against organized dissent. If the central feature of the fascist state is the political alliance or identity of big government and big business, and the power of such an alliance to work its will without significant restraints other than those it chooses to impose on itself, then it minces words to say that an American fascism is possible. Such a fascism may or may not be internally vicious. The point is that its style will be determined essentially by its executives' unchecked will. They will somehow contrive to do what they will determine should be done. The corporate state can plant dynamite in a SNCC [Student Nonviolent Coordinating Committee] office, then stage a police raid to discover this dynamite; it has done this. It can plant narcotics in an SDS office, then stage a raid to discover these narcotics; it has done this. It can tacitly direct its right-wing policemen to stand by while a right-wing gang assaults a few war-protesters and then jail the protesters; it has done this. It can refuse to bring racist murderers to justice and thus produce an effectively state-sponsored Terror; it has done this. Whatever the state decides to do, it can do without check or hindrance. It is alone on the commanding heights of power.

What Is to Be Done?

The central issue must be understood. The one and only basic question which Americans now have to ask themselves is whether or not they want to be politically free. The imperial house of bondage can give them wealth, security, and order; it can give them victories and certify these victories to be authentically glorious. It may even have the grace to let some people live in a subcultist absentia from the political society, sequestered from history in the undergrounds of LSD, suburban sex, pure research, or the quaint little magazines of provisory dissent, anonymously in solitude with like-spirited solitaries. The superstate may even turn a half preoccupied ear to the murmurs of the dispossessed; may give of its bounty to those who will ritually humble themselves before it. But the state cannot give political freedom. It is neither in the nature of the state that it can give political freedom nor in the nature of political freedom that it can be given. Political freedom is not a license to be purchased or petitioned from a higher power. It is not a gift. It does not exist as a fund under the superintendency of privileged offices. Political freedom is in political man, in his life, and it exists when he claims it. It is an elemental condition of the individual will. The state may deny it or obstruct its flow, but the state may neither take it nor give it because it does not lie in the capacities of the state to hold, to possess, so mercurial an entity as the political freedom of men. Only men, not states, can be free, can produce and exhibit freedom.

Whether or not Americans will choose to be free is the transcendent political question, the one question that coordinates and subsumes all the searing issues of foreign and domestic policy. If Americans choose freedom, there can be no totalitarian America, and without a totalitarian America, there can be no American empire.

This central question is not clarified, it is obscured, by our common political categories of left, right, and center; it is not clarified, it is obscured, by the traditional American debate about socialism versus capitalism versus the Keynesian mixed economy. The socialist radical, the corporatist conservative, and the welfare-state liberal are all equally capable of leading us forward into the totalized society. Whether central planning should be coordinated by government or corporate hands is a question whose realism has disappeared. The urgent question is about the locus of power in the community: Is it in the state or is it in the people? And in our American time, our American place, the main principle of the radically humanist politics is this: *Any decision not made by the people in free association, whatever the content of that decision, cannot be good.* If the American humanist must mellow his intransigence and move from his Utopian principle to meet the realities of life in the technological society, it is nevertheless that main principle which sets his goals, gives him his style, and motivates his work; it is that principle which he proceeds to elaborate and enrich through human exchanges in the context of human situations. The humanist does not say: "We shall accept this dismal house of bondage and try to redecorate it." He says rather: "We shall insist on the priority of man's freedom and ground our social invention in the ethic of the social contract freely made." The primary task of the humanist is to describe and help to realize those political acts through which the power of the central authoritarian monolith can be broken and the political life of man reconstituted on the base of the associational, democratic, nonexclusive community. William Appleman Williams puts it this way:

> The core radical ideals and values of community, equality, democracy, and humaneness simply cannot in the future be realized and sustained—nor should they be sought—through more centralization and consolidation. These radical values can most nearly be realized through decentralization and through the creation of many truly human communities. . . . Such decentralization is technologically and economically possible. Such decentralization is essential if democracy is to be maintained and extended. And such decentralization is psychologically and morally mandatory. Our humanity is being pounded and squeezed out of us by the consolidated power of a nationalist corporate welfare capitalism.

This is not merely a leftist's challenge to other leftists. As much as it is in the grain of American democratic populism, it is also in the grain of the American libertarian right.

The right wing in America is presently in a state of almost eerie spiritual disarray. Under one and the same banner, joining the John Birch Society, out on the rifle range with the Minutemen, chuckling through the pages of the *National Review,* the conservative right wing of imperialist, authoritarian, and even monarchist disposition enjoys the fraternity of the libertarian right wing of *laissez faire,* free-market individualism. These two groupings could not possibly have less in common. Why have the libertarians conceded leadership to the conservatives? Why have the traditional opponents of big, militarized, central authoritarian government now joined forces with such a government's boldest advocates?

They have done so because they have been persuaded that there is a clear and present danger that necessitates a temporary excursion from final values. They should know better. They should know that for the totalitarian imperialists there is *always* a clear and present danger, that it is pre-eminently through the ideology of the Foreign Threat, the myth of the tiger at the gates, that frontier and global imperialism and domestic authoritarianism have always rationalized themselves. Three outbursts of exemplary candor on this point:

First, from a 1938 report authored by the United States Office of Naval Intelligence: "Realistically, all wars have been fought for economic reasons. To make them politically and socially palatable, ideological issues have always been invoked. Any possible future war will, undoubtedly, conform to historical precedent."

Second, Senator Arthur Vandenberg's belief that to win their acceptance of a militant and expensive Cold War policy it would be necessary "to scare hell out of the American people."

Third, the testimony of General Douglas MacArthur:

> Talk of imminent threat to our national security through the application of external force is pure nonsense. . . . Indeed, it is a part of the general pattern of misguided policy that our country is now geared to an arms economy which was bred in an artificially induced psychosis of war hysteria and nurtured upon an incessant propaganda of fear. While such an economy may produce a sense of seeming prosperity for the moment, it rests on an illusory foundation of complete unreliability and renders among our political leaders almost a greater fear of peace than is their fear of war.

It would be a piece of great good fortune for America and the world if the libertarian right could be reminded that besides the debased Republicanism of the Knowlands and the Judds there is another tradition available to them—their own: the tradition of Congressman Howard Buffett, Senator Taft's midwestern campaign manager in 1952, who attacked the Truman Doctrine with the words: "Our Christian ideals cannot be exported to other lands by dollars and guns. . . . We cannot practice might and force abroad and retain freedom at home. We cannot talk world cooperation and practice power politics." There is the right of Frank Chodorov, whose response to the domestic Red Menace was abruptly to the point: "The way to get rid of communists in government jobs is to abolish the jobs." And of Dean Russell, who wrote in 1955: "Those who advocate the 'temporary loss' of our freedom in order to preserve it permanently are advocating only one thing: the abolition of liberty. . . . We are rapidly becoming a caricature of the thing we profess to hate." Most engaging, there is the right of the tough-minded Garet Garrett, who produced in 1952 a short analysis of the totalitarian impulse of imperialism which the events of the intervening years have reverified over and again. Beginning with the words, "We have crossed the boundary that lies between Republic and Empire," Garrett's pamphlet unerringly names the features of the imperial pathology: dominance of the national executive over Congress, court, and Constitution; subordination of domestic policy to foreign policy; ascendency of the military influence; the creation of political and military satellites; a complex of arrogance and fearfulness toward the "barbarian"; and, most insidiously, casting off the national identity for an internationalist and "historic" identity—the *republic* is free; the *empire* is history's hostage.

This style of political thought, rootedly American, is carried forward today by the Negro freedom movement and the student movement against Great Society–Free World imperialism. That these movements are called leftist means nothing. They are of the grain of American humanist individualism and voluntaristic associational action; and it is only through them that the libertarian tradition is activated and kept alive. In a strong sense, the Old Right and the New Left are morally and politically coordinate.

Yet their intersection can be missed. Their potentially redemptive union can go unattempted and unmade. On both sides, vision can be cut off by habituated responses to passé labels. The New Left can lose itself in the imported left-wing debates of the thirties, wondering what it ought to say about technocracy and Stalin. The libertarian right can remain hypnotically charmed by the authoritarian imperialists whose only ultimate love is Power, the subhuman brownshirted power of the jingo state militant, the state rampant, the iron state possessed of its own clanking glory. If this happens, if the new realities are not penetrated and a fundamental ideological rearrangement does not take place, then this new political humanism which has shown its courage from Lowndes County to Berkeley will no doubt prove unworthy of more than a footnote in the scavenger histories of our time. And someone will finally have to make the observation that the American dream did not come true, that maybe it was quite an idle dream after all and the people never really had a chance. The superstate will glide onward in its steel and vinyl splendor, tagging and numbering us with its scientific tests, conscripting us with its computers, swaggering through exotic graveyards which it filled and where it dares to lay wreaths, smug in the ruins of its old-fashioned, man-centered promises to itself.

Here stands the modern Western humanist, fruit of a long line, but perhaps already a useless and archaic item, superseded already perhaps by that very unsentimental rationality which he has for so long been pleased to honor. Increasingly estranged from those images of man which once sustained his work and informed his hopes, he slips his fantasies for a moment to wonder if there is not some easy way to recapture what seems to have been so easily lost. There is no use in wondering, however. What seems lost was not really lost; it came to an end. The frontiers are gone. There are no more barbarians to justify the basic conquests and salve the conscience. There is no easy way to make the old dream breathe in this new air, no buttons to find and push. The people are alone, as usual, with themselves. It belongs to Americans to claim again and try to reshape their country. Only the American people can do that. Only the people should.

16

Dehumanization and Repression

Herbert Marcuse

A comfortable, smooth, reasonable, democratic unfreedom prevails in advanced industrial civilization, a token of technical progress. Indeed, what could be more rational than the suppression of individuality in the mechanization of socially necessary but painful performances; the concentration of individual enterprises in more effective, more productive corporations; the regulation of free competition among unequally equipped economic subjects; the curtailment of prerogatives and national sovereignties which impede the international organization of resources? That this technological order also involves a political and intellectual coordination may be a regrettable and yet promising development.

The rights and liberties which were such vital factors in the origins and earlier stages of industrial society yield to a higher stage of this society: they are losing their traditional rationale and content. Freedom of thought, speech, and conscience were—just as free enterprise, which they served to promote and protect—essentially *critical* ideas, designed to replace an obsolescent material and intellectual culture by a more productive and rational one. Once institutionalized, these rights and liberties shared the fate of the society of which they had become an integral part. The achievement cancels the premises.

To the degree to which freedom from want, the concrete substance of all freedom, is becoming a real possibility, the liberties which pertain to a state of lower productivity are losing their former content.

SOURCE: Reprinted from *One-Dimensional Man* by permission of the Beacon Press, copyright © 1964 by Herbert Marcuse.

Independence of thought, autonomy, and the right to political opposition are being deprived of their basic critical function in a society which seems increasingly capable of satisfying the needs of the individuals through the way in which it is organized. Such a society may justly demand acceptance of its principles and institutions, and reduce the opposition to the discussion and promotion of alternative policies *within* the status quo. In this respect, it seems to make little difference whether the increasing satisfaction of needs is accomplished by an authoritarian or a non-authoritarian system. Under the conditions of a rising standard of living, non-conformity with the system itself appears to be socially useless, and the more so when it entails tangible economic and political disadvantages and threatens the smooth operation of the whole. Indeed, at least in so far as the necessities of life are involved, there seems to be no reason why the production and distribution of goods and services should proceed through the competitive concurrence of individual liberties.

Freedom of enterprise was from the beginning not altogether a blessing. As the liberty to work or to starve, it spelled toil, insecurity, and fear for the vast majority of the population. If the individual were no longer compelled to prove himself on the market, as a free economic subject, the disappearance of this kind of freedom would be one of the greatest achievements of civilization. The technological processes of mechanization and standardization might release individual energy into a yet uncharted realm of freedom beyond necessity. The very structure of human existence would be altered; the individual would be liberated from the work world's imposing upon him alien needs and alien possibilities. The individual would be free to exert autonomy over a life that would be his own. If the productive apparatus could be organized and directed toward the satisfaction of the vital needs, its control might well be centralized; such control would not prevent individual autonomy, but render it possible.

This is a goal within the capabilities of advanced industrial civilization, the "end" of technological rationality. In actual fact, however, the contrary trend operates: the apparatus imposes its economic and political requirements for defense and expansion on labor time and free time, on the material and intellectual culture. By virtue of the way it has organized its technological base, contemporary industrial society tends to be totalitarian. For "totalitarian" is not only a terroristic political coordination of society, but also a non-terroristic economic-technical coordination which operates through the manipulation of needs by vested interests. It thus precludes the emergence of an effective opposition against the whole. Not only a specific form of government or party rules makes for totalitarianism, but also a specific system of production and distribution which may well be compatible with a "pluralism" of parties, newspapers, "countervailing powers," etc.

Today political power asserts itself through its power over the machine process and over the technical organization of the apparatus. The government of advanced and advancing industrial societies can maintain and secure itself only when it succeeds in mobilizing, organizing, and exploiting the technical, scientific, and mechanical productivity available to industrial civilization. And this productivity mobilizes society as a whole, above and beyond any particular individual or group interests. The brute fact that the machine's physical (only physical?) power surpasses that of the individual, and of any particular group of individuals, makes the machine the most effective political instrument in any society whose basic organization is that of the machine process. But the political trend may be reversed; essentially the power of the machine is only the stored-up and projected power of man. To the extent to which the work world is conceived of as a machine and mechanized accordingly, it becomes the *potential* basis of a new freedom for man.

Contemporary industrial civilization demonstrates that it has reached the stage at which "the free society" can no longer be adequately defined in the traditional terms of economic, political, and intellectual liberties, not because these liberties have become insignificant, but because they are too significant to be confined within the traditional forms. New modes of realization are needed, corresponding to the new capabilities of society.

Such new modes can be indicated only in negative terms because they would amount to the negation of the prevailing modes. Thus economic freedom would mean freedom *from* the economy—from being controlled by economic forces and relationships; freedom from the daily struggle for existence, from earning a living. Political freedom would mean liberation of the individuals *from* politics over which they have no effective control. Similarly, intellectual freedom would mean the restoration of individual thought now absorbed by mass communication and indoctrination, abolition of "public opinion" together with its makers. The unrealistic sound of these propositions is indicative, not of their utopian character, but of the strength of the forces which prevent their realization. The most effective and enduring form of warfare against liberation is the implanting of material and intellectual needs that perpetuate obsolete forms of the struggle for existence.

The intensity, the satisfaction, and even the character of human needs, beyond the biological level, have always been preconditioned. Whether or not the possibility of doing or leaving, enjoying or destroying, possessing or rejecting something is seized as a *need* depends on whether or not it can be seen as desirable and necessary for the prevailing societal institutions and interests. In this sense, human needs are historical needs and, to the extent to which the society demands the repressive development of the individual, his needs themselves and their claim for satisfaction are subject to overriding critical standards.

We may distinguish both true and false needs. "False" are those which are superimposed upon the individual by particular social interests in his repression: the needs which perpetuate toil, aggressiveness, misery, and injustice. Their satisfaction might be most gratifying to the individual, but this happiness is not a condition which has to be maintained and protected if it serves to arrest the development of the ability (his own and others') to recognize the disease of the whole and grasp the chances of curing the disease. The result then is euphoria in unhappiness. Most of the prevailing needs to relax, to have fun, to behave and consume in accordance with the advertisements, to love and hate what others love and hate, belong to this category of false needs.

Such needs have a societal content and function which are determined by external powers over which the individual has no control; the development and satisfaction of these needs is heteronomous. No matter how much such needs may have become the individual's own, reproduced and fortified by the conditions of his existence; no matter how much he identifies himself with them and finds himself in their satisfaction, they continue to be what they were from the beginning—products of a society whose dominant interest demands repression.

The prevalence of repressive needs is an accomplished fact, accepted in ignorance and defeat, but a fact that must be undone in the interest of the happy individual as well as all those whose misery is the price of his satisfaction. The only needs that have an unqualified claim for satisfaction are the vital ones—nourishment, clothing, lodging at the attainable level of culture. The satisfaction of these needs is the prerequisite for the realization of *all* needs, of the unsublimated as well as the sublimated ones.

For any consciousness and conscience, for any experience which does not accept the prevailing societal interest as the supreme law of thought and behavior, the established universe of needs and satisfactions is a fact to be questioned—questioned in terms of truth and falsehood. These terms are historical throughout, and their objectivity is historical. The judgment of needs and their satisfaction, under the given conditions, involves standards of *priority*—standards which refer to the optimal development of the individual, of all individuals, under the optimal utilization of the material and intellectual resources available to man. The resources are calculable. "Truth" and "falsehood" of needs designate objective conditions to the extent to which the universal satisfaction of vital needs and, beyond it, the progressive alleviation of toil and poverty, are universally valid standards. But as historical standards, they do not only vary according to area and stage of development, they also can be defined only in (greater or lesser) *contradiction* to the prevailing ones. What tribunal can possibly claim the authority of decision?

In the last analysis, the question of what are true and false needs must be answered by the individuals themselves, but only in the last analysis; that is, if and when they are free to give their own answer. As long as they are kept incapable of being autonomous, as long as they are indoctrinated and manipulated (down to their very instincts), their answer to this question cannot be taken as their own. By the same token, however, no tribunal can justly arrogate to itself the right to decide which needs should be developed and satisfied. Any such tribunal is reprehensible, although our revulsion does not do away with the question: how can the people who have been the object of effective and productive domination by themselves create the conditions of freedom?

The more rational, productive, technical, and total the repressive administration of society becomes, the more unimaginable the means and ways by which the administered individuals might break their servitude and seize their own liberation. To be sure, to impose Reason upon an entire society is a paradoxical and scandalous idea—although one might dispute the righteousness of a society which ridicules this idea while making its own population into objects of total administration. All liberation depends on the consciousness of servitude, and the emergence of this consciousness is always hampered by the predominance of needs and satisfactions which, to a great extent, have become the individual's own. The process always replaces one system of preconditioning by another; the optimal goal is the replacement of false needs by true ones, the abandonment of repressive satisfaction.

The distinguishing feature of advanced industrial society is its effective suffocation of those needs which demand liberation—liberation also from that which is tolerable and rewarding and comfortable—while it sustains and absolves the destructive power and repressive function of the affluent society. Here, the social controls exact the overwhelming need for the production and consumption of waste; the need for stupefying work where it is no longer a real necessity; the need for modes of relaxation which soothe and prolong this stupefaction; the need for maintaining such deceptive liberties as free competition at administered prices, a free press which censors itself, free choice between brands and gadgets.

Under the rule of a repressive whole, liberty can be made into a powerful instrument of domination. The range of choice open to the individual is not the decisive factor in determining the degree of human freedom, but *what* can be chosen and what *is* chosen by the individual. The criterion for free choice can never be an absolute one, but neither is it entirely relative. Free election of masters does not abolish the masters or the slaves. Free choice among a wide variety of goods and services does not signify freedom if these goods and services sustain social controls over a life of toil and fear—that is, if they sustain alienation. And the spontaneous reproduction of superimposed needs by the individual does not establish autonomy; it only testifies to the efficacy of the controls.

Our insistence on the depth and efficacy of these controls is open to the objection that we overrate greatly the indoctrinating power of the "media," and that by themselves the people would feel and satisfy the needs which are now imposed upon them. The objection misses the point. The preconditioning does not start with the mass production of radio and television and with the centralization of their control. The people enter this stage as preconditioned receptacles of long standing; the decisive difference is in the flattening out of the contrast (or conflict) between the given and the possible, between the satisfied and the unsatisfied needs. Here, the so-called equalization of class distinctions reveals its ideological function. If the worker and his boss enjoy the same television program and visit the same resort places, if the typist is as attractively made up as the daughter of her employer, if the Negro owns a Cadillac, if they all read the same newspaper, then this assimilation indicates not the disappearance of classes, but the extent to which the needs and satisfactions that serve the preservation of the Establishment are shared by the underlying population.

Indeed, in the most highly developed areas of contemporary society, the transplantation of social into individual needs is so effective that the difference between them seems to be purely theoretical. Can one really distinguish between the mass media as instruments of information and entertainment, and as agents of manipulation and indoctrination? Between the automobile as nuisance and as convenience? Between the horrors and the comforts of functional architecture? Between the work for national defense and the work for corporate gain? Between the private pleasure and the commercial and political utility involved in increasing the birth rate?

We are again confronted with one of the most vexing aspects of advanced industrial civilization: the rational character of its irrationality. Its productivity and efficiency, its capacity to increase and spread comforts, to turn waste into need, and destruction into construction, the extent to which this civilization transforms the object world into an extension of man's mind and body makes the very notion of alienation questionable. The people recognize themselves in their commodities; they find their soul in their automobile, hi-fi set, split-level home, kitchen equipment. The very mechanism which ties the individual to his society has changed, and social control is anchored in the new needs which it has produced.

The prevailing forms of social control are technological in a new sense. To be sure, the technical structure and efficacy of the productive and destructive apparatus has been a major instrumentality for subjecting the population to the established social division of labor throughout the modern period. Moreover, such integration has always been accompanied by more obvious forms of compulsion: loss of livelihood, the administration of justice, the police, the armed forces. It still is. But in the contemporary period, the technological controls appear to be the very embodiment of Reason for the benefit of all social groups and interests—to such an extent that all contradiction seems irrational and all counteraction impossible.

No wonder then that, in the most advanced areas of this civilization, the social controls have been introjected to the point where even individual protest is affected at its roots. The intellectual and emotional refusal "to go along" appears neurotic and impotent. This is the socio-psychological aspect of the political event that marks the contemporary period: the passing of the historical forces which, at the preceding stage of industrial society, seemed to represent the possibility of new forms of existence.

But the term "introjection" perhaps no longer describes the way in which the individual by himself reproduces and perpetuates the external controls exercised by his society. Introjection suggests a variety of relatively spontaneous processes by which a Self (Ego) transposes the "outer" into the "inner." Thus introjection implies the existence of an inner dimension distinguished from and even antagonistic to the external exigencies—an individual consciousness and an individual unconscious *apart from* public opinion and behavior. The idea of "inner freedom" here has its reality: it designates the private space in which man may become and remain "himself."

Today this private space has been invaded and whittled down by technological reality. Mass production and mass distribution claim the *entire* individual, and industrial psychology has long since ceased to be confined to the factory. The manifold processes of introjection seem to be ossified in almost mechanical reactions. The result is, not adjustment but *mimesis:* an immediate identification of the individual with *his* society and, through it, with the society as a whole.

This immediate, automatic identification (which may have been characteristic of primitive forms of association) reappears in high industrial civilization; its new "immediacy," however, is the product of a sophisticated, scientific management and organization. In this process, the "inner" dimension of the mind in which opposition to the status quo can take root is whittled down. The loss of this dimension, in which the power of negative thinking—the critical power of Reason—is at home, is the ideological counterpart to the very material process in which advanced industrial society silences and reconciles the opposition. The impact of progress turns Reason into submission to the facts of life, and to the dynamic capability of producing more and bigger facts of the same sort of life. The efficiency of the system blunts the individuals' recognition that it contains no facts which do not communicate the repressive power of the whole. If the individuals find themselves in the things which shape their life, they do so, not by giving, but by accepting the law of things—not the laws of physics but the law of their society.

I have just suggested that the concept of alienation seems to become questionable when the individuals identify themselves with the existence which is imposed upon them and have in it their own development and satisfaction. This identification is not illusion but reality. However, the reality constitutes a more progressive stage of alienation. The latter has become entirely objective; the subject which is alienated is swallowed up by its alienated existence. There is only one dimension, and it is everywhere and in all forms. The achievements of progress defy ideological indictment as well as justification; before their tribunal, the "false consciousness" of their rationality becomes the true consciousness.

This absorption of ideology into reality does not, however, signify the "end of ideology." On the contrary, in a specific sense advanced industrial culture is *more* ideological than its predecessor, inasmuch as today the ideology is in the process of production itself.[1] In a provocative form, this proposition reveals the political aspects of the prevailing technological rationality. The productive apparatus and the goods and services which it produces "sell" or impose the social system as a whole. The means of mass transportation and communication, the commodities of lodging, food, and clothing, the irresistible output of the entertainment and information industry carry with them prescribed attitudes and habits, certain intellectual and emotional reactions which bind the consumers more or less pleasantly to the producers and, through the latter, to the whole. The products indoctrinate and manipulate; they promote a false consciousness which is immune against its falsehood. And as these beneficial products become available to more individuals in more social classes, the indoctrination they carry ceases to be publicity; it becomes a way of life. It is a good way of life—much better than before—and as a good way of life, it militates against qualitative change. Thus emerges a pattern of *one-dimensional thought and behavior* in which ideas, aspirations, and objectives that, by their content, transcend the established universe of discourse and action are either repelled or reduced to terms of this universe. They are redefined by the rationality of the given system and of its quantitative extension.

The trend may be related to a development in scientific method: operationalism in the physical, behaviorism in the social sciences. The common feature is a total empiricism in the treatment of con-

---

[1] Theodor W. Adorno, *Prismen. Kulturkritik und Gesellschaft.* (Frankfurt: Suhrkamp, 1955), pp. 24 f.

cepts; their meaning is restricted to the representation of particular operations and behavior. The operational point of view is well illustrated by P. W. Bridgman's analysis of the concept of length:[2]

> We evidently know what we mean by length if we can tell what the length of any and every object is, and for the physicist nothing more is required. To find the length of an object, we have to perform certain physical operations. The concept of length is therefore fixed when the operations by which length is measured are fixed: that is, the concept of length involves as much and nothing more than the set of operations by which length is determined. In general, we mean by any concept nothing more than a set of operations; *the concept is synonymous with the corresponding set of operations.*

Bridgman has seen the wide implications of this mode of thought for the society at large:

> To adopt the operational point of view involves much more than a mere restriction of the sense in which we understand "concept," but means a far-reaching change in all our habits of thought, in that we shall no longer permit ourselves to use as tools in our thinking concepts of which we cannot give an adequate account in terms of operations.

Bridgman's prediction has come true. The new mode of thought is today the predominant tendency in philosophy, psychology, sociology, and other fields. Many of the most seriously troublesome concepts are being "eliminated" by showing that no adequate account of them in terms of operations or behavior can be given. The radical empiricist onslaught . . . thus provides the methodological justification for the debunking of the mind by the intellectuals—a positivism which, in its denial of the transcending elements of Reason, forms the academic counterpart of the socially required behavior.

Outside the academic establishment, the "far-reaching change in all our habits of thought" is more serious. It serves to coordinate ideas and goals with those exacted by the prevailing system, to enclose them in the system, and to repel those which are irreconcilable

---

[2] P. W. Bridgman, *The Logic of Modern Physics* (New York: Macmillan, 1928), p. 5. The operational doctrine has since been refined and qualified. Bridgman himself has extended the concept of "operation" to include the "paper-and-pencil" operations of the theorist (in Philipp J. Frank, *The Validation of Scientific Theories* [Boston: Beacon Press, 1954], Chap. II). The main impetus remains the same: it is "desirable" that the paper-and-pencil operations "be capable of eventual contact, although perhaps indirectly, with instrumental operations."

with the system. The reign of such a one-dimensional reality does not mean that materialism rules, and that the spiritual, metaphysical, and bohemian occupations are petering out. On the contrary, there is a great deal of "Worship together this week," "Why not try God," Zen, existentialism, and beat ways of life, etc. But such modes of protest and transcendence are no longer contradictory to the status quo and no longer negative. They are rather the ceremonial part of practical behaviorism, its harmless negation, and are quickly digested by the status quo as part of its healthy diet.

One-dimensional thought is systematically promoted by the makers of politics and their purveyors of mass information. Their universe of discourse is populated by self-validating hypotheses which, incessantly and monopolistically repeated, become hypnotic definitions or dictations. For example, "free" are the institutions which operate (and are operated on) in the countries of the Free World; other transcending modes of freedom are by definition either anarchism, communism, or propaganda. "Socialistic" are all encroachments on private enterprises not undertaken by private enterprise itself (or by government contracts), such as universal and comprehensive health insurance, or the protection of nature from all too sweeping commercialization, or the establishment of public services which may hurt private profit. This totalitarian logic of accomplished facts has its Eastern counterpart. There, freedom is the way of life instituted by a communist regime, and all other transcending modes of freedom are either capitalistic, or revisionist, or leftist sectarianism. In both camps, non-operational ideas are non-behavioral and subversive. The movement of thought is stopped at barriers which appear as the limits of Reason itself.

Such limitation of thought is certainly not new. Ascending modern rationalism, in its speculative as well as empirical form, shows a striking contrast between extreme critical radicalism in scientific and philosophic method on the one hand, and an uncritical quietism in the attitude toward established and functioning social institutions. Thus Descartes' *ego cogitans* was to leave the "great public bodies" untouched, and Hobbes held that "the present ought always to be preferred, maintained, and accounted best." Kant agreed with Locke in justifying revolution *if and when* it has succeeded in organizing the whole and in preventing subversion.

However, these accommodating concepts of Reason were always contradicted by the evident misery and injustice of the "great public bodies" and the effective, more or less conscious rebellion against them. Societal conditions existed which provoked and permitted real dissociation from the established state of affairs; a private as well as political dimension was present in which dissociation could develop into effective opposition, testing its strength and the validity of its objectives.

With the gradual closing of this dimension by the society, the self-limitation of thought assumes a larger significance. The interrelation between scientific-philosophical and societal processes, between theoretical and practical Reason, asserts itself "behind the back" of the scientists and philosophers. The society bars a whole type of oppositional operations and behavior; consequently, the concepts pertaining to them are rendered illusory or meaningless. Historical transcendence appears as metaphysical transcendence, not acceptable to science and scientific thought. The operational and behavioral point of view, practiced as a "habit of thought" at large, becomes the view of the established universe of discourse and action, needs and aspirations. The "cunning of Reason" works, as it so often did, in the interest of the powers that be. The insistence on operational and behavioral concepts turns against the efforts to free thought and behavior *from* the given reality and *for* the suppressed alternatives. Theoretical and practical Reason, academic and social behaviorism meet on common ground: that of an advanced society which makes scientific and technical progress into an instrument of domination.

"Progress" is not a neutral term; it moves toward specific ends, and these ends are defined by the possibilities of ameliorating the human condition. Advanced industrial society is approaching the stage where continued progress would demand the radical subversion of the prevailing direction and organization of progress. This stage would be reached when material production (including the necessary services) becomes automated to the extent that all vital needs can be satisfied while necessary labor time is reduced to marginal time. From this point on, technical progress would transcend the realm of necessity, where it served as the instrument of domination and exploitation which thereby limited its rationality; technology would become subject to the free play of faculties in the struggle for the pacification of nature and society.

Such a state is envisioned in Marx's notion of the "abolition of labor." The term "pacification of existence" seems better suited to designate the historical alternative of a world which—through an international conflict which transforms and suspends the contradictions within the established societies—advances on the brink of a global war. "Pacification of existence" means the development of man's struggle with man and with nature, under conditions where the competing needs, desires, and aspirations are no longer organized by vested interests in domination and scarcity—an organization which perpetuates the destructive forms of this struggle.

Today's fight against this historical alternative finds a firm mass basis in the underlying population, and finds its ideology in the rigid orientation of thought and behavior to the given universe of facts. Validated by the accomplishments of science and technology, justified by its growing productivity, the status quo defies all transcendence. Faced with the possibility of pacification on the grounds of its technical and intellectual achievements, the mature industrial society closes itself against this alternative. Operationalism, in theory and practice, becomes the theory and practice of *containment*. Underneath its obvious dynamics, this society is a thoroughly static system of life: self-propelling in its oppressive productivity and in its beneficial coordination. Containment of technical progress goes hand in hand with its growth in the established direction. In spite of the political fetters imposed by the status quo, the more technology appears capable of creating the conditions for pacification, the more are the minds and bodies of man organized against this alternative.

The most advanced areas of industrial society exhibit throughout these two features: a trend toward consummation of technological rationality, and intensive efforts to contain this trend within the established institutions. Here is the internal contradiction of this civilization: the irrational element in its rationality. It is the token of its achievements. The industrial society which makes technology and science its own is organized for the ever-more-effective domination of man and nature, for the ever-more-effective utilization of its resources. It becomes irrational when the success of these efforts opens new dimensions of human realization. Organization for peace is different from organization for war; the institutions which served the struggle for existence cannot serve the pacification of existence. Life as an end is qualitatively different from life as a means.

Such a qualitatively new mode of existence can never be envisaged as the mere by-product of economic and political changes, as the more or less spontaneous effect of the new institutions which constitute the necessary prerequisite. Qualitative change also involves a change in the *technical* basis on which this society rests—one which sustains the economic and political institutions through which the "second nature" of man as an aggressive object of administration is stabilized. The techniques of industrialization are political techniques; as such, they prejudge the possibilities of Reason and Freedom.

To be sure, labor must precede the reduction of labor, and industrialization must precede the development of human needs and satisfactions. But as all freedom depends on the conquest of alien necessity, the realization of freedom depends on the *techniques* of this conquest. The highest productivity of labor can be used for the perpetuation of labor, and the most efficient industrialization can serve the restriction and manipulation of needs.

When this point is reached, domination—in the guise of affluence and liberty—extends to all spheres of private and public existence, integrates all authentic opposition, absorbs all alternatives. Technological rationality reveals its political character as it becomes the great vehicle of better domination, creating a truly totalitarian universe in which society and nature, mind and body are kept in a state of permanent mobilization for the defense of this universe.

Part Four

Profiles—Assessments of Right and Left

All of the readings that follow combine analytical detachment with critical and sometimes polemical observations about the radical right and the new left. Collectively taken, they embrace the typical nonextremist views to be found among supporters and critics of scholarly repute. It is of particular importance to note the manner in which various conclusions are reached as a reflection of the authors' own premises, both explicit and implicit. Indeed, the "problem" of radicalism should be defined to include the views of those who, as influential writers, help to condition public understanding and responses.

CONTRIBUTORS

Richard Hofstadter: Professor of American history at Columbia University, has lectured widely in the United States and Britain. He is author of *Social Darwinism in American Thought, The American Political Tradition, The Age of Reform, Anti-Intellectualism in American Life, The Paranoid Style in American Politics,* and *The Idea of a Party System.*

David Danzig: Late program director of the American Jewish Committee and was a frequent contributor to *Commentary* and other publications. His writings cover a broad range of topics, including religion, culture, and politics.

David Riesman: Best known for his coauthorship of *The Lonely*

Crowd. He is Henry Ford Professor of Social Science at Harvard University and has also taught at Chicago, Yale, and Johns Hopkins. His other publications include *Thorstein Veblen, Individualism Reconsidered,* and *Conversations in Japan.*

Seymour M. Lipset: Professor of government and social relations at Harvard University, and also research associate at Harvard's Center for International Affairs. He is the author of *Political Man, The First New Nation, The Social Bases of Politics,* and *Agrarian Socialism.* He has taught at the University of California at Berkeley and at Columbia University.

Jack Newfield: A close observer of the culture and politics of the new left. He is the author of *A Prophetic Minority, Robert Kennedy: A Memoir,* and has written a variety of studies and interpretations for the *Village Voice.*

Kenneth Keniston: Professor of psychology in the Department of Psychiatry of Yale Medical School. His articles have appeared in such publications as *The Atlantic Monthly, The American Scholar,* and *Commentary.* He is the author of *The Uncommitted: Alienated Youth in American Society* and *Young Radicals.*

Irving Howe: Late author, historian, and critic, had taught at Brandeis, Princeton, and Stanford universities. He was cofounder and editor of *Dissent* and a frequent contributor to *Partisan Review* and other publications. He has written *Sherwood Anderson: A Critical Biography, Politics and the Novel,* and *Steady Work.*

Nathan Glazer: A sociologist and has taught at the University of California at Berkeley, Smith College, and Columbia University. He is coauthor, with David Riesman, of *The Lonely Crowd,* and his books include *American Judaism, The Social Basis of American Communism,* and *Beyond the Melting Pot* (with D. P. Moynihan).

17

Paranoid Politics

Richard Hofstadter

Let us now abstract the basic elements in the paranoid style. The central image is that of a vast and sinister conspiracy, a gigantic and yet subtle machinery of influence set in motion to undermine and destroy a way of life. One may object that they *are* conspiratorial acts in history, and there is nothing paranoid about taking note of them. This is true. All political behavior requires strategy, many strategic acts depend for their effect upon a period of secrecy, and anything that is secret may be described, often with but little exaggeration, as conspiratorial. The distinguishing thing about the paranoid style is not that its exponents see conspiracies or plots here and there in history, but that they regard a "vast" or "gigantic" conspiracy as *the motive force* in historical events. History *is* a conspiracy, set in motion by demonic forces of almost transcendent power, and what is felt to be needed to defeat it is not the usual methods of political give-and-take, but an all-out crusade. The paranoid spokesman sees the fate of this conspiracy in apocalyptic terms—he traffics in the birth and death of whole worlds, whole political orders, whole systems of human values. He is always manning the barricades of civilization. He constantly lives at a turning point: it is now or never in organizing resistance to conspiracy. Time is forever just running out. Like religious millenarians, he expresses the anxiety of those who are living through the last days and he is sometimes disposed to set a date for the apocalypse. "Time is running out," said Welch in

---

SOURCE: From *The Paranoid Style in American Politics,* by Richard Hofstadter. Copyright 1952, 1954, © 1964, 1965 by Richard Hofstadter. Reprinted by permission of Alfred A. Knopf, Inc.

1951. "Evidence is piling up on many sides and from many sources that October 1952 is the fatal month when Stalin will attack."[1] The apocalypticism of the paranoid style runs dangerously near to hopeless pessimism, but usually stops short of it. Apocalyptic warnings arouse passion and militancy, and strike at susceptibility to similar themes in Christianity. Properly expressed, such warnings serve somewhat the same function as a description of the horrible consequences of sin in a revivalist sermon: they portray that which impends but which may still be avoided. They are a secular and demonic version of adventism.

As a member of the avant-garde who is capable of perceiving the

---

[1] *May God Forgive Us* (Chicago, 1952), p. 73. Dr. Fred C. Schwarz of the Christian Anti-Communism Crusade is more circumspect. In his lectures he sets the year 1973 as the date for the Communists to achieve control of the world, if they are not stopped. Most contemporary paranoid spokesmen speak of a "Communist timetable," of whose focal dates they often seem to have intimate knowledge.

Probably the most spectacular American instance of such adventism is the case of William Miller, who flourished in New York in the 1830s. The offspring of a line of Baptist preachers, Miller became preoccupied with millenarian prophecies, and made calculations which indicated that Christ would come at first in 1843, and then on October 22, 1844, and became the leader of an adventist sect with a considerable following. On the appointed day, Millerites gathered to pray, many abandoned their worldly occupations, and some disposed of their property. The Miller movement waned after the fatal day, but other adventists, more cautious about their use of dates, carried on.

A notable quality in Miller's work was the rigorously logical and systematic character of his demonstrations, as was his militant opposition to Masonry, Catholicism, and other seductions. His lieutenants and followers, A. Whitney Cross has remarked, "found the world beyond rescue, legislatures corrupt, and infidelity, idolatry, Romanism, sectarianism, seduction, fraud, murder, and duels all waxing stronger." Cross argues that the Millerite movement was not so far from the mainstream of American Protestantism as some might think: "The Millerites cannot be dismissed as ignorant farmers, libertarian frontiersmen, impoverished victims of economic change, or hypnotized followers of a maniac thrown into prominence by freak coincidences, when the whole of American Protestantism came so very close to the same beliefs. Their doctrine was the logical absolute of fundamentalist orthodoxy, as perfectionism was the extreme of revivalism. . . . All Protestants expected some grand event about 1843, and no critic from the orthodox side took any serious issue on basic principles with Miller's calculations." *The Burned-Over District* (Ithaca, N.Y., 1950), pp. 320–1; see Ch. 17 for a good account of the Millerite movement.

For the story of an interesting contemporary prophetic cult and some sober reflections on the powerful resistance of true believers to overwhelming disconfirmation, see L. Festinger, H. W. Riecken, and S. Schachter: *When Prophecy Fails* (Minneapolis, 1956).

conspiracy before it is fully obvious to an as yet unaroused public, the paranoid is a militant leader. He does not see social conflict as something to be mediated and compromised, in the manner of the working politician. Since what is at stake is always a conflict between absolute good and absolute evil, the quality needed is not a willingness to compromise but the will to fight things out to a finish. Nothing but complete victory will do. Since the enemy is thought of as being totally evil and totally unappeasable, he must be totally eliminated—if not from the world, at least from the theater of operations to which the paranoid directs his attention.[2] This demand for unqualified victories leads to the formulation of hopelessly demanding and unrealistic goals, and since these goals are not even remotely attainable, failure constantly heightens the paranoid's frustration. Even partial success leaves him with the same sense of powerlessness with which he began, and this in turn only strengthens his awareness of the vast and terrifying quality of the enemy he opposes.

This enemy is clearly delineated: he is a perfect model of malice, a kind of amoral superman: sinister, ubiquitous, powerful, cruel, sensual, luxury-loving. Unlike the rest of us, the enemy is not caught in the toils of the vast mechanism of history, himself a victim of his past, his desires, his limitations. He is a free, active, demonic agent. He wills, indeed he manufactures, the mechanism of history himself, or deflects the normal course of history in an evil way. He makes crises, starts runs on banks, causes depressions, manufactures disasters, and then enjoys and profits from the misery he has produced. The paranoid's interpretation of history is in this sense distinctly personal: decisive events are not taken as part of the stream of history, but as the consequences of someone's will. Very often the enemy is held to possess some especially effective source of power: he controls the press; he directs the public mind through "managed news"; he has unlimited funds; he has a new secret for influencing the mind (brainwashing); he has a special technique for seduction (the Catholic confessional); he is gaining a stranglehold on the educational system.

This enemy seems to be on many counts a projection of the self: both the ideal and the unacceptable aspects of the self are attributed to him. A fundamental paradox of the paranoid style is the imitation of the enemy. The enemy, for example, may be the cosmopolitan

---

[2] The systems are diametrically opposed: one must and will exterminate the other." Edward Beecher: *The Papal Conspiracy Exposed and Protestantism Defended* (Boston, 1855), p. 29.

intellectual, but the paranoid will outdo him in the apparatus of scholarship, even of pedantry. Senator McCarthy, with his heavily documented tracts and his show of information, Mr. Welch with his accumulations of irresistible evidence, John Robison with his laborious study of documents in a language he but poorly used, the anti-Masons with their endlessly painstaking discussions of Masonic ritual —all these offer a kind of implicit compliment to their opponents. Secret organizations set up to combat secret organizations give the same flattery. The Ku Klux Klan imitated Catholicism to the point of donning priestly vestments, developing an elaborate ritual and an equally elaborate hierarchy. The John Birch Society emulates Communist cells and quasi-secret operation through "front" groups, and preaches a ruthless prosecution of the ideological war along lines very similar to those it finds in the Communist enemy. Spokesmen of the various Christian anti-Communist "crusades" openly express their admiration for the dedication, discipline, and strategic ingenuity the Communist cause calls forth.[3]

David Brion Davis, in a remarkable essay on pre–Civil War "counter-subversive" movements, has commented on the manner in which the nineteenth-century nativist unwittingly fashioned himself after his enemy:

> As the nativist searched for participation in a noble cause, for unity in a group sanctioned by tradition and authority, he professed a belief in democracy and equal rights. Yet in his very zeal for freedom he curiously assumed many of the characteristics of the imagined enemy. By condemning the subversive's fanatical allegiance to an ideology, he affirmed a similarly uncritical acceptance of a different ideology; by attacking the subversive's intolerance of dissent, he worked to eliminate dissent and diversity of opinion; by censuring the subversive for alleged licentiousness, he engaged in sensual fantasies; by criticizing the subversive's loyalty to an organization, he

---

[3] This has now become a fashionable trend in more respectable quarters. Stephen Shadegg, known for his success in Senator Goldwater's senatorial campaigns, writes: "Mao Tse-tung . . . has written a valuable book on the tactics of infiltration. In it he says: 'Give me just two or three men in a village and I will taken the village.' In the Goldwater campaigns of 1952 and 1958 and in all other campaigns where I have served as a consultant I have followed the advice of Mao Tse-tung." *How to Win an Election* (New York, 1964), p. 106. Writing about cold-war strategy, Goldwater himself declares: "I would suggest that we analyze and copy the strategy of the enemy; theirs has worked and ours has not." *Why Not Victory?* (New York, 1962), p. 24.

sought to prove his unconditional loyalty to the established order. The nativist moved even farther in the direction of his enemies when he formed tightly-knit societies and parties which were often secret and which subordinated the individual to the single purpose of the group. Though the nativists generally agreed that the worst evil of subversives was their subordination of means to ends, they themselves recommended the most radical means to purge the nation of troublesome groups and to enforce unquestioned loyalty to the state.[4]

Much of the function of the enemy lies not in what can be imitated but in what can be wholly condemned. The sexual freedom often attributed to him, his lack of moral inhibition, his possession of especially effective techniques for fulfilling his desires give exponents of the paranoid style an opportunity to project and freely express unacceptable aspects of their own minds. Priests and Mormon patriarchs were commonly thought to have especial attraction for women, and hence licentious privilege. Thus Catholics and Mormons—later Negroes and Jews—lent themselves to a preoccupation with illicit sex. Very often the fantasies of true believers serve as strong sado-masochistic outlets, vividly expressed, for example, in the concern of anti-Masons with the alleged cruelty of Masonic punishments. Concerning this phenomenon, Davis remarks:

> Masons disemboweled or slit the throats of their victims; Catholics cut unborn infants from their mothers' wombs and threw them to the dogs before their parents' eyes; Mormons raped and lashed recalcitrant women, or seared their mouths with red-hot irons. This obsession with details of sadism, which reached pathological proportions in much of the literature, showed a furious determination to purge the enemy of every admirable quality.[5]

Another recurring aspect of the paranoid style is the special significance that attaches to the figure of the renegade from the enemy cause. The anti-Masonic movement seemed at times to be the creation of ex-Masons; it certainly attached the highest significance and gave the most unqualified credulity to their revelations. Similarly anti-Catholicism used the runaway nun and the apostate priest, anti-Mormonism the ex-wife from the harem of polygamy; the avant-

---

[4] David Brion Davis: "Some Themes of Counter-Subversion: An Analysis of Anti-Masonic, Anti-Catholic, and Anti-Mormon Literature," *Mississippi Valley Historical Review*, XLVII (September, 1960), 223.
[5] *Ibid.*, p. 221.

garde anti-Communist movements of our time use the ex-Communist. In some part the special authority accorded the renegade derives from the obsession with secrecy so characteristic of such movements: the renegade is the man or woman who has been in the secret world of the enemy, and brings forth with him or her the final verification of suspicions which might otherwise have been doubted by a skeptical world. But I think there is a deeper eschatological significance attached to the person of the renegade: in the spiritual wrestling match between good and evil which is the paranoid's archetypal model of the world struggle, the renegade is living proof that all the conversions are not made by the wrong side. He brings with him the promise of redemption and victory.

In contemporary right-wing movements a particularly important part has been played by ex-Communists who have moved rapidly, though not without anguish, from the paranoid left to the paranoid right, clinging all the while to the fundamentally Manichean psychology that underlies both. Such authorities on communism remind one of those ancient converts from paganism to Christianity of whom it is told that upon their conversion they did not entirely cease to believe in their old gods but converted them into demons.

A final aspect of the paranoid style is related to that quality of pedantry to which I have already referred. One of the impressive things about paranoid literature is precisely the elaborate concern with demonstration it almost invariably shows. One should not be misled by the fantastic conclusions that are so characteristic of this political style into imagining that it is not, so to speak, argued out along factual lines. The very fantastic character of its conclusions leads to heroic strivings for "evidence" to prove that the unbelievable is the only thing that can be believed. Of course, there are highbrow, lowbrow, and middlebrow paranoids, as there are likely to be in any political tendency, and paranoid movements from the Middle Ages onward have had a magnetic attraction for demi-intellectuals. But respectable paranoid literature not only starts from certain moral commitments that can be justified to many non-paranoids but also carefully and all but obsessively accumulates "evidence." Paranoid writing begins with certain defensible judgments. There *was* something to be said for the anit-Masons. After all, a secret society composed of influential men bound by special obligations could conceivably pose some kind of threat to the civil order in which they were suspended. There was also something to be said for the Protestant principles of individuality and freedom, as well as for the nativist desire to develop in North America a homogeneous civilization. Again, in our time innumerable decisions of the Second World War and the cold war can be faulted, and it is easy for the suspicious to believe that such decisions are not simply the mistakes of well-meaning men but the plans of traitors.

The typical procedure of the higher paranoid scholarship is to start with such defensible assumptions and with a careful accumulation of facts, or at least of what appear to be facts, and to marshal these facts toward an overwhelming "proof" of the particular conspiracy that is to be established. It is nothing if not coherent—in fact, the paranoid mentality is far more coherent than the real world, since it leaves no room for mistakes, failures, or ambiguities. It is, if not wholly rational, at least intensely rationalistic; it believes that it is up against an enemy who is as infallibly rational as he is totally evil, and it seeks to match his imputed total competence with its own, leaving nothing unexplained and comprehending all of reality in one overreaching, consistent theory. It is nothing if not "scholarly" in technique. McCarthy's 96-page pamphlet *McCarthyism* contains no less than 313 footnote references, and Mr. Welch's fantastic assault on Eisenhower, *The Politician,* is weighed down by a hundred pages of bibliography and notes. The entire right-wing movement of our time is a parade of experts, study groups, monographs, footnotes, and bibliographies. Sometimes the right-wing striving for scholarly depth and an inclusive world view has startling consequences: Mr. Welch, for example, has charged that the popularity of Arnold Toynbee's historical work is the consequence of a plot on the part of Fabians, "Labour Party bosses in England," and various members of the Anglo-American "liberal establishment" to overshadow the much more truthful and illuminating work of Oswald Spengler.[6]

What distinguishes the paranoid style is not, then, the absence of verifiable facts (though it is occasionally true that in his extravagant passion for facts the paranoid occasionally manufactures them), but rather the curious leap in imagination that is always made at some critical point in the recital of events. John Robison's tract on the Illuminati followed a pattern that has been repeated for over a century and a half. For page after page he patiently records the details he has been able to accumulate about the history of the Illuminati. Then, suddenly, the French Revolution has taken place, and the Illuminati have brought it about. What is missing is not veracious infor-

---

[6] *The Blue Book of The John Birch Society* (n.p., 1961), pp. 42–3.

mation about the organization, but sensible judgment about what can cause a revolution. The plausibility the paranoid style has for those who find it plausible lies, in good measure, in this appearance of the most careful, conscientious, and seemingly coherent application to detail, the laborious accumulation of what can be taken as convincing evidence for the most fantastic conclusions, the careful preparation for the big leap from the undeniable to the unbelievable. The singular thing about all this laborious work is that the passion for factual evidence does not, as in most intellectual exchanges, have the effect of putting the paranoid spokesman into effective two-way communication with the world outside his group—least of all with those who doubt his views. He has little real hope that his evidence will convince a hostile world. His effort to amass it has rather the quality of a defensive act which shuts off his receptive apparatus and protects him from having to attend to disturbing considerations that do not fortify his ideas. He has all the evidence he needs; he is not a receiver, he is a transmitter.

Since I have drawn so heavily on American examples, I would like to emphasize again that the paranoid style is an international phenomenon. Nor is it confined to modern times. Studying the millennial sects of Europe from the eleventh to the sixteenth century, Norman Cohn finds, in his brilliant book *The Pursuit of the Millennium*, a persistent psychological complex that closely resembles what I have been considering—a style made up of certain marked preoccupations and fantasies: "the megalomanic view of oneself as the Elect, wholly good, abominably persecuted yet assured of ultimate triumph; the attribution of gigantic and demonic powers to the adversary; the refusal to accept the ineluctable limitations and imperfections of human existence, such as transience, dissention, conflict, fallibility whether intellectual or moral; the obsession with inerrable prophecies . . . systematized misinterpretations, always gross and often grotesque . . . ruthlessness directed towards an end which by its very nature cannot be realised—towards a total and final solution such as cannot be attained at any actual time or in any concrete situation, but only in the timeless and autistic realm of phantasy."[7]

---

[7] *The Pursuit of the Millennium* (London, 1957), pp. 309–10; see also pp. 58–74. In the Middle Ages millenarianism flourished among the poor, the oppressed, and the hopeless. In Anglo-American experience, as Samuel Shepperson has observed, such movements have never been confined to these classes, but have had a more solid middle-class foundation. "The Comparative Study of Millenarian Movements," in Sylvia Thrupp (ed.): *Millennial Dreams in Action* (The Hague, 1962), pp. 49–52.

The recurrence of the paranoid style over a long span of time and in different places suggests that a mentality disposed to see the world in the paranoid's way may always be present in some considerable minority of the population. But the fact that movements employing the paranoid style are not constant but come in successive episodic waves suggests that the paranoid disposition is mobilized into action chiefly by social conflicts that involve ultimate schemes of values and that bring fundamental fears and hatreds, rather than negotiable interests, into political action. Catastrophe or the fear of catastrophe is most likely to elicit the syndrome of paranoid rhetoric.

In American experience, ethnic and religious conflicts, with their threat of the submergence of whole systems of values, have plainly been the major focus for militant and suspicious minds of this sort, but elsewhere class conflicts have also mobilized such energies. The paranoid tendency is aroused by a confrontation of opposed interests which are (or are felt to be) totally irreconcilable, and thus by nature not susceptible to the normal political processes of bargain and compromise. The situation becomes worse when the representatives of a particular political interest—perhaps because of the very unrealistic and unrealizable nature of their demands—cannot make themselves felt in the political process. Feeling that they have no access to political bargaining or the making of decisions, they find their original conception of the world of power as omnipotent, sinister, and malicious fully confirmed. They see only the consequences of power—and this through distorting lenses—and have little chance to observe its actual machinery. L. B. Namier once said that "the crowning attainment of historical study" is to achieve "an intuitive sense of how things do not happen."[8] It is precisely this kind of awareness that the paranoid fails to develop. He has a special resistance of his own, of course, to such awareness, but circumstances often deprive him of exposure to events that might enlighten him. We are all sufferers from history, but the paranoid is a double sufferer, since he is afflicted not only by the real world, with the rest of us, but by his fantasies as well.

---

[8] L. B. Namier: "History," in Fritz Stern (ed.): *The Varieties of History* (New York, 1956), p. 375.

18

The Politics of Right-wing Fundamentalism

David Danzig

Early in February of this year a group of leading Protestant ministers and laymen in Dallas, Texas, were invited to form the core of a local chapter of "Christian Citizen," a new national organization whose announced aim is to train Christians in the techniques of practical politics. The founder of Christian Citizen, Mr. Gerri von Frellick (a Denver real estate developer and a Southern Baptist lay leader), spelled out the program of his movement as primarily an educational one whose purpose is to foster Christian principles in the nation's government and to combat "an increasing sense of futility and apathy in America." Qualifications for membership require only that the recruits must "give testimony of their personal experience with Christ" and must "accept the Bible as the infallible word of God." Once having joined, the "Christian Citizen" will be given an extensive training period at the precinct level and then go to work in the political party of his choice. The organization itself, according to von Frellick, will not endorse any candidate or take partisan stands on controversial issues. Appropriate action will be left to the "graduates" who will organize Christians to vote as a bloc and thus "participate effectively in the nation's political life." It is von Frellick's expectation that the movement will eventually become influential enough to "take over a majority of the precincts in this country."

As to actual political objectives, von Frellick has insisted that these are open and unspecified, the ideology of Christian Citizen being that "the democratic process has room for all viewpoints." When ques-

SOURCE: David Danzig, "The Radical Right and the Rise of the Fundamentalist Minority," *Commentary* (April, 1962). Copyright © 1962 by the American Jewish Committee. Reprinted by permission.

tioned about his position on certain key leaders and groups of the much publicized "radical right," von Frellick said that Dr. Fred C. Schwarz's Christian Anti-Communist Crusade was a "terrific" organization and "doing a fabulous job." He also said that the John Birch Society has "made a tremendous contribution to alerting the American people to the problem of Communism." The main difference which the Denver realtor finds between his organization and these others is that they lack "a positive approach"—whereas Christian Citizen can be "a means of launching an offensive in the ideological struggle with Communism."

Behind the vague and pious slogans, then, what we have here is the most recent formation of a cell nucleus in the growing organism of the extreme right. Christian Citizen also offers a particularly clear example of the relation of the more extreme wing of Protestant fundamentalism to the new ultra-conservative movement—a relationship that has frequently been overlooked or scanted by writers in their haste to explain the movement in purely political terms and to find its roots in the same general rightist tendencies that produced the politics of Father Coughlin or of Senator McCarthy or Senator Goldwater, as the case may be. While it is true, of course, that Senator McCarthy is taken by the John Birch Society as its second great martyr, there are some significant differences between McCarthyism and the new radical right—one of the most decisive of which has precisely to do with the connection between this radical right and extreme Protestant fundamentalism.

Fundamentalism, when noticed at all by our popular journals, is usually patronized as a colorful fragment of an older, vanishing way of life. But the truth is that fundamentalism is a growing socio-religious force in America. While its more moderate wing has been attempting to work out a position of "classic orthodoxy" in theology and an over-all *modus vivendi* with liberal Protestantism (particularly of the National Council of Churches variety), its more extreme wing, defined in good part by a belligerent opposition to liberal Protestantism and deep hostility to the NCC, has by no means lost ground. It is only of this latter group that we shall be speaking in the following pages.

Fundamentalism is not a sect or a denomination or a specific church; it is a rigorously orthodox point of view which completely dominates some Protestant denominations and has adherents in many others, including even the Episcopal Church. Among its basic doctrines are the inerrancy of the Bible, salvation by faith alone, and the pre-millennial return of Christ. On religious questions, it takes a stand against any attempts at revisionism and modernism. This emphasis upon literalness and purity of doctrine makes the fundamentalist look upon pragmatism in the social world with the same suspiciousness and distaste with which he views revisionism in religious doctrine. His commitment to Biblical prophecy, moreover, results in an anti-historicist perspective which readily supports the conspiracy theory of social change. Given all this, and given the association that came to be developed between the "Protestant ethic" and the ideology of nineteenth-century capitalism, it is not surprising that fundamentalism should always have had a strong disposition to regard the revisions of this ideology (which were partly inspired by Protestant liberals) as the work of heretics and atheistic radicals, infected with and spreading false doctrines in a conspiratorial manner.*

In fundamentalist eyes, departures from nineteenth-century capitalism have carried with them the corruption of virtually sanctified socio-economic doctrines and have consequently helped to undermine the Christian society. Thus, the fundamentalist's apocalyptic conception of the world as strictly divided into the saved and the damned, the forces of good and the forces of evil, has readily lent itself to reactionary political uses. Fundamentalism today supports a superpatriotic Americanism; the conflict with Communism is not one of power blocs but of faiths, part of the unending struggle between God and the devil. The danger of Communism, therefore, is from within—from the corrosion of faith by insidious doctrines. That is to say, by "collectivism"—the modern fundamentalist's secular counterpart of atheism.

The inherently conservative bent of fundamentalism has been further reinforced in America by regional factors. The fundamentalist population has always been located predominantly in the South, the border states, the Middle West, and in several Western states. It was partly as a spokesman for this population that William Jennings Bryan could talk of the East as "enemy territory," and express their economic plight in the fundamentalist imagery of the "cross of gold" speech. In Bryan, as later in Huey Long, the hatred of finance capi-

---

* In his *History of Fundamentalism,* Stewart Cole speaks of fundamentalism as "the organized determination of conservative churchmen to continue the imperialistic culture of historic Protestantism, within an inhospitable civilization dominated by secular interests and a progressive Christian idealism."

talism, or "Wall Street," by a rural population could produce the reforming spirit of Populism without appreciably liberalizing the impacted prejudices of fundamentalist social attitudes. As H. Richard Niebuhr has said:

> The fundamentalist movement was related in some localities to ... intense racialism or sectionalism. With them it shared antagonism to changes in the mores which the war [World War I] and its consequences, the rise to power of previously submerged immigrant or racial groups and other social processes, brought forth. The political effectiveness of fundamentalism was due in part to this association and *to the support which it gave to political leaders,* who found in it a powerful symbolism representative of the antagonism of political and economic minorities against the eastern or northern urban industrial majority.

The influence of fundamentalist ideas on the political and social life of these regions is seen in the fact that the states in which the movement predominated were the ones that passed—or nearly passed—statutes forbidding the teaching of evolution in the schools and that first enacted prohibition laws. Similarly, fundamentalism's ancient and unregenerate hostility to Catholicism was in good part responsible for the heavy losses which the Democrat Al Smith suffered in 1928 in these regions.

The states that repudiated Darwinism and Al Smith are today prominent among those nineteen that have passed "Right to Work" laws. Since World War I the social base of fundamentalism has shifted markedly, though few political writers have apparently noticed the shift. Its constituency is no longer mainly made up of sharecroppers and poorly educated villagers. Many fundamentalist churches are modern and imposing, financed by wealthy oilmen from Texas and Oklahoma and prosperous farmers in the wheat and corn belts. Rich and influential lay leaders such as J. Howard Pew and von Frellick now make their influence felt in the power structure of the community and state. The fundamentalists also operate a vast network of colleges, training schools, Bible institutions, Bible prophecy conferences, prayer meetings, and study groups. They have many large publishing houses which blanket small towns with conservative tracts and pamphlets. An increase in Protestant orthodoxy has added members to their churches at a more rapid rate than the liberal churches have been able to show. Though still more numerous in the small sects and local churches such as the Pentecostal and Seventh-

Day Adventists* and among the Southern Baptists, the fundamentalists, in some areas, are also found in the Presbyterian and Methodist churches and, to a lesser degree, in the Episcopal and Congregationalist ones. For example, the members of a Congregationalist church in Los Angeles and an Episcopal church in Fort Worth, both cities with powerful fundamentalist traditions, are likely to have a stronger affinity with these traditions than with those practiced by their sister church memberships in the large New England cities.

Population movements, affluence, and mass culture have all, of course, obscured some of the distinct regional features of fundamentalism. But it would be a mistake to view the more prosperous and integrated surfaces of contemporary fundamentalism as indicating any real loss or modification of its identity. Though it has become increasingly middle-class, this has not changed its profoundly conservative character, and its vast wealth and growing respectability have mainly served to broaden the base of its traditional antagonism to modern reform capitalism. Its local and regional character has insulated it from the influence of religious pluralism; still mainly Anglo-Saxon, it has preserved—unlike Catholicism and liberal Protestantism—an ethnic homogeneity that shields it from the liberalizing social adjustments invariably created by contending ethnic interests.

With the continuing world crisis, fundamentalism is finding a new political relevance for its doctrines and an arena in which it can exert its growing influence. As *Christian Century,* the leading organ of liberal Protestantism, observed recently: "Now the fundamentalists have apparently decided that the time has come to break out of their isolation and to contend for the soul of American Protestantism." A special target of theirs has been the National Council of Churches—the citadel of modern Protestantism. On the whole the attacks have come in the rural areas rather than the large cities, by means of local media rather than national. (One exception was an Air Force manual charging that the National Council of Churches was infiltrated by Communism, which had the effect of driving the Fourth Baptist Church of Wichita, Kansas—the largest local church in the Baptist convention—to withdraw from the convention in protest of its affiliation with the Council.) In those regions populated with churches, schools, publishing houses, and study groups that are dominated by fundamentalists, liberal Protestantism has been subjected to an ava-

---

* Many of these small sects are affiliated with the National Association of Evangelicals which claims a total membership of about ten million.

lanche of bigotry and calumny exceeded in intensity only by the worst period of anti-Catholic propaganda.

In analyzing the motives behind these attacks, Dr. Truman B. Douglas, formerly vice-president of the Board of Home Missions of the Congregational Churches, has explained that "what they really want is to silence the witness of the Church *on all social problems and issues.* . . ." That is to say, on all social issues and problems other than Communism. However, as we began by indicating, the fundamentalist mentality and temperament—in the extreme, unregenerate forms that we are discussing [here]—is unable to view the threat of Russian or Chinese Communism in pragmatic and realistic ways. For the fundamentalist mind the great menace of Communism is less in its military power than in its *doctrines,* and the main threat of these doctrines is not that they operate abroad but at home. Like the "papists" of America who, the fundamentalist continues to believe, have never ceased in their insidious and cunningly concealed attempts to undermine the faith and institutions of Protestant America and to deliver the nation up to Rome, the Communists today are everywhere at work disseminating under such subterfuges as "liberalism" and "middle-of-the-road progressivism" the heretical doctrines of collectivism that are poisoning American faith and subverting its social order. Instead of a puissant and pure Christian America marching resolutely toward its apocalyptic encounter with the Soviet anti-Christ, the nation, drugged with false doctrines and blinded by traitorous leaders, is being carried down the road to appeasement and, eventually, capitulation.

It is not surprising to discover, then, that Robert Welch, who has built his organization to fight a conspiracy which numbers President Eisenhower among its members, should have come from a strong fundamentalist background, or that John Birch himself first prepared for his martyrdom in China by being suspended from college because of the extremist zeal of his fundamentalist activities. Much of the affinity of fundamentalism for what is today called the radical right derives from the attempt to wed Protestant zeal and reactionary animus which developed and took shape during the New Deal years. The leader of one such group, the Christian Freedom Foundation, wrote a diatribe which was titled *The Menace of Roosevelt.* During the same period of the middle 1930s, an organization called Spiritual Mobilization was established "to check the trend toward pagan statism." In coming out of their "isolation," as the *Christian Century* puts it, the fundamentalists are not only "competing for the soul of

Protestantism" but are also trying to reassert the traditional cultural and political supremacy of conservative Protestantism. Its leaders—men like the Reverend Billy [James] Hargis, the Reverend Fred C. Schwarz, the Reverend James Fifield—are no less aware than the late Senator McCarthy was of the demagogic possibilities inherent in an anti-Communist crusade. But they enjoy an advantage that McCarthy did not have: a massive potential following which is prepared to accept the belief that a restoration of the influence of the old-time religion must be accompanied by a return to the pre–New Deal era of free enterprise and isolationism if the country is to be purged of its disabling doses of collectivism and internationalism. Thus the fundamentalist movement provides both potent political images and popular support to rally other disaffected Americans of different backgrounds who nonetheless feel that they, as well as the nation as a whole, have been losing power, and who are united not only in their hostility to Communism but in their anti-minority, anti-city, anti-labor, and anti-international attitudes.

The election of a Catholic to the Presidency has signalled the change in America from a Protestant nation with a prevailing Anglo-Saxon tradition to a pluralistic nation with a Protestant tradition. The defeats that the South has been suffering in civil rights mark the demise of white supremacy in its own sectional stronghold. Given current population trends, increasing urbanization, the organizational growth of minority groups, these changes are not likely to be reversed. Not long ago a leading figure in Spiritual Mobilizers, who also heads a large and wealthy Los Angeles church, articulated part of what the fundamentalist position amounts to in socio-ethnic terms when he reportedly said, "We are not going to give the city away to the Jews, Negroes, and Mexicans." Such cities as Houston, Miami, and Los Angeles were always fundamentalist strongholds, but the fact that they are now also centers of rightist politics is at least partly to be explained in terms of local responses to a growing Catholic minority, a growing Jewish community, and rapidly increasing Negro or Spanish-speaking minorities.

While the election of Kennedy reflected a decline in bigotry in some quarters, his campaign stimulated a recrudescence of it in others; . . . . The fundamentalists' reaction to the ascendancy of pluralism is double-sided. As Anglo-Saxon Protestants, in the main, they are reacting to the loss of the political dominance that came from their majority position. As *fundamentalist* Protestants, however, they are a particularly fervent and committed religious *minority* and one growing in wealth and numbers and ambition. As such, they are behaving more and more like other important minorities in America— demanding more time and space in the media, and devoting more energy to organizing their constituencies for social and political action. Whatever else may develop, it is abundantly clear that the Protestant fundamentalists have now taken their place among the other distinct groups—the Catholics, liberal Protestants, Jews, Negroes, and secular humanists—that make up the pluralistic socio-religious pattern of America.

In trying to convince the community that America's interest will best be served through their leadership, many fundamentalist religious and lay leaders have been moving into the seats of power which have opened on the radical right. Insofar as militant anti-Communism today has a socio-religious cast, fundamentalism has replaced Catholicism as the spearhead of the movement.* None of this is to say, of course, that the radical right has become identified with the aspirations of a single group—it would hardly have got off the ground if it had. The radical right cuts across all groups in varying degrees, and no doubt there is still a hard core of Catholic McCarthyites who have followed his sanctified image into the radical right movement. Father John F. Cronin, the author of the pamphlet issued [in March of 1962] by the NCWC attacking the new "extremists of the right," was indeed quoted by the New York *Times* as saying that "quite a few Catholics" belong to the John Birch Society.

But supporters of Senator McCarthy were, on the whole, a much more variegated and dispersed group than the constituency of the radical right today seems to be. Though many Catholics found in the Senator an expression of their militant anti-Communism, Mc-

---

* Father Robert A. Graham, among others, has called attention to this change in a recent issue of *America:* "It was not so long ago that Catholics were regarded as the most active foes of Communism. This can no longer be said today. Dr. Fred C. Schwarz's anti-Communist Christian Crusade is of predominantly Baptist inspiration. The National Education Program of Dr. George S. Benson [of the Church of Christ] is another fundamentalist operation. It is no accident that the key centers of the John Birch Society are in the fundamentalist South and Southwest." An even more authoritative indication of the fact that the new radical right does not lean on a predominantly Catholic base is the campaign begun [in March of 1962] by the National Catholic Welfare Conference—the central administrative body of the American bishops—to discourage participation by Catholics in extreme anti-Communist movements.

Carthyism never became a "Catholic movement." It drew the bulk of its support from the traditional "isolationist block"—pro-German and anti-British—who had opposed an alliance with Communist Russia against Nazi Germany. McCarthy also had a sizable following in the large cities, in the national veterans' organizations, and in working-class groups—particularly those with roots in countries now behind the Iron Curtain.

From his famous first speech in Wheeling, West Virginia, McCarthy clearly played up to the minority groups, who were attracted by his hard anti-Communism, which they saw as posing no threat to the economic gains they had made during the New Deal. For the most part, McCarthy managed to attack New Deal liberalism for allowing itself to be infiltrated by Communists, without directly challenging the policies and practices of reformed capitalism that had been achieved by the Democratic coalition and had come to be supported by the middle-of-the-road consensus in America. Seen in historical perspective, McCarthyism was the final phase in the repudiation of our wartime alliance with Russia; the charges of treason and disloyalty were aimed vengefully by those who had always considered Stalin a greater menace than Hitler against those who had taken the opposite position and engineered the alliance with Russia, and who might therefore be held responsible for the postwar predicaments which had flowed from that alliance. However, McCarthyism was virtually devoid of social and economic content as well as religious inspiration, and so lacked stable bases of local, popular support. With an all but inevitable logic, McCarthy was forced to play out his role in the national arena where his main concerns lay. Once his performance there had been discredited by the changes in international policy that were already in progress when his star appeared on the horizon, and by his unchecked hostility to the executive branch that was now in the hands of his own party, McCarthy collapsed. And with no further issues and grass-roots support which his followers could exploit, McCarthyism, in effect, collapsed with him.

The radical right, as we have been seeing, is a very different affair, one with a definite political, economic, and social purpose, and able to capitalize on the growing power of an important religious group which has long felt the denial of its rightful share in shaping the policies of the nation. To be sure, fundamentalist conservatism is today by no means a monolithic ideology. Even as von Frellick was attempting to recruit prominent ministers and lay leaders in Dallas for Christian Citizen, a leader of the Baptist General Convention of

Texas was publicly reminding them of the recent recommendation of the Convention that "Baptists . . . exercise caution when asked to support efforts to mobilize Christians into a political power." But despite this recommendation, and despite warnings by other Baptists and moderate fundamentalists, it remains clear that large numbers of fundamentalists *are* being "mobilized" and that their religious and regional conservatism is converting readily into the ideology of the radical right and swelling the chorus of reactionary and apocalyptic voices in the land.

The main strength and appeal of fundamentalist conservatism lies in its nativist nationalism. In the "gray atmosphere" of America's tense, cautious international power struggle with the Soviet Union in a nuclear age—an atmosphere made even more troubled by the rise of the minorities within the society—its program of "Americanism" becomes a way of explaining the nation's loss of supremacy and autonomy; it also provides a set of crusading directives for the road to Armageddon that dispels uncertainty and discharges both national tensions and local frustrations. On the international scene, it identifies America's "decline" and the Communist ascendancy with the loss of the West's four-hundred-year monopoly of power and with the passing of Anglo-Saxon dominance. The immense strengthening of America's world position since the war counts for nothing in the light of our failure to assume the world dominance which Great Britain has relinquished. The shock which followed Sputnik has doubtless helped to bring on the somewhat delayed discovery by certain people in the hinterlands that the American century had been lost, just as the Supreme Court decision on desegregation and the election of Kennedy woke many of the same people to the fact that political power in America was also passing out of their hands.

The appeal of the new nativist nationalism, however, need not remain confined to the rabid—as McCarthyism, being a form of revenge politics, necessarily was. The redistribution of power both abroad and at home has disheartened many moderate people—those who gladly might have settled for less than a monopoly if they could be sure that the Russians (and the Chinese) would do likewise, and who might have accepted the claims of the racial, religious, and ethnic minorities (and of labor), so long as these did not encroach upon their own lives, and so long as their own interests continued to be dominantly represented. Feeling that all of this is no longer the case, the nativist segment of the Protestant population becomes a prey of those who would like to replace the pluralistic orientation which has led America to a precarious co-existence by a doctrinaire, chauvinistic Americanism seeking to achieve a *"Pax Americana."* In Protestant fundamentalism, imbued with nationalism—not unlike the case of pre-World War II German Lutheranism—many formerly moderate people find a powerful rationale and symbolism for this complex of attitudes. The practical program to support the "Americanist" effort in foreign affairs has the further attraction of asking for the abolition of the welfare state, which the Protestants in question see as benefiting mainly the minorities whose rise to prominence has begun to threaten their control within the society and reshape their America in a different image. Thus they are susceptible to a program which, by calling for a return to a nineteenth-century type of capitalism and an end to collaboration with our allies on an equal basis, will bring into power those native groups who can restore their traditional position in the scheme of things. It is on such anxieties and impulses that the radical right has battened.

Whoever has taken the radical right as amounting to nothing more than the fulminations of a few crackpots, or the temporary prominence of the lunatic fringe achieved mainly by publicity, would do well to ponder the matter further. More thought had better be taken, also, by those who have concluded that since the radical right is unlikely to take over America, it can be disregarded as a growing power bloc and a potential influence for harm.

While it is probably true that the new-found strength of reactionary ideas cannot be said to indicate a turn toward conservatism in the population at large, it does seem to indicate that American conservatism is being pulled to the right. This in itself represents a gain for the ultras. But what gives them an even greater potentiality for influence is the fact that they operate at the local and state levels, where a minimum of pressure can exert a maximum of effect, and where there is no necessity for taking the risk of an all-or-nothing gamble—as McCarthy, working at the national level only, was forced to do. This does not mean that the new ultras are interested only in local affairs. On the contrary, as a distinct and now politically self-conscious minority within the pluralistic pattern, they are demanding a greater voice in the shaping of national policy, which they hope to achieve through a strategy of interlocking local pressures. (The effectiveness of such a strategy can be seen from the enormous amount of attention Manager Mitchell attracted through his attack on public welfare programs in the city of Newburgh; a similar attack in Congress would probably have fallen flat.)

So far as foreign policy is concerned, there is even an advantage to the ultras in being an out-of-power faction: they can conduct their programs with wild irresponsibility, blanketing the country with small undercover cells, repressing free discussion, and imposing a doctrinaire conformity. The effect of all this is to reduce the government's opportunities for a flexible handling of delicate problems such as we now face in Germany, in the UN, in Africa. Perhaps most important of all, the ultras make it very difficult for the country to dissociate itself from the imperialism and white supremacy in which the Anglo-Saxon world has figured so prominently in the past. It is ironic, if not yet tragic, that having more or less united the Western world around the belief that the best way to oppose Communism is through the promotion of social reform and the development of international pluralism, America should now be the scene of a nativist movement which would substitute for this idea a belligerent nationalism, one whose socio-religious mystique is not very different from that with which certain European nations recently experimented and in so disastrous a fashion.

19

America Moves to the Right

David Riesman

When Barry Goldwater was defeated by a large majority in the electoral college in 1964, many liberals and radicals concluded that the right wing had been similarly defeated. I thought then that they were too euphoric, overlooking the substantial numbers who had voted not only for the Republican party but specifically for Goldwater, and especially the many enthusiastic young people who brought to the Goldwater crusade an intensity of passion, an anarchic attitude toward bigness in government and, often, in business, and a quasi-conspiratorial view of its enemies similar to what we see now on the extreme left. The left and the right, of course, differ very much in the objects of their compassion and concern: the left cares about the non-white world, about the weak and powerless and the victims of militarism at home and abroad; the crusaders of the right, far less compassionate to begin with, are concerned about William Graham Sumner's original forgotten man: the middling white man who works hard, pays taxes, likes sports more than ideas, and finds the modern world bewildering. (There are also a number of extremely wealthy, though provincial, sponsors of right-wing thought who, as Daniel Bell has observed, nevertheless feel dispossessed because they have more wealth than standing or understanding.) On the right wing, there are a number of people who are psychologically predisposed to authoritarianism, admiring the strong and despising the weak, fiercely chauvinistic vis-à-vis their race, their country, their definition of the American way. However, people of this dispensation,

SOURCE: David Riesman, "America Moves to the Right," *New York Times Magazine,* October 27, 1968. Reprinted by permission of the author.

although more than sufficient to staff a totalitarian regime, account for only a fraction of the support for right-wing political candidates. How, then, is one to explain the persistence and growth of right-wing sentiment in America, to the point at which a quarter of our young people have become supporters of George Wallace, a brilliant demagogue where Goldwater was genial and perhaps the most capable right-wing politician since Huey Long?

To begin with, it must be recognized that the United States through most of its history has been a profoundly conservative country. However, the conservative majority for much of our national existence has been apathetic, reasonably generous and good-natured, and willing to put up with change if it did not come too fast and if it did not appear to threaten the majority's definition of what America stood for and what they themselves represented. Revisionist historians of Jacksonian America (Richard Hofstadter, Lee Benson, Marvin Meyers) have argued that, despite Populist rhetoric, neither Jackson nor his followers were radicals, nor did their movement have radical consequences, even for the civil service. Lincoln was no radical, nor was Woodrow Wilson, nor yet Franklin Roosevelt. Indeed, even in the Depression of 1929 and subsequent years, Communists, Trotskyites, and national-Populists were mistaken in supposing that vast unemployment and an apparent failure of capitalism offered opportunities to mobilize people for revolutionary political change. On the whole, Americans have favored equality of opportunity, not equality of result, although there has been a slowly increasing willingness to put a floor under misery, if not a ceiling over aspiration and accomplishment.

The conservative majority has not been especially interested in politics, particularly at the national level. It has distrusted politicians, by which is meant professional politicians, not generals or celebrities whose previous reputations made it possible for them to appear to be above politics. Some national leaders, and many members of national elites, have been liberal or even radical; their views have gradually influenced Americans without ever establishing a permanent liberal hegemony. What has resulted is a blend of traditions: a conservatism about American values coupled with an interest in innovation and, when people have felt unthreatened, a certain measure of mutual tolerance for different ways of life. Correspondingly, when cumulative changes have presented the conservative majority with definitions of American life sharply at odds with their own, the result has often been what Professor Joseph Gusfield terms symbolic crusades to extirpate the strange and the stranger and to set the country back on the right track.

Gusfield points out, for example, that the temperance movement was a way in which Protestant small-town America defined beer-drinking Germans in Milwaukee or whisky-drinking Irishmen in Boston not as an interesting contribution to cultural pluralism but as a threat to their America, just as the hippies appear to some today not as an exotic curiosity but as a threat to masculine dominance and family stability. Even when the national climate is moderately liberal, many such battles are fought locally, with the victory going to the conservatives. There are, for instance, the many recent referenda on the fluoridation of water in New England and elsewhere. Fluoridation comes to be defined as an interference with God's water, a conspiracy between the Communist party and the aluminum company to poison good Americans. Beyond that, it is seen as one more example of the intrusion of the national scientific elite into local affairs—and the vote against fluoridation has often been a vote against those well-educated, smooth people who have come into one's town and who seem to understand the modern world and even profit from it.

The natives can score similar victories over such people (and over the young as well) by voting down school bond issues or school budgets; such negative votes have been endemic in the last few years. To understand them better, one has to appreciate the fact that geographic and social mobility have the effect of forcing change on those who stay put as well as those who move. Stay-putters feel threatened by new people who come from elsewhere to run the new light industries, teach at the new colleges, preach at the more liberal Catholic and Protestant churches, and otherwise bring the tolerant messages of the college-educated, national upper–middle class to previously isolated locales—messages which include staying up later at night, treating children more permissively, spending more on their education, and introducing foreign movies. Hence a vote against fluoridation or a school bond issue may express resentment against a style of life that is costlier and at the same time more articulately defended than that of the indigenous stay-at-homes; such a vote also may be a gesture of impotent defiance against the big and feared powers: big government, big business, big labor—and the media. In the South, a similar politics of resentment has operated on the issue of race and in many communities has permitted a counter-establishment to develop in opposition to traditional moderate upper-class and upper–middle-class paternalistic whites who do not feel endangered by Negroes but who can be pushed out of authority by less affluent segregationists.

It is only under certain conditions, such as an unsatisfactory war, that these local pockets of right-wing and defensive conservatism coalesce into any kind of national movement. Father Coughlin represented such a movement at the time of the Depression, Senator Joseph McCarthy at the time of the Korean War. Like George Wallace today, and like Huey Long, the late Joseph McCarthy espoused some Populist attitudes, speaking on behalf of the little people against all the big powers, eventually including the Army itself. Opportunistically, he sought victims, not an agenda for change or even an effort to turn America back to the point where older people could feel that things made sense again. Joseph McCarthy helped to throw liberals and the left off balance by bullying individuals and by making dramatically visible the extent of resistance to change. Furthermore, as a Republican Irish Catholic, he helped cement a new tacit alliance of Catholic and Protestant fundamentalism—an alliance that became still more evident in the Kennedy–Nixon election, when a minority of conservative Catholics opposed Kennedy and allied themselves with Southern Baptists; it is often forgotten how near they came to winning, how tenuous Kennedy's victory was.

It has been almost as difficult for the various fragments on the extreme right to unite as for those on the extreme left, thanks to the suspiciousness and distrust that is one of the characteristics of right-wing attitudes. Among many other groups, the John Birch Society has been one which, as it were, could keep in storage some of the more well-to-do secular fundamentalists during a period when the right wing was on the defensive nationally, even while the society's members could be given practice in domestic counter-insurgency in crusades against UNESCO or Earl Warren or Polish hams in supermarkets. Its extreme economic conservatism and aura of wealth deprived the society of the Populist support that Joseph McCarthy had. Its weight, along with that of other endemic right-wing sects, could be felt only locally. However, at a time when the less well-to-do working class and the lower–middle class—stirred up by the Negro revolution, South and North, and by its liberal and radical white supporters—are ready to respond to someone like Wallace, who speaks to them directly as one of them, the wealthier and already organized right-wing cadres can serve as clusters of influence, political mobilization, and financial backing. George Wallace is building a mass movement as Joseph McCarthy never did.

The right wing and the more apathetic conservatives, despite what might divide them in the realm of fiscal policy, tend to react similarly to the widespread and not wholly unrealistic feeling that there is no one in charge in America—that the country faces dissolution and anarchy. Of course, they are not aware how much they contribute to this anarchy themselves, seeing only the blacks and the militants on the left as the source of dissension.

As I have stated, the majority of conservative Americans are not repressive or fanatical. But they want to feel that the country is manageable and can be governed; they will accept progress if it does not cost too much, either in taxes or in altered symbolic values. Some of this majority were prepared to rally to Senator Eugene McCarthy, had he been nominated, because they liked his calm and respected his individualism. Indeed, many Midwestern farmers and many people who had supported Goldwater admired Eugene McCarthy, and some who had supported him in the primaries will surely vote for George Wallace. Wallace and Nixon give many voters a sense of an ability to take charge, to recognize problems of order, even though they do not lay claim to a great deal of inventiveness, a quality which no candidate now possesses.

It is not that most Americans are themselves convinced that they have the right answers to our national problems, or indeed that there are answers. There is a great deal of fluidity, uneasiness, and temporizing. In this situation, the tactical advantage is decisive. On the national scene, the liberals have had that advantage for the last decade. They profited from the growing dissatisfaction with President Eisenhower, from the great accomplishment of the test-ban treaty and the partial *détente* it symbolized, from the massive defeat of Goldwater, from the energy with which President Johnson attacked the country's domestic problems early in his administration. The fruits of sustained prosperity, increased education, and the more sophisticated national media were visible all over America. Despite the war in Vietnam, a climate of unprecedented openness prevailed.

In this climate, previously submerged and apparently docile groups were able to reveal latent attitudes that shocked and offended those who once enjoyed patronizing them. This was true of Negroes, South and North, and more recently of a minority of demonstrating and extremely visible college students. As Professor S. M. Lipset has pointed out, the tactics of civil disobedience used by black and white militants were first practiced by dissident segregationists opposing the integration of Southern schools, buses, or other public facilities—

usually violently rather than nonviolently, and always in disobedience to Federal if not local law. (George Wallace is clearly ready to take his movement to the streets—the streets that the radicals in Chicago at the time of the Democratic Convention said belonged to the people, without realizing that other people vastly outnumbering them could make the same claim.)

Both the suppressed blacks and the previously less political students have behaved as emancipated minorities generally do, with the heightened momentum that readily leads to euphoric excess; they are defiant and exuberant and they promulgate millennial claims. Demographic changes have brought these minorities together in numbers large enough to score tactical victories over vulnerable, understaffed university and city administrations. Many adult and young radicals are provincial, living in settings in which they are exposed to the like-minded, more conscious of the supposedly more pure on their left than of the vaguely sensed differences among conservative and right-wing Americans. Furthermore, many radical students have taken comfort from a feeling of identification with student demonstrators the world over, ignoring the differences among national situations. Similarly, some of the black militants see in the colored peoples of the Third World the source of eventual leverage, even within America. Yet these international connections, tenuous as they are, have increased anxieties on the right and opened many in the middle to an upsurge of nationalistic fears. Numbers of McCarthy supporters who felt betrayed because of the defeat of the Vietnam peace plank at Chicago have failed to appreciate that much recent opposition to the Vietnam War is not based on moral-political revulsion, but rather on impatience with civilian restraints on military initiative and a feeling of being misled by the Administration. (Naturally, the conservatives who have come around to weariness with the Vietnam War are not grateful to the radical students and others who helped make opposition to the war visible and less flamboyant opposition to it increasingly respectable.)

When the extreme right behaves with very bad manners or extravagant brutality, it is apt to offend the conservative majority, as Joseph McCarthy offended many and as Southern segregationist mobs often offended local as well as national leaders. There comes a point when, for many Americans, the political process loses its entertainment value and comes to be regarded as unsettling and a drain on energies. Political acquiescence may leave invisible scars, but after a while political agitators, like screaming children, may come to be resented, no matter how well one understands their causes. It is at this point that the calls for law and order, if not themselves too strident, strike home. Along with the rhetoric of traditional American virtue and patriotism, the right wing shares with the conventional conservative majority a nostalgic sense of our past. However, this past is far more violent than most Americans recognize; in fact there is less domestic violence now than in earlier periods. Some black militants *talk* more violent games against whites than they play, for in this they can draw on a long American, and especially Southern and Negro, tradition of evangelical exhortation. But some radical students, perhaps more literal-minded in this respect, take the rhetoric seriously and seek not to be outdone in militancy; in general, there is a temptation among whites to attend to the more strident black leaders and not the more pragmatic ones (who themselves share some of the feelings the militants voice). Some extreme militants have a stake in proving that all whites are equally to be distrusted, and thus they assault the reservoirs of sympathy that exist for the Negro among conservative white Americans.

The result is that the conservative majority attributes the rising national noise level to the radical left and to the liberal, educated upper–middle class, which appears to tolerate if not to sponsor the radicals. The life of the blue-collar working class and the lower–middle white-collar class tends to be a neighborhood life, with friendships based on family and propinquity, savings based on real estate, and much dependence on public facilities (like schools) and semipublic ones (like churches and taverns). These people often feel themselves caught in a pincers movement between the Negroes or Puerto Ricans pressing into their neighborhoods from below and the upper-class and upper–middle-class anti-Puritan snobs who admire the poor and defiant, not the square and inhibited. (Many of the poor are square and inhibited, too, but the tradition of Western romanticism closes its eyes to this.) Policemen, schoolteachers, social workers, factory foremen, and lower-level civil servants are all men in the middle, caught between their often-unruly clients and the liberal and tolerant mandates of the national elite and its media. (These mandates sometimes suffer from a credibility gap, as when they appear to deny the everyday experience of Negro crime, picturing the oppressed as victims and rarely as victimizers.)

Among the hippies and their hangers-on, there are many splinter groups, but most of them come from the affluent strata and appear to denigrate the American insistence that in a democracy everyone must strive to get ahead; they reject the advantages desperately sought by those who have risen from the working class to the lower–middle class. Hence, although some hippies celebrate the value of toil, they cannot pose as members of the "poor but honest" class who disturb nobody; on the contrary, as played up by the mass media, they contribute their share to the politics of polarization.

Some hippies share with the radicals and with many liberals the widely prevalent assumption that the country is already post-industrial, that there is no serious problem of keeping the economy going but only of redirecting its energies. This seems far-fetched to those who do not yet feel secure in the affluence they see around them, which they define as an American prerogative. Many understandably feel helpless in the face of strikes that cripple a city's transport, hospitals, schools, or telephone service. I often see our society as a series of vast traffic jams, to which each idiosyncratic individual contributes his own weight, complaining about that of the others. To unsnarl America, to keep it productive, to make it so productive that it can satisfy the claims of the disinherited without aggravating the malaise of the most recent, still-undernourished heirs, is no mean task. The many intellectuals who reject industrialism and bureaucracy are tacitly assuming that it is no trick at all to keep our society's 200 million people alive, functioning and productive, and some of their discourse suggests that they would prefer a smaller country of noble frontiersmen. At this point society depends upon the ethic of production to keep going. Someday it may be possible to reject the blessings production provides, but that day cannot come until the blessings are universal, until they are fully at hand. I was mistaken in thinking at one time that abundance was assured, even though I recognized that our measure of it has depended since 1939 on a war-preparedness economy.

As vested interests can sabotage production in the economy, so each locale, each ethnic group and ideological position has in effect had its own deterrent in national politics. The anarchic right wing seeks Federal funds for its projects, but resists Federal control. In foreign affairs, however, it is the captive of its own chauvinism, and with the decline in right-wing isolationism, there have obviously been insufficient deterrents to adventurous and expensive foreign and military policies; Federal action has had many powerful friends and, despite generally declining xenophobia, few organized opponents. And since the right wing in the United States always tacitly cooperates with the right wing and militarists elsewhere, the influence of our right wing domestically grows when, for example, the Soviet military insists on the invasion of Czechoslovakia to secure the Warsaw Pact; such cooperation has also imperiled the nuclear nonproliferation treaty and other measures of arms control.

Nevertheless, despite the unintentional assistance given American chauvinism by nationalists elsewhere, the patriotic fervor of Americans has continued to decline throughout the century. America is a more open society than it has ever been. Leftist radicals point to the repression of dissent against the Vietnam War, as in the trial of Dr. Spock or in the prosecution or reclassification of draft resisters. Yet compared to the way opposition to earlier wars was treated, opposition to the somewhat tangential and patiently escalated war in Vietnam has not evoked fierce community pressures. There is little censure of those who avoid the draft, even though there is opprobrium for men who express opposition to America as well as to the war. The relative coolness and equanimity with which the majority of Americans accepted the Soviet invasion of Czechoslovakia is an indication of maturity (and, to some degree, of indifference) inconceivable a decade earlier. Even vis-à-vis Communist China—and despite fanaticism there—there is less fanaticism now in the United States than there was when Quemoy and Matsu seemed almost fighting words.

What Communist adversaries have not succeeded in doing to strengthen the American right wing, the provocative left is accomplishing in another tacit alliance of extremes. Some on the left regard contemporary America as basically fascist and want to develop the latent film that has already, in their view, been exposed. "America couldn't be worse" is a frequent refrain. Little do they know. Some indeed do not want to know, since the excitement and solidarity of the politics of confrontation tend to blind them to their own destructiveness. Others vastly overestimate the potential power of militant students, militant professionals and housewives, and militant blacks. They are not even aware that the Young Americans for Freedom are at least four times as numerous as the Students for a Democratic Society. There is a penchant for the theater of confrontation in which the good guys can make the bad guys look even badder on television—and radicalize still more potential good guys from the vapid, timid middle class. In the civil rights movement, this tactic succeeded with a great many liberal students and professional people, upper-middle class housewives, and clergymen. But the dramas of Selma and Birmingham that helped mobilize these minorities also set in motion efforts at school and neighborhood integration which have heightened the enthusiastic support for George Wallace among young voters, both in the South and in the North, many of whom were in school when efforts at integration began.

An absolute morality tends to be characteristic of people whose experience of life has not included the give-and-take of wide human contacts and the mutual tolerance and sense for compromise that these often, but not invariably, encourage. Idealistic young people both on the right and on the left are outraged at an America that does not live up to its ideals as their parents and other significant adults interpret—and evade—them. Both extremes are concerned with the quality of American life. Some on the right want more order (at least for others), and some on the left want more experimentalism, not only for themselves but for others as well. On neither side is there a uniform view as to the lineaments of a more desirable future. But this diversity gets lost when judged from the other side of the right–left dividing line. Thus, many Americans of the right, center, and left who want more participation in decision-making for the common man may have in mind quite different forms of representation, orders of decision, and national priorities. When questions about these matters are turned into issues of absolute morality, where ememies are those who do not share an identical view, tactics tend also to escalate. Sometimes the tactics escalate before the goals do, requiring more elevated and demanding goals to justify the means already employed.

Speaking now only of the left, white radicals in many academic and other settings are engaged in competition with black militants as to who is more militant, more uncompromising, more total in his rejection of an America that has fallen from grace. But on the whole, both militant and moderate black leaders remain more political: there are specific things they want, and—while their dignity and powers of territoriality cannot be quickly redeemed, their schools enlightened, their dwellings made more habitable—some accommodation can be made to their demands. In contrast, the demands of the New Left and of more moderate professionals and housewives tend to be qualitative and inchoate. They want Americans to be more open to experience, less driven, less bound by birth to a particular gender, class, color, or nationality. They want institutions to consider not only the products or services they turn out, but also the people in them; by emphasizing process as well as product, they seek to subordinate traditional goals of efficiency or harmony and to promote instead more complicated goals of personal autonomy—an autonomy that, as I have suggested, can sometimes become more anarchic than responsive. When these ideals are stated as absolute demands, rather than as aims to be approximated over time, the effect is sometimes to aggravate the right without much helping the left. For example, America is condemned as being racist, thus forcing on people introspection concerning their attitudes—an introspection often confused by the fact that most Negroes are lower-class, while most Americans seek democratically not to be class conscious. One consequence of calling people racists who consider themselves reasonably decent and humane may well be that they will conclude: "So be it; I am a racist and will follow leadership that respects and justifies me as I am."

Incremental gains won over a long period by careful work—and capable of being easily erased by an explosion, whether nuclear or political—seem like no gains at all to impatient young people of all chronological ages. I think that one must live simultaneously on two levels: the level on which one works for incremental gains and another on which one develops the faith and vision by which to judge those gains and to evaluate both what has been accomplished and where shortcomings remain. But a sense of moral urgency has led many people on the left to an attitude a little like that of the 1930s, when left-wing radicals found in the near target of the liberals an enemy who shared enough of their own values to be despised for not sharing them *à outrance*. Thus the radicals today [1968] make a target of Vice-President Humphrey and only rarely bother with Nixon, where their attacks would not sting or provoke dramatic response. (Black militants and their white allies do attack George Wallace, and—as he has often recognized—make votes for him; when challenged about this, they are apt to say that things couldn't be worse, when in reality things have gotten so much better that the blacks are liberated from inhibition and calculation.)*

I recall talking in 1964 with some Berkeley students active in the Free Speech Movement who were elated at the way in which they had been able to mobilize support and to gain many of their ends on the campus. I told them that they should also take into account the likelihood that they could make Ronald Reagan governor—maybe President of the United States. This prospect delighted them, for they preferred Reagan to Governor Edmund Brown as more real, less hy-

---

* The radicals of the right have a similar tropism which leads them to attack with special venom conservatives who appear complacent and hypocritical—President Eisenhower, for instance, or Secretary of State John Foster Dulles.

pocritical; Reagan would make clear where he stood. Many on the left seem quite as dedicated to a politics of style and mood as do those on the right.

Yet the argument for caution has itself to be used with caution. Any liberal who counsels radicals to his left against revolutionary tactics in a situation where the only revolution that seems probable will come from the right is likely to be reminded that, in the period when Joseph McCarthy flourished, many timid liberals sacrificed the left without mollifying the radical right. The question of tactics is always an arguable one, and it is possible that self-restraint in the face of the right-wing danger may provoke and encourage the right. The extreme right, as we have already seen, is often in the anomalous position of being stronger than it feels. It feels persecuted because many positions of influence in Washington, New York, and Hollywood are outside its control, but Goldwater's 27 million votes represent an enormous potential base to which the right wing can appeal. Yet many on the left, both black and white, make no assessment of their potential strength or that of their adversaries before plunging into battle. Some with whom I have talked justify this by saying not only that there is little to lose but also that prudence and calculation are less attractive and human than impulse and spontaneity, so why not express themselves, even in dubious battle? One difficulty with this cavalier approach is that the victims may be others than themselves, so that indulgence in spontaneity and a lack of calculation for oneself may have long-range consequences that limit the spontaneity of others.

In the 1930s, German refugees asked people like me whether America would go fascist, whether it could happen here. My response was generally to raise the paradox that it could not happen here because in part it had already: one could not overturn a system which was not a system, which chaotically gave representation to fascist and anti-fascist tendencies alike and which was sufficiently anarchic to make difficult the dominance of any authoritarian group. But this very disorderliness can breed its own antibodies. It can lead Americans to arm themselves individually while refusing to pay higher taxes for better and more professional police. Private weapons have not reduced crime any more than private air conditioners have reduced air pollution. Most of our domestic problems are so difficult that we do not even know how to begin to resolve them; Eugene McCarthy's unhysterical campaign appeared to recognize this, which won him followers among some conservatives and liberals while failing to attract many who believed that grave national problems needed to be attacked by charisma as well as by competence. In his best moments, McCarthy sought to liberate energies and hopes so that one could discover problems and begin to cope with them, although in the aftermath of what many mistakenly regarded as his defeat, some former followers have succumbed to desperation and vindictiveness toward the disorganized Democratic party rather than resuming work at the precinct level. George Wallace comfortably puts the blame for the malaise and fears of his followers on "pseudo-intellectuals" and "Communist traitors"—nothing that a good tank or billy club could not cure. The essence of demagogy is this notion that problems are simple and enemies easily identifiable . . .

* * *

My own view of America is that we grow slowly more civilized, though not at a rate guaranteed to prevent catastrophe. The upper-middle, educated classes become more tolerant, less xenophobic, more willing to endure complexity. The corporate executives who in 1964 turned against Goldwater because he was too provincial, muscular, and brash may reluctantly in 1968 vote for Nixon as the only man with a chance to keep America sufficiently together so that its problems can be worked on, its production maintained, its moral poise not totally shattered. Even now, more Americans are confused than are dogmatic and fanatical; more Americans are decent than are sadistic and niggardly. It is my impression from studying public-opinion polls that, except among the most militant, firm ideological polarities of left and right have not crystallized; rather the Vietnam War and the race issue overlap and combine with different constituencies to create political constellations that may not be permanent. Undoubtedly, Wallace's national showing helps make legitimate the myriad local campaigns which the right wing continuously wages. Yet other than shooting looters and bombing Haiphong, there is no coherent national right-wing program; a new long-term right-wing hegemony—as opposed to a traditional conservative one—has not been forged.

If the war should continue, a violent push to the right is likely to ensue, both abroad and at home. But if we can somehow make peace in Vietnam and survive the present era, we may discover that America's development toward further openness has been only temporarily halted.

20

Supporters of the Birch Society

Seymour M. Lipset

The analysis of the supporters of the John Birch Society presents some special problems . . . Because it lacks a nationally known leader, espouses a virulent and extremist ideology which gives rise to attacks on the moderate leaders of both major parties as Communists, and upholds an economic program promoting the interests and values of the small stratum of moderately well-to-do businessmen and professionals, it has appealed to a much smaller segment of the general public than did [Father] Coughlin or [Joseph] McCarthy. Further, the Society is only dimly known to many people. For example, a Gallup Survey that inquired into attitudes toward the John Birch Society in the beginning of 1962 found that over two-thirds of those interviewed had not heard of it, or else had no opinion of it (Table 1). Among those who did express opinions, negative judgments outnumbered positive ones by five to one: 5 per cent favored the Society and 26 per cent opposed it. These results were obtained four years after the Society was first organized, and over a year after it began to receive widespread attention in the general press, as well as sharp criticism from liberal political leaders and journals.

Because the bulk of the national sample had no opinion on the Birchers, certain limitations are imposed in drawing conclusions from the data. Comparisons between population sub-groups must be interpreted with extreme caution, since they may at times be quite misleading. In analyzing support for the Birchers in terms of such

SOURCE: Seymour M. Lipset, "Three Decades of the 'Radical Right,'" in D. Bell (ed.), *The Radical Right* (New York: Anchor Books, Inc., 1963), pp. 421–439. Reprinted by permission of the author.

TABLE 1 *Opinion of a National Sample on the Birch Society—February, 1962*
(GALLUP)

Favorable to the Society	5%
Unfavorable	26
No Opinion	27
Have Not Heard of the Society	42
	100%
	(1616)

categories, it is necessary to compare such small percentages as 3 per cent pro-Birch among Democrats and 7 per cent among Republicans. Such comparisons are made all the more difficult because the proportion of respondents without opinions varies widely from sub-group to sub-group, following the pattern typically associated with political knowledge, opinion, and participation.

As Table 2 shows, the proportion without an opinion is 44 per cent among those who went to college, but 85 per cent among the grammar-school-educated. Further examination of the table discloses that the college-trained have a higher proportion of Birch supporters —and also Birch opponents—than do the grade-school-educated. To take another example, professionals appear much more pro-Birch than farmers, if one looks only at the percentage of the two occupations that is favorable to the Society; however, 60 per cent of the professionals expressed an opinion, as contrasted with 15 per cent of the farmers. (To emphasize the differing contributions of various population sub-groups to opinion, both pro and con, on the Birch Society, Table 3 is included, based on the same data as Table 2, but showing the relative contribution of sub-groups to the pro-Birch and anti-Birch groups, rather than the opinion distribution of the sub-groups on the Birch issue.)

The low level of opinion on the Society has additional implications for an analysis of Birch support. These concern the extent of possible latent support. One cannot assume that, because the low-income element (family income under $4000) of the population divided 4 to 1 against the Birchers in 1962, the same division of opinion would obtain at a time when, perhaps, a majority of these persons will know of, and have views regarding, the Birchers. At the time of the Gallup Survey, only 20 per cent of low-income respondents had an opinion on the organization. One cannot guess whether the balance of judgment would remain the same if 50 per cent—or

TABLE 2 *Attitudes Toward Birch Society by Selected Characteristics in Per Cent—February, 1962*

(GALLUP)

Characteristics	Pro	Con	Don't Know Haven't Heard	N
PARTY				
Democrat	3%	21	76	(787)
Independent	5	34	61	(368)
Republican	7	28	65	(444)
RELIGION				
Protestant	4	24	72	(1108)
Catholic	5	27	68	(390)
Jewish	6	48	46	(54)
REGION				
Northeast	4	34	62	(460)
Midwest	4	20	76	(538)
South	4	19	77	(359)
West	7	35	58	(259)
EDUCATION				
Grade	2	13	85	(428)
High	5	25	70	(889)
College	8	48	44	(294)
INCOME				
Low	4	16	80	(509)
Medium	5	24	71	(605)
High	6	39	55	(483)
SEX				
Men	5	30	65	(784)
Women	4	22	74	(820)
OCCUPATION				
Professional	9	51	40	(166)
Business, executive	6	33	61	(176)
Clerical, sales	7	34	57	(193)
Skilled labor	5	19	76	(258)
Unskilled, service	3	18	79	(381)
Farmer	1	14	85	(173)
Non–labor force	5	22	73	(235)
Non-manual	7	39	54	(535)
Manual	4	19	77	(639)
AGE				
21–29	5	23	72	(232)
30–49	3	29	68	(700)
50 and over	6	23	71	(623)
TOTAL SAMPLE	5	26	69	(1616)

80 per cent—of this group had opinions to offer. In short, under different conditions arising either within the country or outside it, and with different policies and techniques pursued by the Society itself,

TABLE 3 *Characteristics of Birch Supporters and Opponents in Per Cent—February, 1962*

(GALLUP)

Characteristics	Total Sample	Pro-Birch	Anti-Birch	Don't Know, Haven't Heard
PARTY				
Democrat	49%	33%	40%	54%
Independent	23	24	30	20
Republican	28	43	30	26
RELIGION				
Protestant	72	66	66	74
Catholic	25	30	27	24
Jewish	3	4	7	2
REGION				
Northeast	28	25	37	25
Midwest	34	32	25	36
South	22	21	16	26
West	16	22	22	13
EDUCATION				
Grade	27	13	13	33
High	55	57	53	57
College	18	30	34	12
INCOME				
Low	32	24	20	37
Medium	38	38	35	39
High	30	38	45	24
SEX				
Men	49	57	57	45
Women	51	43	43	55
OCCUPATION				
Professional	11	20	21	6
Business, executive	11	13	15	10
Clerical, sales	12	17	16	10
Skilled labor	16	16	12	18
Farmer	11	1	6	13
Non–labor force	15	17	13	16
Unskilled, service	24	16	17	27
Non-manual	34	50	52	26
Manual	40	32	29	45
AGE				
21–29	15	15	13	15
30–49	45	33	51	44
50 and over	40	52	36	41
	100%	100%	100%	100%
N	(1616)	(76)	(416)	(1124)

the Birchers may come to the attention of segments of the population they are not presently reaching, and the relative distribution of supporters and opponents within different analytic categories may become quite different.

Given these difficulties in interpreting the results of the national survey, I shall not discuss them in great detail. It is possible, however, to specify some of the factors that are associated with opinion toward the Society by concentrating on an analysis of attitudes within the one state in the Union in which the Society has become an important election issue and source of controversy—California. The California Poll, a state-wide survey organization, reports that in January, 1962, 82 per cent of a sample of 1100 Californians had heard of the Society. The national Gallup Survey, cited earlier, which was taken at about the same time, indicates that among respondents in the three Pacific Coast states, 79 per cent had heard of the Society as contrasted with 58 per cent in the nation as a whole.[1] The salience of the Birch issue in California in 1962 can hardly be disputed: at the time, two California congressmen were avowed members of the organization; the attorney general of the state issued a detailed report on the Society that was extensively reported and discussed in the newspapers; the Republican Assembly, meeting to endorse candidates for the 1962 primaries, spent considerable time debating the Party's position with respect to the Society; and both gubernatorial candidates, Governor Edmund Brown and former Vice-President Nixon, vied in attacking the Birchites.[2]

Given the salience of the Birch issue in California politics, and the high degree of public knowledge of the organization, findings for the state of California may be interpreted with somewhat greater confidence than the national data. The January, 1962, California Poll permitted the construction of [this] measure of Birch support and opposition . . . : The Poll inquired first whether respondents would be more or less likely to vote for a gubernatorial candidate who welcomed Birch Society support, and second whether they would be more or less likely to vote for a candidate who rejected the Society's en-

---

[1] The wording of the question in the two surveys was similar but not identical, since the California Poll item read: "Have you heard anything about a political group called the John Birch Society?" The Gallup query did not include the word "political."

[2] It should be noted, however, that this does not mean that Californians are more in favor of the Birch Society than those in other parts of the country. Actually, among those with opinions, there are proportionately more pro-Birchers in the Midwest and in the South than in the Far West.

dorsement. From responses on these two questions, respondents were divided into three groups: those who were sympathetic to the Birch Society on at least one question; those who said that the Birch issue would not affect their vote; and those who were unsympathetic to the Birch Society on one or both questions. A fourth group contained those who did not have an opinion on either question, together with persons who had never heard of the Society. Table 4 gives the distribution among California respondents in these four categories.

It is clear that in California, as in the nation as a whole, the bulk of those with opinions about the Birchers were hostile. Among the national sample, as we have seen, unfavorable replies outnumbered

TABLE 4 *Attitudes Toward the Birch Society Among Californians—January, 1962*

(CALIFORNIA POLL)

Favorable	6%
Neutral	15
Unfavorable	41
No Opinion[a]/ Never Heard	38
	100%
N	(1186)

[a] No Opinion includes 2 per cent who gave contradictory responses.

favorable by a magnitude of five to one (26 per cent to 5 per cent); in California, the negative exceeded the positive by seven to one (41 per cent to 6 per cent). Exact comparisons are, of course, impossible since the questions posed were so different. Moreover, it might be argued that the neutral category in California, those who reported that it made no difference whether a candidate was pro-Birch Society or not—the anti–anti-Birchers, so to speak—were "soft on Birchism." In spite of the propaganda emphasizing the anti-democratic propensities of the Birch Society and its attacks on Eisenhower and other major figures as Communists or dupes, these persons were still willing to say that a candidate's involvement in the Birch Society would not prejudice them against him.

An examination of the data reported in Tables 5 and 6 points up a number of factors associated with Birch support in California. A supporter of the Society is more likely to be a Republican than a Democrat, to live in southern California, to be better educated, and to be in a higher economic category. Occupational variations as such

TABLE 5 *Attitudes Toward Birch Society by Selected Characteristics in Per Cent—January, 1962*

(CALIFORNIA POLL)

Characteristics	Pro	Neut.	Con	DK/HH[a]	Total	N
PARTY						
Democrat	3%	11	45	41	100%	(673)
Republican	10	21	36	33	100	(468)
RELIGION						
Protestant	6	17	39	38	100	(769)
Catholic	6	11	42	41	100	(273)
Jewish	4	6	63	27	100	(67)
REGION						
No. California	3	13	37	47	100	(499)
So. California	8	17	44	31	100	(687)
EDUCATION						
Grade School	2	15	25	58	100	(127)
High School	4	13	36	47	100	(594)
1-2 Coll./Trade	8	16	50	26	100	(230)
3+ College	11	17	55	17	100	(235)
ECON. LEVEL						
Low	5	11	36	48	100	(306)
Medium	5	17	42	36	100	(639)
High	10	14	47	29	100	(240)
SEX						
Men	7	17	42	34	100	(590)
Women	5	13	40	42	100	(595)
OCCUPATION						
Professional	6	15	53	25	100	(162)
Exec./Mgr.	7	18	47	28	100	(71)
Self-empl. business	4	20	39	37	100	(67)
Cler./Sales	6	13	47	34	100	(191)
Skilled	4	12	42	42	100	(203)
Unskilled & service	5	12	34	49	100	(258)
Farm	17	29	20	34	100	(35)
Ret'd, etc.	8	17	37	38	100	(174)
Non-manual	6	15	48	31	100	(492)
Manual	5	12	37	46	100	(461)
AGE						
21-29	6	15	39	40	100	(226)
30-49	6	13	47	34	100	(538)
50 and over	6	17	35	42	100	(421)
TOTAL SAMPLE	6	15	41	38	100	(1186)

[a] Abbreviations for "Don't know, Haven't heard."

do not seem to be significantly related to attitudes toward the Birchers, with the exception of the fact that the small group of farmers in the sample seem to be the most strongly pro-Birch among the vocational categories. Differences between religious groups are small, al-

TABLE 6 *Characteristics of Birch Supporters Contrasted with Birch Opponents in Per Cent—January, 1962*

(CALIFORNIA POLL)

Characteristics	Total Sample	Pro-Birch	Neutral	Anti-Birch	DK/HH
PARTY					
Democrat	59%	28%	45%	64%	64%
Republican	41	72	55	36	36
RELIGION					
Protestant	69	71	79	66	70
Catholic	25	25	19	25	26
Jewish	6	5	2	9	4
REGION					
No. California	42	22	36	38	53
So. California	58	78	64	62	47
EDUCATION					
Grade School	11	4	11	7	16
High School	50	34	46	43	62
1–2 Coll./Trade	19	26	20	23	14
3+ College	20	36	23	27	8
ECON. LEVEL					
Low	20	21	20	22	33
Medium	54	44	61	55	52
High	26	35	19	23	15
SEX					
Men	50	57	57	51	45
Women	50	43	43	49	55
OCCUPATION					
Professional	14	14	15	18	9
Business	12	11	15	13	10
Cler./Sales	17	15	15	19	15
Skilled	17	12	15	17	19
Unskilled & service	22	20	18	18	28
Farm	3	8	6	1	5
Ret'd, etc.	15	20	17	14	15
Non-manual	43	40	45	50	34
Manual	39	32	33	35	47
AGE					
21–29	19	19	19	18	20
30–49	45	47	39	52	41
50 and over	36	34	42	30	39
	100%	100%	100%	100%	100%
	N (1186)	N (73)	N (176)	N (488)	N (449)

though Catholics are somewhat less likely to back the Birch Society than are Protestants.

Since party identification appears so crucial in determining attitude toward the Birch Society, it is possible that some of the above-mentioned relationships are indirectly a consequence of political affiliation. For example, the political commitment of Protestants and Catholics varies greatly. In California, Protestants divide 50–50 in allegiance to the major parties, whereas among Catholics, Democrats outnumber Republicans 4 to 1. These results suggest that the Democratic commitment of Catholics may account for their slightly greater opposition to the Birch Society. And in fact we find that when religious groups are compared *within* party categories Catholics are slightly more likely to favor the Birch Society than are Protestants[3] (Table 7).

TABLE 7 *Relationship of Party Affiliation and Religion to Attitude Toward John Birch Society in California, in Per Cent—January, 1962*

(CALIFORNIA POLL)

Party and Religion	Pro	Neutral	Con	Don't Know or Never Heard	Total	N
Democrats						
Protestants	2%	14	41	43	100%	(387)
Catholics	4	8	44	44	100	(206)
Republicans						
Protestants	10	21	37	32	100	(380)
Catholics	14	21	32	33	100	(57)

When the effect of education on attitudes toward the Birch Society is analyzed within party groups, the data suggest little difference among Democrats according to education. If anything, better-educated Democrats are more likely to be more anti-Birch. Among Republicans, however, greater education is associated with being pro-Birch. To a considerable extent these variations would seem to be a product of socio-economic status. That is, with increasing economic level, Republicans are more disposed to support the Birch Society, while Democrats at higher-status levels are somewhat more inclined to oppose the organization than their less-privileged party brethren (Table 8).

The data clearly reflect the strong connection between attitudes toward the Birch Society and basic party commitment—a relationship that is hardly surprising, given the tenor of the organization. Basically, the Birch Society appeals most to well-to-do Republicans, and

---
[3] The same pattern occurs in the national Gallup data.

TABLE 8 *Relationship of Party Affiliation and Economic Level to Attitudes Toward the Birch Society in California, in Per Cent—January, 1962*

(CALIFORNIA POLL)

Party and SES[a]	Pro	Neutral	Con	Don't Know or Never Heard	Total	N
Democrats						
High	3%	12	50	35	100%	(109)
Medium	3	11	49	37	100	(358)
Low	3	11	36	50	100	(218)
Republicans						
High	18	14	45	23	100	(126)
Medium	8	25	33	34	100	(274)
Low	6	15	32	47	100	(68)

[a] Abbreviated for socio-economic status.

somewhat more to the Catholics among them than to the Protestants. These findings suggest that the Society's appeal is most effective among those to whom economic conservatism and fear of Communism are crucial issues.

Evidence for this interpretation may be drawn from an analysis of attitudes toward the Birch Society as related to preferences among likely contenders for the G.O.P. presidential nomination in 1964, and as related to opinions on the importance of the threat of internal Communism. (The first comparison is made only for Republicans.) Among Republicans who supported the Birch Society, almost three-fifths (59 per cent) favored Senator Goldwater for President in 1964 (Table 9). Conversely, while former Vice-President Nixon was

TABLE 9 *Opinion Toward the Birch Society According to Preferred Republican Presidential Choice for 1964 Among California Republicans—January, 1962*

(CALIFORNIA POLL)

Preferred Candidate	Pro	Neutral	Con	Don't Know, Never Heard	Total Sample
Rockefeller	4%	15%	23%	21%	19%
Nixon	25	38	38	33	35
Romney	8	11	4	7	7
Goldwater	59	22	23	18	25
Don't Know	4	14	12	21	14
	100%	100%	100%	100%	100%
N	(48)	(96)	(170)	(154)	(468)

the leading candidate among the other categories, Republicans who opposed the Birch Society contained a larger proportion of Rockefeller backers than did any other opinion groups. Examined in terms of the attitudes of the supporters of the different candidates, the data show that 71 per cent of the Rockefeller partisans were anti-Birch, as contrasted with 56 per cent of the Nixon supporters, and 45 per cent of the Goldwater advocates. Clearly, Birchism and general political conservatism were strongly related among California Republicans in 1962.

Among followers of both parties, attitudes toward the Birchers are influenced by views on the importance of internal Communism as a

TABLE 10 *Birch Opinion Related to Perception of Domestic Communist Threat Among Californians—January, 1962*

(CALIFORNIA POLL)

Perception of Communist Threat	Attitudes on Birch Society				Total Sample
	Pro	Neutral	Con	Don't Know, Haven't Heard	
High	75%	53%	48%	50%	51%
Medium	21	33	32	37	33
Low	4	14	20	13	16
	100%	100%	100%	100%	100%
N	(67)	(173)	(471)	(407)	(1118)

threat to the nation. Three-fourths of Birch supporters see the danger of domestic Communism as great, as contrasted with slightly more than half of the neutral group and a little less than half of the anti-Birch element. Those perceiving minimal threat from internal Communism constitute 4 per cent of the pro-Birchers, 14 per cent of the neutrals, and 20 per cent of the anti-Birchers (Table 10). (The same relationship between Birch opinion and perceived threat holds when Republicans and Democrats are taken separately, although Republicans more often than Democrats perceive the threat as high.)

There is also a difference between supporters and opponents of the Society who agree that the internal Communist threat is great in their opinion of the adequacy of existing agencies dealing with the problem. Approximately three-fifths of the Society's opponents who agree that domestic Communism is a major problem feel that it is not being adequately dealt with, as compared with four-fifths of the Society's supporters. Thus, those who like the Society differ sharply from those who dislike it in their evaluation of the extent of the threat and the way it is being handled. Considering both opinions together, we find that twice the proportion of the former group (60 per cent) feels that the threat is great and that it is being inadequately handled, compared to the latter (30 per cent).

Neither the national Gallup Survey nor the California Poll included questions concerning attitudes on issues other than those reported above. However, a questionnaire study conducted in the San Francisco Bay Area in the spring of 1962, primarily for the purpose of studying opinions on peace issues, included a question on the John Birch Society and other attitudes relevant to this investigation. Though designed to secure a representative sample of the Bay Area population, the survey suffered from defects not uncommon in surveys utilizing self-administered questionnaires as opposed to interviews—that is, a heavy bias in the direction of responses by the better-educated.[4] Forty-seven per cent of those who answered the questionnaire had at least some college education, and two-thirds were engaged in non-manual occupations. It is impossible, therefore, to draw any reliable conclusions from this survey as to the social characteristics of Birch supporters in the San Francisco region. But since the study did contain a number of attitude items on a variety of issues, and because the social characteristics of Birch supporters and opponents corresponded on the whole with the findings of the California Poll, a brief report on its results seems warranted.[5]

Of particular interest in this survey were a number of questions dealing with attitudes toward minority ethnic and religious groups. Respondents were asked, "In choosing your friends and associates, how do you feel about the following types of people?" Response categories were, "Would rather not deal with," "Feel some reservations about dealing with," and "Feel the same about them as others." It was found that those approving the Birch Society (9 per cent) tend to be more prejudiced against Negroes and Mexicans than those who opposed the organization.[6] The pro-Birch group is also some-

---

[4] The questionnaires were left at the homes of those chosen in the sample, to be filled out by the respondent and picked up the following day.

[5] The survey indicated that Bay Area Birch supporters are more likely to be Republicans than Democrats, college-educated rather than less schooled, and white Christians rather than members of racial or religious minorities. Thus, of the white, Christian, college-trained Republicans in the sample, 16 per cent reported themselves generally favorable to the Birchers. No Jews or Orientals and only 4 per cent of the Negroes queried were pro-Birch.

[6] Only white Christians were included in these comparisons, since the findings would presumably have been distorted by the inclusion of the minorities in ratings of their own groups.

what more hostile to Orientals and Jews than the opposing element, but the differences are relatively minor. The findings hold when respondents of differing educational attainment are treated separately, indicating that, despite the greater prejudice of the less-educated generally, Birch supporters tend to show more prejudice than Birch opponents.

TABLE 11 *Prejudice Toward Ethnic and Religious Minorities According to Opinion on Birch Society*

(WHITE CHRISTMAS ONLY)[a]

Prejudiced Toward:	Proportion Expressing Prejudice Among:	
	Pro-Birch Group	Anti-Birch Group
Negroes	53%	37%
Mexicans	38	27
Orientals	22	17
Jews	15	11
Jehovah's Witnesses	44	40
N	(42)	(303)
Catholics[b]	7	8
N	(26)	(193)

[a] Data presented through the courtesy of Robert Schutz, of the Northern California Lobby for Peace, and Thomas Tissue, graduate assistant in sociology.
[b] Only responses by Protestants are presented—N = 26 Pro-Birch, N = 193 Anti-Birch.

Supporters of the Birch Society are less willing to grant civil liberties to Communists, atheists, and pacifists than those unfavorable to the organization; they are also less likely to feel that search warrants should be required of police entering a house, more likely to favor censorship of "crime comic books," and more likely to deny the right of public meetings to those opposing "our form of government." However, it is important to note that degree of education tends to have a much greater effect on attitude than does opinion of the Birch Society. For example, college-educated Birch *supporters* are more inclined to allow Communists to speak in their community than are Birch *opponents* who have not attended college (38 per cent versus 28 per cent). Supporters of the Society also exhibit more prejudice toward Negroes and Mexicans, although they do not register a significantly higher degree of anti-Semitism than the population at large. In all likelihood, more refined and comprehensive analysis of various sorts of ethnic and religious prejudice will be necessary before definitive conclusions may be reached regarding the relationship, or relationships, of these phenomena to current forms of right-wing extremism.

Thus far, I have omitted any discussion of the fact that the Birch Society is much stronger in southern than in northern California. In fact, the data from the California Poll survey discussed here and a later one completed in May, 1962 (too late to be analyzed and reported in detail here), indicate that California support for the Society is largely a phenomenon of the south. It has even less backing in northern California than in most other sections of the country.

The explanation for the variations between the two sections would seem to lie largely in certain differences in their community structure. Northern California, centered around San Francisco, is the old, established part of the state. It was the original dominant center of population. Los Angeles and southern California have emerged as major population centers only since World War I, and their really rapid mass growth occurred after 1940. Although northern California has continued to increase in population, its major center, San Francisco, has grown little for many decades. There are many old families in the Bay Area who represent four and five generations of wealth, the descendants of those who made their money in mining, commerce, or railroads in the first decades after statehood, from 1850 to 1880. Wealth in Los Angeles, on the other hand, is almost exclusively *nouveaux riches,* and the well-to-do there possess the attitudes toward politics and economics characteristic of this stratum. They are more likely to back the rightist groups that oppose the welfare state, the income tax, and trade unions, and, lacking political and cultural sophistication, are more prone to accept conspiracy interpretations of the strength behind liberal or welfare measures. There is little that is stabilized or institutionalized in southern California. New, rapidly expanding centers of population lack a traditional leadership structure accustomed to the responsibilities of running community institutions and supportive of the rights of various groups to share in community decisions and authority. Ethnic and racial tensions are high in the south, and whereas in the north community leaders cooperate to repress any potential conflict, in the south there is little cooperation to ease such tensions.

Some evidence for the hypothesis that the strength of the Birch Society in southern California (and in Arizona, Texas, and Florida, as well) is related to the tensions of population growth and community integration may be found in the second (May) California Poll. This survey inquired among those not native to the state as to when they moved to California. When respondents are divided between those who have been in the state more, or less, than 15 years, the data indicate that a larger proportion of the supporters of the Society (39 per cent) are among those who migrated to the state since World War II than is true among opponents (29 per cent). Unfortunately, there are no available data that bear directly on the political effects of social mobility, that is, the extent to which the experience of a change in socio-economic position, up or down the social hierarchy, is related to these political issues. The California Poll data do clearly suggest, however, that respondents whose educational and occupational attainments are not congruent—*e.g.,* manual workers who went to college, or those in high-status positions with little education—are more likely to be pro-Birch than others within their strata whose statuses on these two stratification dimensions are roughly similar. These findings (based unfortunately on far too few cases of Birch supporters to be significant) are in line with the assumption that social mobility and/or status discrepancies predispose those involved in such experiences to accept extremist forms of politics.

The support the John Birch Society has received is seemingly somewhat different from [certain other] radical-rightist movements discussed earlier. As compared to them, it has drawn more heavily from ideological conservatives, those committed to the Republican Party, and, within the ranks of the Republicans, from among the more well-to-do and better-educated.[7] Twenty-two per cent of high economic level, college-educated Republicans in the California Poll are favorable to the Birchers, as compared with 6 per cent in the sample as a whole.[8] As a group advocating economic conservatism, the

---

[7] Stories reported in the California press concerning internal conflicts within the Republican Party and the attitudes of wealthy Republicans toward contributing to Nixon's campaign suggest that the Party is troubled by the fact that support for the Birch Society is much greater among Party activists and wealthy contributors than among the Republican electorate. Recent evidence from analysis of national data indicates that local Republican leaders around the country tend to be considerably more conservative than the rank and file of the G.O.P. See Herbert McClosky, Paul J. Hoffman, and Rosemary O'Hara, "Issue Conflict and Consensus Among Party Leaders and Followers," *American Political Science Review,* 54 (1960), pp. 406–27; see, especially, pp. 422–24.

[8] Similar conclusions concerning differences between the support of [Joseph] McCarthy and of the Birch Society drawn from survey data have recently been suggested in a report of a comparative study of mail attacking senatorial critics of the radical right (Senator Fulbright for his opposition to McCarthy and Senator Kuchel for his attacks on the Birch Society). The report states that "only 15 per cent of the McCarthyite mail could—charitably, at best—be described as reasonable in tone, substance, or literacy." However, the "Birch mail is much more moderate in tone than McCarthy mail, even though it may be as extremist in objective. It is better written and better reasoned.

Society naturally has little appeal for the economically deprived. It is difficult to see a movement with so little popular appeal—and with so conspiratorial a view of the American political process—making headway among the general population. But the considerable progress it has made among well-to-do Republicans who can afford to support their political convictions financially may mean that the Birch Society will be able to maintain the impression of a powerful mass-supported group for some time to come.[9]

. . . The great bulk of the mail came from people who acknowledge membership in the Birch Society or from sympathizers. . . . Many of the writers seem genuinely concerned over the rise of Communism. . . . But many of them seem more aroused over social-welfare legislation, income taxes, and foreign aid than they are over Communism." (See Herman Edelsberg, "Birchites Make Polite Pen Pals," *The A.D.L. Bulletin,* April, 1962, pp. 7–8.)

Presumably the differences in style and tone of the letters reflected the variation in the class and educational levels of the supporters of both tendencies.

[9] Various journalistic accounts indicate that the Birch Society includes among its members the heads of a number of medium-size corporations, such as independent oil companies, and manufacturing concerns. Such men . . . also supported McCarthy, and they are often willing to back up their antagonism to "creeping socialism" with heavy contributions.

21

A Prophetic Minority

Jack Newfield

A new generation of radicals has been spawned from the chrome womb of affluent America. The last lingering doubts that the Silent Generation had found its voice vanished forever on April 17, 1965, when more than 20,000 of this new breed converged on the nation's capital to protest against the war in Vietnam. It was the largest antiwar demonstration in the history of Washington, D.C.—and it had been organized and sponsored by a student organization—SDS.

Assembled in the warm afternoon sunshine that Saturday were the boys and girls who had "freedom rode" to Jackson, Mississippi; who had joined the Peace Corps and returned disillusioned; tutored Negro teen-agers in the slums of the great cities; vigiled against the Bomb; rioted against the House Un-American Activities Committee; risked their lives to register voters in the Black Belt; and sat-in for free speech at the University of California at Berkeley.

They were the new generation of American radicals, nourished not by the alien cobwebbed dogmas of Marx, Lenin, and Trotsky, but by the existential humanism of Albert Camus, the anticolonialism of Frantz Fanon, the communitarian anarchism of Paul Goodman, the poetic alienation of Bob Dylan, and the grass-roots radicalism of that "prophetic shock minority" called SNCC [Student Nonviolent Coordinating Committee]. They were there not to protest anything so simple as war or capitalism. They came to cry out against the hypocrisy called Brotherhood Week, assembly lines called colleges, manipulative

SOURCE: Reprinted by permission of The World Publishing Company from *A Prophetic Minority* by Jack Newfield. An NAL Book. Copyright © 1966 by Jack Newfield.

hierarchies called corporations, conformity called status, lives of quiet desperation called success.

They heard Joan Baez sing Dylan's sardonic poem, "With God on Our Side," and cheered spontaneously when she sang, "Although they murdered six million, in the ovens they fried/Now they too have God on their side."

They sang "Do What the Spirit Say Do," the latest freedom hit to come out of the jails and churches of the South, an indication perhaps of their deepest concern—human freedom and expression. Thus, Freedom now, "Oh Freedom," freedom ride, free university, freedom school, Free Speech Movement, and the Freedom Democratic Party.

And the 20,000 listened to the visionary voices of the New Radicalism.

Staughton Lynd, a romantic, a Quaker, and a revolutionary, told them:

> We are here today in behalf of Jean-Paul Sartre . . . we are here to keep the faith with those of all countries and all ages who have sought to beat swords into ploughshares and to war no more.

They heard Bob Parris, SNCC's humble visionary, who told them:

> Listen and think. Don't clap, please. . . . Don't use Mississippi as a moral lightning rod. Use it as a looking glass. Look into it and see what it tells you about all of America.

And they listened to Paul Potter, the tense, brilliant, twenty-four-year-old former president of SDS, who said:

> There is no simple plan, no scheme or gimmick that can be proposed here. There is no simple way to attack something that is deeply rooted in the society. If the people of this country are to end the war in Vietnam, and to change the institutions which create it, then the people of this country must create a massive social movement—and if that can be built around the issue of Vietnam, then that is what we must do.
>
> By a social movement I mean more than petitions and letters of protest, or tacit support of dissident Congressmen; I mean people who are willing to change their lives, who are willing to challenge the system, to take the problem of change seriously.
>
> By a social movement I mean an effort that is powerful enough to make the country understand that our problems are not in Vietnam, or China or Brazil or outer space or at the bottom of the ocean, but here in the United States. What we must begin to do

is build a democratic and humane society in which Vietnams are unthinkable. . . .

Then, after three hours of speeches and freedom singing, the 20,000 stood in the lengthening shadow of the Washington Monument, linked arms, and, swaying back and forth, sang the anthem of their movement. Reaching out to clasp strange hands were button-down intellectuals from Harvard and broken-down Village hippies; freshmen from small Jesuit schools and the overalled kamikazes of SNCC; curious faculty members and high-school girls; angry ghetto Negroes and middle-aged parents, wondering what motivates their rebellious children; all together, singing and feeling the words, "Deep in my heart/ I do believe/ We shall overcome someday."

The SDS march, which had drawn twice the participation everyone, including its sponsors, had expected, suddenly illuminated a phenomenon that had been growing underground, in campus dorms, in the Mississippi delta, in bohemian subcultures, for more than five years. It was the phenomenon of students rejecting the dominant values of their parents and their country; becoming alienated, becoming political, becoming active, becoming radical; protesting against racism, poverty, war, Orwell's *1984,* Camus's executioner, Mills's Power Elite, Mailer's Cancerous Totalitarianism; protesting against irrational anti-Communism, nuclear weaponry, the lies of statesmen, the hypocrisy of laws against narcotics and abortion; protesting against loyalty oaths, speaker bans, HUAC [House on Un-American Activities Committee], *in loco parentis*—and finally, at Berkeley, protesting against the computer, symbol of man's dehumanization by the machine; in sum, protesting against all those obscenities that form the cryptic composite called the System.

In the weeks immediately following the SDS march the mass media suddenly discovered that the Brainwashed Generation, as poet Karl Shapiro had tagged the campus catatonics of the 1950s, had become a protest generation, that a cultural and sociological revolution had taken place while they had been preoccupied with the Bogart cult, J. D. Salinger, and baseball bonus babies. Within an eight-week period, *Time, Newsweek, The Saturday Evening Post, The New York Times Magazine, Life,* and two television networks all popularized the New Left. They smeared it, they psychoanalyzed it, they exaggerated it, they cartooned it, they made it look like a mélange of beatniks, potheads, and agents of international Communism; *they did everything but explain the failures in the society that called it into being.*

The New Radicalism is pluralistic, amorphous, and multilayered. Its three political strands—anarchism, pacifism, and socialism—mingle in different proportions in different places. It's different in every city, on every campus. In Berkeley there is a strong sex-drug-literary orientation. In New York there is a politically sophisticated component. In the South there is extra emphasis on the nonviolent religious element.

At its surface, *political* level, the New Radicalism is an anti-Establishment protest against all the obvious inequities of American life. It says that Negroes should vote, that America should follow a peaceful, noninterventionist foreign policy, that anti-Communism at home has become paranoid and destructive, that the poverty of forty million should be abolished. It is a series of individual criticisms many liberals can agree with.

At its second, more complex level, this new movement is a *moral* revulsion against a society that is becoming increasingly corrupt. The New Radicals were coming to maturity as McCarthy built a movement based on deceit and bullying, as Dulles lied about the CIA's role in the 1954 Guatemala *coup,* as Eisenhower lied to the world about the U-2 flight over the Soviet Union, as Adlai Stevenson lied to the UN about America's support of the Bay of Pigs invasion, as Charles Van Doren participated in fixed quiz shows on television, as congressmen and judges were convicted for bribery. They saw the organs of masscult[ure] lie about their movement, the clergy exile priests for practicing brotherhood, older men red-bait their organizations. Feeling this ethical vacuum in the country, the New Radicals have made morality and truth the touchstones of their movement. Like Gandhi, they try to "speak truth to power." Their politics are not particularly concerned with power or success, but rather with absolute moral alternatives like love, justice, equality, and freedom. Practical, programmatic goals are of little interest. They want to pose an alternate vision, not just demand "more" or "better" of what exists. They don't say welfare programs should be better subsidized; they say they should be administered in a wholly different, more dignifying way. They don't say Negroes need leaders with better judgment; they say Negroes should develop spokesmen from their own ranks.

At its third, subterranean level, the New Radicalism is an *existential* revolt against remote, impersonal machines that are not responsive to human needs. The New Radicals feel sharply the growing totalitarianization of life in this technological, urban decade. They feel powerless and unreal beneath the unfeeling instruments that control their lives. They comprehend the essentially undemocratic nature of the military-industrial complex; the Power Elite; the multiversity with its IBM course cards; urban renewal by technocrats; canned television laughter; wire taps; automation; computer marriages and artificial insemination; and, finally, the mysterious button somewhere that can trigger the nuclear holocaust.

The New Radicals are the first products of liberal affluence. They have grown up in sterile suburbs, urban complexes bereft of community, in impersonal universities. They are the children of economic surplus and spiritual starvation. They agree with C. Wright Mills when he writes, "Organized irresponsibility, in this impersonal sense, is a leading characteristic of modern industrial societies everywhere. On every hand the individual is confronted with seemingly remote organizations; he feels dwarfed and helpless before the managerial cadres and their manipulated and manipulating minions."

And they can only chant "amen" to Lewis Mumford, who observed in *The Transformations of Man,* [that] modern man has already depersonalized "himself so effectively that he is no longer man enough to stand up to his machines."

From their fury at arbitrary power wielded by impersonal machines (governments, college administrations, welfare bureaucracies, draft boards, television networks) come some of the New Radicals' most innovative ideas. Participatory democracy—the notion that ordinary people should be able to affect [effect] all the decisions that control their lives. The idea that social reformation comes from organizing the dispossessed into their own insurgent movements rather than from forming top-down alliances between liberal bureaucratic organizations. The insistence on fraternity and community inside the movement. The passion against manipulation and centralized decision-making. The reluctance to make the New Left itself a machine tooled and fueled to win political power in the traditional battle pits. The concept of creating new democratic forms like the Mississippi Freedom Democratic Party, the Newark Community Union Project, and the *Southern Courier,* a newspaper designed to represent the Negroes of the Black Belt rather than the white power structure or the civil rights organizations. It is its brilliant insight into the creeping authoritarianism of modern technology and bureaucracy that gives the New Radicalism its definitive qualities of decentralism, communitarianism, and existential humanism.

Historically, the New Radicals' forebears are the Whitman–Emerson–Thoreau transcendentalists, and the Joe Hill–Bill Haywood Wobblies. Like the IWW mill strikers at Lawrence, Massachusetts, in 1912, the New Left wants "bread and roses too."

A prophetic minority creates each generation's legend. In the 1920s it was the expatriate quest for personal expression. In the 1930s it was radical social action. In the 1940s it was the heroism of the trenches. In the 1950s it was the cultivation of the private self. Now, halfway through the decade, it is once again the ideal of social action that is *defining a generation*.

By this I mean specifically that in fifteen years Bob Dylan's poems will be taught in college classrooms, that Paul Booth, Julian Bond, and Stokely Carmichael will be the leaders of adult protest movements, that the Beatles movies will be revived in art houses, and that Tom Hayden, Norman Fruchter, Robb Burlage, Bob Parris, and Carl Oglesby will be major social critics. But I also mean to emphasize that the New Left has, and always will have, only a fraction of the whole truth, just as the Freudians, the Symbolists, the Marxists, and the Impressionists possessed only a fragment of the truth. But it is the fragment glimpsed by this generation.

The legend of the 1930s turned to ashes in Washington, Moscow, and Madrid before the decade was over. It is entirely possible that the New Left can meet such a tragic end as well. The possibility of political fissures exists in any movement. This one could split over tactics like the Bolsheviks or Mensheviks, or over morality like Sartre and Camus. Black nationalism may yet poison it, and unfocused activism may exhaust it. But I doubt it.

In the immediate future, the impulse to rebel will continue to grow among marginal groups like students, Negroes, migrant farm workers, intellectuals, and white-collar workers. This will happen because the generators of dissent—war, bureaucracy, guilt-producing affluence, racism, hypocrisy, moral rot—are enduring in the fabric of American society. If the Vietnam war is settled, there will be another one in Thailand, or Angola, or Peru. If Bobby Baker is jailed, there will be another fast-buck politician exposed. If the killers of Goodman, Chaney, and Schwerner are convicted, there will be other atrocities in the South.

All this means that the New Left—and the other sections of the society in motion—will grow and become even more uncomfortably radical. My own hunch is that SDS will be the chief repository of this radical mood, that SNCC's time has passed, its gifts taken without adequate acknowledgment. I also suspect the Hereditary Left will not grow much, because it is too weighted down with the moral bankruptcy of Communism, and because it misses completely this generation's indictment of impersonal bureaucracies and the existential void of the middle class. Primarily, the New Left will become increasingly the umbrella under which indigenous, decentralized movements will grow. Grass-roots insurgencies, such as the grape strike in California, Berkeley's Vietnam Day Committee, the NCUP [Newark Community Union Project] project in Newark, the Lowndes County Freedom Organization in Alabama, Dick Gregory's campaign for mayor of Chicago, independent community committees against the war in Vietnam, and campus protests against the draft like those at Chicago and CCNY, are the shadows of the future. National organizations are not the style of anarchists and improvisers.

Beneath this nation's gleaming surface of computers, Hilton hotels, and superhighways, there are latent volcanoes of violence. These volcanoes have erupted tragically in Birmingham, Mississippi, and Dallas in 1963; in Harlem and Rochester in 1964; in Watts and Selma in 1965; and in Watts and in Mississippi again in 1966. Riot and assassination are symptoms of the disease in our society below the Disneyland façade. The New Radicals will rub these hidden sores until they bleed, or until the Great Society begins to heal the one in five who are poor, and the millions who are voteless, powerless, victimized, and mad.

But two yawning pitfalls stretch out before the New Left, diluting the chances of its growth. One is the rising tide of domestic McCarthyism, which is parelleling the escalation of the war in Vietnam. The other is the culture's spongelike genius for either absorbing or merchandising all dissent.

* * *

There has always been a latent anti-intellectual strain to the American character, as Richard Hofstadter documented in his Pulitzer Prize–winning book, *Anti-intellectualism in American Life.* The country's repudiation of Adlai Stevenson and the upsurge of McCarthyism in the 1950s were the latest expression of attitudes that go back to the Alien and Sedition Acts and the Salem witch trials. Now, as the Vietnam war grows more bloody, the stalemate more frustrating, there seems to be a resurgence of paranoid know-nothing sentiment throughout the country. My fear is that if the war drags on, and there are 400,000 American troops in Vietnam at the start of 1967, then all of America will begin to close down, just as the nation turned in on itself during the Korean War, or as France became repressive during the last stages of its seven-year conflict with Algeria. If this happens, then all bets are off on the future of the New Left. Its elite will be drafted, its organizations pilloried and red-baited, its idealism shattered, its mentality turned underground.

The first smell of this new McCarthyism is already in the air, burning the nostrils and poisoning the lungs.

In October of 1965 Congress enacted a law that made the burning of a draft card punishable by five years in jail and a five-thousand-dollar fine. A few weeks later, Attorney General Katzenbach announced the Justice Department was investigating SDS. In January of 1966 the Georgia state legislature refused to seat the democratically elected Julian Bond because of his opposition to the Vietnam war. In February, Congressman Olin E. Teague of Texas introduced legislation making all antiwar protests illegal; he characterized the demonstrators as "beatnik types and pseudo-intellectuals." A few days later the Michigan state legislature adopted a resolution banning Communists from speaking on campuses in the state. On March 3, the Justice Department petitioned the Subversive Activities Control Board to order the Du Bois Clubs to register as a Communist-front organization. Within forty-eight hours the clubs' national headquarters was blown up, and its members beaten up on a Brooklyn street, and then arrested by police. On March 26, antiwar marches in Oklahoma City and Boston were broken up by hooligans, and in New York, twenty thousand marchers were pelted with rotten eggs, and assailed by the *Daily News* as "dupes of the communists." On March 31, four young draft-card burners were savagely beaten on the steps of a Boston courthouse by a mob of teen-agers, while police looked on and newsreel photographers jostled each other for close-ups of the pummeling. On April 8, the VDC [Vietnam Day Committee] headquarters in Berkeley was bombed. On May 15, a crazed gunman killed a member of the YSA [Young Socialist Alliance] in Detroit. On June 5, a sniper waiting in ambush shot James Meredith near Hernando, Mississippi.

The other pitfall blocking the path of the New Left is the culture's skill at amiably absorbing all manner of rebels and turning them into celebrities. To be a radical in America today is like trying to punch your way out of a cage made of marshmallow. Every thrust at the jugular draws not blood, but sweet success; every hack at the roots draws not retaliation, but fame and affluence. The culture's insatiable thirst for novelty and titillation insures LeRoi Jones television interviews, Norman Mailer million-dollar royalties, and Paul Goodman fat paychecks as a government consultant. Yesterday's underground becomes today's vaudeville and tomorrow's cliché. If the draft, superpatriots, and the Justice Department don't wreck the New Left, masscult may kill it with kindness and then deposit its carcass in the cemetery of celebrities, alongside of Baby Jane Holzer, Liberace, and Jack Kerouac.

Already there are signs that the middle class enjoys being flogged by the New Radicals, while ignoring their criticisms and ideas. Magazines like *Esquire, Mademoiselle,* and *Playboy* have printed glowing accounts of the New Left. Publishing houses have handed out thousands of dollars to the New Radicals for books they know will indict America root and branch—but will return a handsome profit. Government agencies like the Peace Corps and the Office of Economic Opportunity have offered several of the most gifted members of the New Left lucrative jobs.

This paradox of radical ideas creating celebrities can be an insidious process. It is hard to nurse your anger if you're getting two thousand dollars to spill it out on national television. And it is hard to think creatively, or to organize effectively, if you are deluged with a stream of speaking engagements, interviews, and symposia. The danger of becoming performers subsidized to goose a decadent middle class is a real one for the New Left.

Directly toward these twin pitfalls—the escalating war in Vietnam and an endlessly absorptive culture—the New Radicals will march, just as they marched into Mississippi, Sproul Hall, and the urban slums of the North. They will continue to challenge the gods because they are cursed with the passion of Ahab and the innocence of Billy Budd. And because no one else is doing the marching.

The New Radicalism began with a request for a cup of coffee. In six years it has become a new way of looking at the world and a vision of a new kind of politics. It has given a whole generation what William James called "the moral equivalent of war."

To demand any more of this generation is to deny the responsibility of the last one—and the possibility of the next.

22

Studies in Radical Commitment

Kenneth Keniston

Any interviewer who in effect asks a group of young men and women "How did you come to be what you are?" almost inevitably elicits answers that somewhat artificially integrate and sum up an ongoing process. Such answers must be seen as provisional and preliminary, as progress (or non-progress) reports, as time-slices across a moving flow. Yet such statements are useful, for in them the crucial themes of past and present life are often interwoven. . . .

One young woman, when I asked her if she had ever considered abandoning her work in the Movement [New Left], replied:

> No, I've really been very happy. This is one of the things I feel very positive about. . . . One of the things I've learned in the last two years is that you don't need very much to live on. . . . It gives me a completely different perspective on what it is that I decide to go into. I wouldn't mind having a car, but I would have to learn to drive first. I can think of ways to enjoy a nice way of life, but I don't feel obsessed with it. . . .
>
> I sort of feel myself to be open and I feel very happy. It is like I have built a whole new world. It has been a very good transition. I feel like I have a solid foundation. . . . I just saw a friend of mine from ten years ago the other day, and it was very difficult to talk to her. . . . You realize that the people you want to be your friends are people where you don't have to go through the whole process of justifying why you're doing what you're doing. . . . You end up eliminating a lot of your old friends. . . . The kind of people who get involved in the Move-

SOURCE: From *Young Radicals,* copyright © 1968, by Kenneth Keniston. Reprinted by permission of Harcourt, Brace & World, Inc.

ment are really people who have a strong need for friendship. ... I don't feel as politically conscious as maybe I should. Maybe I'm approaching things much more pragmatically. How do you build something? How do you get things done?[1]

In this statement about herself, she introduces issues that will recur in these interviews: her relationship to middle-class monetary and success values, her feeling of openness to the future, her gradual entry into the Movement and her loss of her past friends, her need for friendship, her sense of ideological inadequacy, and finally—and perhaps most important—the questions with which she approaches her own future and the future of the Movement.

For this young woman, as for all of her fellow workers in Vietnam Summer,[2] personality and politics are impossible to separate. Again and again, they stressed the personal origins of political beliefs, and the effects of political involvement in their personal lives. For many, political involvement had been a major catalyst for personal change:

> It was only when I first began to do my first political activity, which was—I can't remember, a boycott or peace work or something—but I really started to move personally. I started to put my mind to a project, an activity, a way of thinking. I really started to work hard in terms of learning how to do that stuff. ... I really put my personality into it. That's what I've been doing ever since. I obviously sublimate a lot of stuff into political activity.

Not only does this young radical underline the personal component of his political life, but he clearly indicates that a major part of the meaning of his radical commitment lies in its role in helping to start "to move personally." Another, summarizing his political development, said:

> The politics came after the people. There was always a personal relationship first. And the most important thing of what

---

[1] All of the quotations in the text are from the young radicals I interviewed in Vietnam Summer. I have changed many personal, organizational, and place names. My own comments or amplifications are noted by brackets. I have used ellipses to indicate deletions from the original spoken narratives. Some quotations have been edited to eliminate unnecessary redundancy or to increase clarity. Apart from these minimal changes, they reflect accurately the spoken style of those I interviewed.

[2] [Vietnam Summer was organized in 1967 by New Leftists as a large and far-reaching group dedicated to "organizing new constituencies" to oppose American involvement in Southeast Asia.—Ed.]

you were going to do with a person was personal, not political. The political development came from that background, and from the reading I did.

Here again, the inseparability of the personal, especially the interpersonal, and the political is underlined.

As a rule, formal elaborated and dogmatic ideological considerations were seldom discussed in these interviews; they rarely formed a major part of the radical's presentation of himself to me. No doubt, had I been a political scientist inquiring about political philosophy, statements of formal ideology could have been obtained. But to give great emphasis to such statements would, I believe, falsify the personal position of these radicals, which rests on a set of time-honored principles rather than on any elaborately rationalized ideology. One interviewee, for example, volunteered:

> One of the things that makes it difficult for me to trace where I came from is the fact that I don't have an ideology. If I did, if I knew precisely, I mean if I had clear political goals—well, I have something of an analysis of why certain things happen, and why certain things must happen. But it's not very tightly formulated and I'm very flexible about it. If I did have a rigid view, I would be better able to look back and say, "This is where this and that came from." . . . But I think it's better this way. It's more real, it ties in, it forces you to bring yourself together more as a unified thing rather than to say, "Here are my politics, Dr. Keniston, and this is where they came from. Now if you want to talk to me about a person, that is something else." But things really are together, and that's real. It's so— Things really *are* together.

And another noted in a similar vein:

> I have never been an ideologue. I always have been a guy who winds up, in terms of ideology, taking it for the excitement of it and really examining it, but I have a lot of difficulty in putting together broad theories. I feel much more humble, I think, than other people do. I think I'm probably wrong about that, but it was always the organizing things that I felt the most at home with. . . .

Formal statements of rationalized philosophy, articulated interpretations of history and political life, and concrete visions of political objectives were almost completely absent in the interviews (and in this respect, as in many others, this is a typically American group). But what did emerge was a strong, if often largely implicit, belief in a set of basic moral principles: justice, decency, equality, responsibility, nonviolence, and fairness. The issue of "tactics," too, was often discussed—the utility of demonstrations, community organizing, electoral politics, or "resistance" as instrumentalities for the New Left. But the primary orientation to basic principles, although one of the most important issues in their lives, was so taken for granted by them (and to a large extent at the time by me as well) that it was rarely emphasized in these young radicals' summaries of themselves. And questions about tactics seemed to them so much a pragmatic matter of effectiveness that they did not include them in their self-descriptions.

Convinced that the personal and the political were linked, and emphatically anti-ideological in their ideologies, these young men and women usually emphasized the personal satisfaction they derived from Movement activities. One individual, when asked why he planned to persist as a radical, said:

> Part of it is that it's something that I do well. I wouldn't like to have to get up at 9:00 o'clock every morning and finish work at 5:30 and be under somebody's authority. [Laughs] . . . and then one is contemporary with the mainstreams of society. One feels on top of things.

Another spoke in comparable terms about the "motion in the Movement":

> I've had a lot of help, because you know there's motion in the Movement. There are people doing things, there are things happening, there are all kinds of exciting people. That helps. That helps a lot.

Still another sustaining force for some of these young radicals is the conviction that they are part of a rising tide of radicalism that is increasingly required by modern American society. For example, one young man, after having discussed his own father's growing impatience with American society, said:

> It's happening now on a national basis, some of the people who are old liberals in the analysis of American society are increasingly radical. For example, Gunnar Myrdal, who back in the fifties had a kind of "growing pains" analysis—you know, America is young and is having growing pains—his analysis is different now: something has got to be done. And I found this also among people like my father, intellectual types, that they are getting the same type of response. A lot of people of your

generation or my father's generation, and from your discipline, are getting drawn into political activities.

One prime source of satisfaction in the radical's commitment, then, derives from the feeling of contemporaneity, of being in motion with others, and of involvement with a changing, growing tide of radicalism.

For others, the satisfactions of Movement work come partly from a feeling of continuity with the values of the personal and collective past. One young man from a radical family summarized his recent development as follows:

> It just seems to me that what happened was that I saw a different way of relating to people. When I started to look around at things, I felt that political activity was a vehicle for that. But it wasn't until last year that I really started feeling that I've come all the way back round full circle. Politics was no longer a vehicle, but this was *the thing*. And then I said to myself, "My God, it never *was* a vehicle. This is what you *were*. This is where you're *at*. This is where you've come from. This is how you're made up. And you aren't supposed to be doing anything else. You shouldn't feel badly about not doing this or not doing that. This is what you *are*."
>
> It's just, you know, a nice feeling. It's very, very supportive, both that emotional and intellectual feeling. It helps you on. It's not something that happens once and there's beautiful flowing music. But once you get that feeling, it's there, and when the time comes and you start getting into the dumps, you can say, "Look, this is what you were made to do."

Another young man, this one not from a radical family, described a strong sense of continuity to the basic values of his family:

> I had a good solid family, no parental trouble among themselves or with the kids. My old man is very straight with the kids. That's been very important, because it has kept in the back of my mind all the time concepts like responsibility, seriousness: "If you're going to work on this, you can't just do it on weekends." I have this whole complex of ideas about carrying through with what you start, being serious about it, being confident about it. I really never could have come close to just flipping out and becoming totally alienated. . . . It doesn't seem to me that simple. All capitalists don't beat their wives, all workers are not hopeless charlatans. . . . That kind of thing was in the back of my mind, nagging at me: "You're not involved, you're not doing anything.". . .

> The values I got from my family, the ones that I've kept, are good. I've pared them and peeled them to fit my own style, but there is a good continuity here. I mean it's a new generation, but there's a lot from my old generation that can't be minimized. Otherwise, I might have flipped out or something like that, or just turned myself off altogether.

This young man, from a relatively apolitical background, links his involvement in the Movement and his escape from "just flipping out and becoming totally alienated" to his continuity with the values of his family.

No summary can characterize the satisfactions of Movement work: for each individual, they are numerous and complex. To return to a central theme in radical development, the crucial sustaining force in the radical commitment is probably an underlying sense of acting on one's basic principles. One individual, for example, who grew up in a religious family, argued that his "basic rhetoric" is a theological one, now translated into secular terms:

> I don't get upset about sexual things, and I don't get upset about religious things. But I feel that honesty, among yourselves, is necessary. I feel that people should fulfill their commitments. I feel that one has to be serious, and able to work hard.... I feel those kinds of things. It's not that I'm against pot smoking or having great dances or wasting time or watching television—I love all those things.... But my vision had always been that all of a sudden a million people would march on Washington, singing "A Mighty Fortress Is Our God," and the government would come tumbling down. I would feel much more identified with that than if a million people marched on Washington singing "The Internationale."...
>
> If I let down all of my defenses, I would wind up being Billy Graham or Elmer Gantry. That would be my first impulse, to say, "That's immoral." My basic rhetoric is a very theological one..... Maybe if I were born three or four hundred years earlier, I'd be a preacher. I'd say that the people should reform, that they should stop being sinners, that they should realize that the world has to be built on different foundations—"Tis the final conflict," "Let each man take his place." [Laughs] ... My initial thing is to get up and preach to people and expect them to follow me. That's where my impulse is, to speak out to the world.

Here the underlying appeal to moral principle is clearly stated: the call to sinners to reform and repent. He went on to note, however,

"My problem is that the basic rhetoric is one that's irrelevant. ... [It] just doesn't work."

Still another, in the course of discussing whether he should buy a friend's Volkswagen microbus, indicated the importance of his underlying moral commitment:

> It may cost me three hundred dollars, and I *had* been going to give that money to a political organization. I may buy it anyway—I think I probably will. It will be nice to have a microbus, and I will have a long life to give money away to political organizations.
> [K. K.: But it's a conflict for you.] Right. [Pause] But right now, it looks like there aren't many more kinds of possessions I would like to have. I don't believe people should go crazy and work sixteen hours a day because the revolution isn't coming tomorrow. It's wrong not to live until then. But I feel very strongly that people with a lot of money should give it. That comes from the same kind of value—you absolutely must do what's good for everyone, not what's good for yourself. It would be impossible for me to do that. ... I'm not uncommitted. I have meaning in my life, that's not the problem. I have other problems, but that's not one of them. ... And that's something (it's certainly true that I got it from my parents) that was very valuable.

In asserting that "you absolutely must do what's good for everyone," and in connecting this value to his parents, this young man affirmed both his moral commitment and his link to his past.

Another aspect of the radical commitment involves a sense of having "grown up" through involvement in the Movement. Many noted how much they had changed, in ways they liked, since their involvement in the New Left:

> I started off being very insecure in terms of what I was thinking and what I was saying. I usually felt I was wrong, and that I should follow other people's directions. But then, over the last years, I have realized that I am usually right. ... It's not a matter of whether my predictions are right, whether Bobby Kennedy will run or not. ... But I feel much more secure in myself, and I am much more willing at this point to project my alternatives onto people, and to push them very hard. I am more willing now to have people follow my direction and to take responsibility for it. That means the possibility of failure

and getting people angry at you and all kinds of things. That was a very big struggle within myself. . . .

Finally, being committed to the Movement means being involved with other people, not being alone, being part of a meaningful group. The radical, as a member of a small political minority, must continually remind himself and be reminded that he is not alone. One individual, for example, said:

> You get these periodic shots in the arm that are very essential. Just like the parties around here. You'd think that in this place you wouldn't feel isolated. But after you get back to your apartment or to wherever you live, you see how few you are, and it gets to be very discouraging. There are billions of *them* out there, and we can't even move the students, we can't even get 10 per cent of the students. But then, you have a party after the meeting on Thursday night, and you get sixty guys who you really like that are radical, and you say, "All right, sixty is enough." You feel reinspired and reinvigorated. It's the same thing with national meetings. You get people together and they give you a shot in the arm. You figure there are some other people around, and you're ready to go back to your own turf and do something yourself.

In raising the issue of helpless isolation ("There are billions of *them* out there"), and then dispelling it by discussing the importance of personal contact with others in the Movement, this young man pointed to a crucial theme in the political lives and personal histories of most of his fellows.

Yet whatever the sense of solidarity in the New Left, membership in a small, fragmented, struggling, and largely unsuccessful radical movement is clearly difficult to sustain. And sustaining most of those I interviewed was their basic feeling of self-respect or adequacy, a feeling they usually traced back to their families. One young woman, when I asked her how she managed to keep going when times were bad, said:

> I don't know. I always had the feeling in the family that I was better than [my siblings]. I was smarter than they were, I didn't have to study as hard, that my mother liked me best. . . . That's a terrible thing to think at times, and I felt guilty about it. And then my mother was very supportive. She was always very supportive, and even though I didn't always trust her, I always fell back to her. If I needed her, she was there. A lot of times I

still do that now. . . . And I've been lucky because there has always been somebody there who had said the things that need to be said when I'm in a slump. Those have been my friends and my parents—my mother—even though she has all these bad things, when I'm down in the dumps, she is there, even now. I don't go to her any more, but when I was a kid I always did.

Another, describing himself in general, said:

I'll tell you this much—I have . . . a funny kind of self-confidence. And what it did was probably to accentuate even more my need for what I'm doing now. That is to say, "See, boob, you can really finish something; you can work on it and you can really see it through." And then you can say, "Well, that's good, let's look at what it was you finished, let's look at the part you played, what you did."

For all of their self-confidence and commitment to radicalism, these young men and women also have abundant self-doubts. Some of these are intimate and personal. One young man, discussing the undesirable aspects of his parents' relationship with each other, said:

I find that I seem to be duplicating that relationship. I seem to be just moving irrationally into that, using my parents' relationship as a model for my relationship with Judy. In a sense, she puts more value—I do too, but I don't move naturally in that direction—on a *relationship* between people. And I put much more emphasis on the family being an arena from which you go out and do things . . . for instance, my father doesn't do any work around the house, and Judy gets angry at me because I don't take out the garbage or wash the dishes. It's not that I don't think I should, it's just that I've never seen it like that before. . . . That makes me very upset because I consider my father a failure.

This young man's most pressing self-doubts center on his fear of being like his father, a fear that is unusually intense in him, but that has echoes in others with whom he worked.

Others questioned their competence for the work they set out to do. One, discussing the aftereffects of a recent meeting that depressed him, said:

I began to question a lot in terms of myself, about where I am in the Movement. Every so often that happens. The whole question came up of which tools I have at my disposal to do the job I want to do. Sometimes I feel that they are very very lacking. . . . I feel I should read more, but I feel I have worked so long and I'm so exhausted that I just can't. Or I read something that's nonpolitical. I'm very very shoddy about it. It's very depressing to me, because I used to like to read like crazy when I was younger and I was in college. But now I don't. . . . I've never read a basic economics book. How about that?

It may be very odd—I say odd because I can't find a better word —I really knew a hell of lot for an eighteen- or nineteen-year-old kid. . . . In terms of politics, I had been doing a lot of reading. I knew a pretty good deal. The problem is that (this may not be true) I haven't made three years' progress in three years' time in certain areas of knowledge. I have developed very well certain abilities, really pushed them almost to the limit of their development at this stage of my life. Yet there are other things which I need to have as a background. I need things that would give me more perspective to help me analyze what it is I've done and what it is I need to do. I need to know more about economics to know how that functions. I want to do more reading in history . . . for example, labor history. I don't know about that. I think if you have a radical perspective, you really should. I just don't have those things.

But for all of their personal and political self-doubts, and for all of the changes that have occurred in their lives in recent years, the most impressive feature of the radical commitment in these young men and women is a sense of continuity most of them feel with their pasts. One young man, discussing his parents' desire that he return to school, said:

This summer they were talking about "Are you thinking about going back to school? We're proud of you and of what you're doing, and we don't want to push you, but let's sit down and talk about this." And I said, "Hey, great, let's *do* talk about it." I'm looking forward to really trying to explain to them the kinds of things I feel, that I am a very personal embodiment of what they are, what they created in a son, and what they brought me up to be. The thing I want to say to them is, "If you feel you've made a mistake, then tell me so. But *I* feel this is the way you brought me up. This is the way you and all the other influences that you put before me in life, that you provided for me—directly and indirectly—[that you] helped make me." I'd like to sit down and really talk with them.

Here again, two important issues are joined: the inner conflict between the Movement and the Academy [University], and the view of radicalism as an outgrowth of the core values of the past.

To these young men and women, then, being a radical means many things. It of course means a general commitment to the general goals and tactics of the New Left. But for all, this commitment is more personal and moral than dogmatic or formally ideological; and in telling me, a psychologist, who they were, they invariably underlined the connection between the private and the political in their lives. Being a radical means a commitment to others, to a Movement "in motion," and to some kind of effort to create a viable radicalism in America. The radical commitment rests on a set of basic moral principles and instincts more than on any formal and elaborated philosophy. And these principles were invariably felt to be continuous with the people and the principles of the personal past. Finally, being a radical meant being open to an indeterminate future.

23

New Styles in "Leftism"

Irving Howe

The "new leftist" appears, at times, as a figure embodying a style of speech, dress, work, and culture. Often, especially if white, the son of the middle class—and sometimes the son of middle-class parents nursing radical memories—he asserts his rebellion against the deceit and hollowness of American society. Very good; there is plenty to rebel against. But in the course of his rebellion he tends to reject not merely the middle-class ethos but a good many other things he too hastily associates with it: the intellectual heritage of the West, the tradition of liberalism at its most serious, the commitment to democracy as an indispensable part of civilized life. He tends to make style into the very substance of his revolt, and while he may, on one side of himself, engage in valuable activities in behalf of civil rights, student freedom, etc., he nevertheless tacitly accepts the "givenness" of American society, has little hope or expectation of changing it, and thereby, in effect, settles for a mode of personal differentiation.

Primarily that means the wish to shock, the wish to assault the sensibilities of a world he cannot overcome. If he cannot change it, then at least he can outrage it. He searches in the limited repertoire of sensation and shock: for sick comics who will say "fuck" in night clubs; for drugs that will vault him beyond the perimeters of the suburbs; for varieties, perversities, and publicities of sex so as perhaps to create an inner, private revolution that will accompany—or replace?—the outer, public revolution.

But the "new leftist" is frequently trapped in a symbiotic relation-

SOURCE: Copyright © 1965 by Irving Howe. Reprinted from his volume, *Steady Work*, by permission of Harcourt, Brace & World, Inc.

ship with the very middle class he rejects, dependent upon it for his self-definition: quite as the professional anti-Communist of a few years ago was caught up with the Communist Party which, had it not existed, he would have had to invent—as indeed at times he did invent. So that for all its humor and charm, the style of the "new leftist" tends to become a rigid anti-style, dependent for its survival on the enemy it is supposed to panic. *Épater le bourgeois*—in this case, perhaps *épater le père*—is to acquiesce in a basic assumption of at least the more sophisticated segments of the middle class: that values can be inferred from, or are resident in, the externals of dress, appearance, furnishings, and hairdos.

Shock as he will, disaffiliate as he may choose, the "new leftist" discovers after a while that nothing has greatly changed. The relations of power remain as before, the Man still hovers over the scene, the "power structure" is unshaken. A few old ladies in California may grow indignant, a DA occasionally arrest someone, a *Village Voice* reporter arrange an interview; but surely that is all small change. And soon the "new leftist" must recognize that even he has not been greatly transformed. For in his personal manner he is acting out the dilemmas of a utopian community, and just as Brook Farm had to remain subject to the laws of the market despite its internal ethic of co-operation, so must he remain subject to the impress of the dominant institutions despite his desire to be totally different.

Victimized by a lack of the historical sense, the "new leftist" does not realize that the desire to shock and create sensations has itself a long and largely disastrous history. The notion, as Meyer Schapiro has remarked, that opium is the revolution of the people has been luring powerless intellectuals and semi-intellectuals for a long time. But the damnable thing is that for an almost equally long time the more sophisticated and urban sectors of the middle class have refused to be shocked. They know the repertoire of sensationalism quite as well as the "new leftist"; and if he is to succeed in shocking them or even himself, he must keep raising the ante. The very rebel who believes himself devoted to an absolute of freedom and looks with contempt upon any mode of compromise is thereby caught up in the compulsiveness of his escalation: a compulsiveness inherently bad enough, but rendered still more difficult, and sometimes pathetic, by the fact that, alas, each year he gets a year older.

Let me amend this somewhat. To say that the urban middle class has become jaded and can no longer be shocked is not quite correct. No; a kind of complicity is set up between the outraged and/or amused urban middle class and the rebels of sensation. Their mutual dependency requires that each shock, to provide the pleasures of indignation, must be a little stronger (like a larger dose) than the previous one. For the point is not so much that the urban middle class can no longer be shocked as that it positively yearns for and comes to depend upon the titillating assaults of its cultural enemies. So that when a new sensation (be it literary violence, sexual fashion, intellectual outrage, high-toned pornography, or sadistic denunciation) is provided by the shock troops of culture, the sophisticated middle class responds with outrage, resistance, and anger—*for upon these initial responses its pleasure depends*. But then, a little later, it rolls over like a happy puppy on its back, moaning, "Oh baby, *épatez* me again, harder this time, tell me what a sterile impotent louse I am and how you are so tough and virile, how you're planning to murder me, *épatez* me again . . ."

Thus a fire-eating character like LeRoi Jones becomes an adjunct of middle-class amusement, and, to take an enormous leap upward in talent and seriousness, a writer like Norman Mailer becomes enmeshed with popular journalism and publicity.

The whole problem was anticipated many years ago by Trotsky when, writing about the Russian poet Esenin, he remarked that the poet thought to frighten the bourgeoisie by making scenes but, as it turned out, the bourgeoisie was delighted, it adored scenes.

One thing alone will not delight the bourgeoisie: a decrease in income, a loss in social power, a threat to its property.

There is another sense in which cultural style dominates the behavior of the "new leftists." Some of them display a tendency to regard political—and perhaps all of—life as a Hemingwayesque contest in courage and rectitude. People are constantly being tested for endurance, bravery, resistance to temptation, and if found inadequate, are denounced for having "copped out." Personal endurance thus becomes the substance of, and perhaps even a replacement for, political ideas.

Now this can be a valid and serious way of looking at things, especially in extreme situations: which is, of course, what Hemingway had in mind. Among civil rights workers in the deep South such a vision of life reflects the ordeal they must constantly face; they *are* under extreme pressure and their courage *is* constantly being tested. Yet their situation cannot be taken as a model for the political life of the country as a whole. If one wants to do more than create a tiny group of the heroic, the tested, and the martyred, their style of work will not suffice. If one wants to build a movement in which not everyone need give "the whole of their lives," then the suspicion and hostility such an outlook is bound to engender toward the somewhat less active and somewhat less committed can only be damaging. For in effect, if not intent, it is a strategy of exclusion, leaving no place for anyone but the vanguard of the scarred.

It is, at times, a strategy of exclusion in a still more troubling sense: it reduces differences of opinion to grades of moral rectitude. If, for example, you think Martin Luther King or Bayard Rustin were wrong in regard to certain tactical matters, if you disagree with what Rustin proposed at the Democratic National Convention in 1964 and what King did in Selma, then you call into question their loyalty and commitment: you charge them with "copping out" or "fooling with the power structure." This approach makes it impossible to build a movement and, in the long run, even to maintain a sect.

The "new leftists" feel little attachment to Russia. Precisely as it has turned away from the more extreme and terroristic version of totalitarianism, so have they begun to find it unsatisfactory as a model: too Victorian, even "bourgeois." Nor are they interested in distinguishing among kinds of anti-Communism, whether of the right or left.

When they turn to politics, they have little concern for precise or complex thought. A few years ago the "new leftists" were likely to be drawn to Communist China, which then seemed bolder than Khrushchev's Russia. But though the Mao regime has kept the loyalty of a small group of students, most of the "new leftists" seem to find it too grim and repressive. They tend to look for their new heroes and models among the leaders of underdeveloped countries. Figures like Lumumba, Nasser, Sukarno, Babu, and above all Castro attract them, suggesting the possibility of a politics not yet bureaucratized and rationalized. But meanwhile they neglect to notice, or do not care, that totalitarian and authoritarian dictatorship can set in even before a society has become fully modernized. They have been drawn to charismatic figures like Lumumba and Castro out of a distaste for the mania of industrial production which the Soviet Union shares with the United States; but they fail to see that such leaders of the underdeveloped countries, who in their eyes represent spontaneity and anarchic freedom, are themselves—perhaps unavoidably—infused with the same mania for industrial production.

Let me specify a few more of the characteristic attitudes among the "new leftists":

1. *An extreme, sometimes unwarranted, hostility toward liberalism.* They see liberalism only in its current version, institutional, corporate, and debased; but avoiding history, they know very little about the elements of the liberal tradition which should remain valuable for any democratic socialist. For the "new leftists," as I have here delimited them, liberalism means Clark Kerr, not John Dewey; Max Lerner, not John Stuart Mill; Pat Brown, not George Norris. And thereby they would cut off the resurgent American radicalism from what is, or should be, one of its sustaining sources: the tradition that has yielded us a heritage of civil freedoms, disinterested speculation, humane tolerance.

2. *An impatience with the problems that concerned an older generation of radicals.* Here the generational conflict breaks out with strong feelings on both sides, the older people feeling threatened in whatever they have been able to salvage from past experiences, the younger people feeling the need to shake off dogma and create their own terms of action.

Perhaps if we all try to restrain—not deny—our emotions, we can agree upon certain essentials. There are traditional radical topics which no one, except the historically minded, need trouble with. To be unconcerned with the dispute in the late twenties over the Anglo-Russian Trade Union Committee or the differences between Lenin and Luxembourg on the "national question"—well and good. These are not quite burning problems of the moment. But *some* of the issues hotly debated in the thirties do remain burning problems: in fact, it should be said for the anti-Stalinist left of the past several decades that it anticipated, in its own somewhat constricted way, a number of the problems (especially, the nature of Stalinism) which have since been widely debated by political scientists, sociologists, indeed, by all people concerned with politics. The nature of Stalinism and of post-Stalinist Communism is not an abstract or esoteric matter; the views one holds concerning these questions determine a large part of one's political conduct: and what is still more important, *they reflect one's fundamental moral values.*

No sensible radical over the age of thirty (something of a cut-off point, I'm told) wants young people merely to rehearse his ideas, or mimic his vocabulary, or look back upon his dusty old articles. On the contrary, what we find disturbing in some of the "new leftists" is that, while barely knowing it, they tend to repeat somewhat too casually the tags of the very past they believe themselves to be transcending. But we do insist that in regard to a few crucial issues, above all, those regarding totalitarian movements and societies, there should be no ambiguity, no evasiveness.

So that if some "new leftists" say that all the older radicals are equally acceptable or equally distasteful or equally inconsequential in their eyes; if they see no significant difference between, say, Norman Thomas and Paul Sweezy such as would require them to regard Thomas as a comrade and Sweezy as an opponent—then the sad truth is that they have not at all left behind them the old disputes, but on the contrary, are still completely in their grip, though perhaps without being quite aware of what is happening to them. The issue of totalitarianism is neither academic nor merely historical; no one can seriously engage in politics without clearly and publicly defining his attitude toward it. I deliberately say "attitude" rather than "analysis," for while there can be a great many legitimate differences of analytic stress and nuance in discussing totalitarian society, morally there should be only a candid and sustained opposition to it.

3. *A vicarious indulgence in violence, often merely theoretic and thereby all the more irresponsible.* Not being a pacifist, I believe there may be times when violence is unavoidable; being a man of the twentieth century, I believe that a recognition of its necessity must come only after the most prolonged consideration, as an utterly last resort. To "advise" the Negro movement to adopt a policy encouraging or sanctioning violence, to sneer at Martin Luther King for his principal refusal of violence, is to take upon oneself a heavy responsibility—and if, as usually happens, taken lightly, it becomes sheer irresponsibility.

It is to be insensitive to the fact that the nonviolent strategy has arisen from Negro experience. It is to ignore the notable achievements that strategy has already brought. It is to evade the hard truth expressed by the Reverend Abernathy: "The whites have the guns." And it is to dismiss the striking moral advantage that nonviolence has yielded the Negro movement, as well as the turmoil, anxiety, and pain—perhaps even fundamental reconsideration—it has caused among whites in the North and the South.

There are situations in which Negroes will choose to defend themselves by arms against terrorist assault, as in the Louisiana towns where they have formed a club of "Elders" which patrols the streets peaceably but with the clear intent of retaliation in case of attack. The Negroes there seem to know what they are doing, and I would not fault them. Yet as a matter of general policy and upon a nationwide level, the Negro movement has chosen nonviolence: rightly, wisely, and heroically.

There are "revolutionaries" who deride this choice. They show a greater interest in ideological preconceptions than in the experience and needs of a living movement; and sometimes they are profoundly irresponsible, in that their true interest is not in helping to reach the goals chosen by the American Negroes, but is rather a social conflagration which would satisfy their apocalyptic yearnings even if meanwhile the Negroes were drowned in blood. The immediate consequence of such talk is a withdrawal from the ongoing struggles. And another consequence is to manufacture a cult out of figures like Malcolm X, who neither led nor won nor taught, and Robert Williams, the Negro leader who declared for violence and ended not with the Negroes in Selma, or at their strike in the hospitals of Westchester County, or on the picket line before the Atlanta Scripto plant (places where the kind of coalition we desire between Negro and labor was being foreshadowed), but by delivering short-wave broadcasts from Cuba.

4. *An unconsidered enmity toward something vaguely called the Establishment.* As the term "Establishment" was first used in England, it had the value of describing—which is to say, delimiting—a precise social group; as it has come to be used in the United States, it tends to be an all-purpose put-down. In England it refers to a caste of intellectuals with an Oxbridge education, closely related in values to the ruling class, and setting the cultural standards which largely dominate both the London literary world and the two leading universities.

Is there an Establishment in this, or any cognate, sense in the United States? Perhaps. There may now be in the process of formation, for the first time, such an intellectual caste; but if so, precise discriminations of analysis and clear boundaries of specification would be required as to what it signifies and how it operates. As the term is currently employed, however, it is difficult to know who, besides those merrily using it as a thunderbolt of opprobrium, is *not* in the Establishment. And a reference that includes almost everyone tells us almost nothing.

5. *An equally unreflective belief in "the decline of the West"*—apparently without the knowledge that, more seriously held, this belief has itself been deeply ingrained in Western thought, frequently in the thought of reactionaries opposed to modern rationality, democracy, and sensibility.

The notion is so loose and baggy, it means little. Can it, however, be broken down? If war is a symptom of this decline, then it holds for the East as well. If totalitarianism is a sign, then it is not confined to the West. If economics is a criterion, then we must acknowledge, Marxist predictions aside, that there has been an astonishing recovery in Western Europe. If we turn to culture, then we must recognize that in the West there has just come to an end one of the greatest periods in human culture—that period of "modernism" represented by figures like Joyce, Stravinsky, Picasso. If improving the life of the workers is to count, then the West can say something in its own behalf. And if personal freedom matters, then, for all its grave imperfections, the West remains virtually alone as a place of hope. There remains, not least of all, the matter of racial prejudice, and here no judgment of the West can be too harsh—so long as we remember that even this blight is by no means confined to the West, and that the very judgments we make draw upon values nurtured by the West.

But is it not really childish to talk about "the West" as if it were some indivisible whole we must either accept or reject without amendment? There are innumerable strands in the Western tradition, and our task is to nourish those which encourage dignity and freedom. But to envisage some global apocalypse that will end in the destruction of the West is a sad fantasy, a token of surrender before the struggles of the moment.

6. *A crude, unqualified anti-Americansim, drawing from every possible source, even if one contradicts another: the aristocratic bias of Eliot and Ortega, Communist propaganda, the speculations of Tocqueville, the* ressentiment *of postwar Europe, etc.*

7. *An increasing identification with that sector of the "third world" in which "radical" nationalism and Communist authoritarianism merge.* Consider this remarkable fact: In the past decade there have occurred major changes in the Communist world, and many of the intellectuals in Russia and Eastern Europe have re-examined their assumptions, often coming to the conclusion, masked only by the need for caution, that democratic values are primary in any serious effort at socialist reconstruction. Yet at the very same time most of

the "new leftists" have identified not with the "revisionists" in Poland or Djilas in Yugoslavia—or even Tito. They identify with the harder, more violent, more dictatorial segments of the Communist world. And they carry this authoritarian bias into their consideration of the "third world," where they praise those rulers who choke off whatever weak impulses there may be toward democratic life.

About the problems of the underdeveloped countries, among the most thorny of our time, it is impossible even to begin to speak with any fullness here. Nor do I mean to suggest that an attack upon authoritarianism and a defense of democracy exhausts consideration of those problems; on the contrary, it is the merest beginning. But what matters in this context is not so much the problems themselves as the attitudes, reflecting a deeper political-moral bias, which the "new leftists" take toward such countries. A few remarks:

a. Between the suppression of democratic rights and the justification or excuse the "new leftists" offer for such suppression there is often a very large distance, sometimes a complete lack of connection. Consider Cuba. It may well be true that United States policy became unjustifiably hostile toward the Castro regime at an early point in its history; but how is this supposed to have occasioned, or how is it supposed to justify, the suppression of democratic rights (including, and especially, those of all other left-wing tendencies) in Cuba? The apologists for Castro have an obligation to show what I think cannot be shown: the alleged close causal relation between United States pressure and the destruction of freedom in Cuba. Frequently, behind such rationales there is a tacit assumption that in times of national stress a people can be rallied more effectively by a dictatorship than by a democratic regime. But this notion—it was used to justify the suppression of political freedoms during the early Bolshevik years—is at the very least called into question by the experience of England and the United States during the Second World War. Furthermore, if Castro does indeed have the degree of mass support that his friends claim, one would think that the preservation of democratic liberties in Cuba would have been an enormously powerful symbol of self-confidence; would have won him greater support at home and certainly in other Latin American countries; and would have significantly disarmed his opponents in the United States.

b. We are all familiar with the "social context" argument: that for democracy to flourish there has first to be a certain level of economic development, a quantity of infrastructure, and a coherent national culture. As usually put forward in academic and certain authoritarian-left circles, it is a crudely deterministic notion which I do not believe to be valid: for one thing, it fails to show how the suppression of even very limited political–social rights contributes, or is *in fact* caused by a wish, to solve these problems. (Who is prepared to maintain that Sukarno's suppression of the Indonesian Socialists and other dissident parties helped solve that country's economic or growth problems?) But for the sake of argument let us accept a version of this theory: let us grant what is certainly a bit more plausible, that a full or stable democratic society cannot be established in a country ridden by economic primitivism, illiteracy, disease, cultural disunion, etc. The crucial question then becomes: can at least some measure of democratic rights be won or granted?—say, the right of workers to form unions or the right of dissidents within a single-party state to form factions and express their views? For if a richer socioeconomic development is a prerequisite of democracy, it must also be remembered that such democratic rights, as they enable the emergence of autonomous social groups, are also needed for socioeconomic development.

c. Let us go even further and grant, again for the sake of argument, that in some underdeveloped countries authoritarian regimes may be necessary for a time. But even if this is true, which I do not believe it is, then it must be acknowledged as an unpleasant necessity, a price we are paying for historical crimes and mistakes of the past. In that case, radicals can hardly find their models in, and should certainly not become an uncritical cheering squad for, authoritarian dictators whose presence is a supposed unavoidability.

The "new leftists," searching for an ideology by which to rationalize their sentiments, can now find exactly what they need in a remarkable book recently translated from the French, *The Wretched of the Earth*. Its author, Frantz Fanon, is a Negro from Martinique who became active in the Algerian revolution. He articulates with notable power the views of those nationalist-revolutionaries in the underdeveloped countries who are contemptuous of their native bourgeois leadership, who see their revolution being pushed beyond national limits and into their own social structure, who do not wish to merge with or become subservient to the Communists yet have no strong objection in principle to Communist methods and values.

Fanon tries to locate a new source of revolutionary energy: the peasants who, he says, "have nothing to lose and everything to gain." He deprecates the working class: in the Western countries it has been bought off, and in the underdeveloped nations it constitutes a tiny "aristocracy." What emerges is a curious version of Trotsky's theory of permanent revolution, concerning national revolts in the backward countries which, to fulfill themselves, must become social revolutions. But with one major difference: Fanon assigns to the peasants and the urban declassed poor the vanguard role Trotsky had assigned to the workers.

What, however, has really happened in countries like Algeria? The peasantry contributes men and blood for an anticolonial war. Once the war is won, it tends to disperse, relapsing into local interests and seeking individual small-scale ownership of the land. It is too poor, too weak, too diffuse to remain or become the leading social force in a newly liberated country. The bourgeoisie, what there was of it, having been shattered and the working class pushed aside, what remains? Primarily the party of nationalism, led by men who are dedicated, uprooted, semieducated, and ruthless. The party rules, increasingly an independent force perched upon and above the weakened classes.

But Fanon is not taken in by his own propaganda. He recognizes the dangers of a preening dictator and has harsh things to say against the Nkrumah type. He proposes, instead, that "the party should be the direct expression of the masses," and adds, "Only those underdeveloped countries led by revolutionary elites who have come up from the people can today *allow* the entry of the masses upon the scene of history." (Emphasis added.)

Fanon wants the masses to participate, yet throughout his book the single-party state remains an unquestioned assumption. But what if the masses do not wish to "participate"? And what if they are hostile to "the"—always "the"—party? Participation without choice is a burlesque of democracy; indeed, it is an essential element of a totalitarian or authoritarian society, for it means that the masses of people act out a charade of involvement but are denied the reality of decision.

The authoritarians find political tendencies and representative men with whom to identify in the Communist world; so do we. We identify with the people who have died for freedom, like Imre Nagy, or who rot in prison, like Djilas. We identify with the "revisionists," those political *marranos* who, forced to employ Communist jargon, yet spoke out for a socialism democratic in character and distinct from both Communism and capitalism. As it happens, our friends in the

Communist world are not in power; but since when has that mattered to socialists?

In 1957, at the height of the Polish ferment, the young philosopher Leszek Kolakowski wrote a brief article entitled "What Is Socialism?" It consisted of a series of epigrammatic sentences describing what socialism is not (at the moment perhaps the more immediate concern), but tacitly indicating as well what socialism should be. The article was banned by the Gomulka regime but copies reached Western periodicals. Here are a few sentences.

Socialism is not

> A society in which a person who has committed no crime sits at home waiting for the police.
>
> A society in which one person is unhappy because he says what he thinks, and another happy because he does not say what is in his mind.
>
> A society in which a person lives better because he does not think at all.
>
> A state whose neighbors curse geography.
>
> A state which wants all its citizens to have the same opinions in philosophy, foreign policy, economics, literature and ethics.
>
> A state whose government defines its citizens' rights, but whose citizens do not define the government's rights.
>
> A state in which there is private ownership of the means of production.
>
> A state which considers itself solidly socialist because it has liquidated private ownership of the means of production.
>
> A state which always knows the will of the people before it asks them.
>
> A state in which the philosophers and writers always say the same as the generals and ministers, but always after them.
>
> A state in which the returns of parliamentary elections are always predictable.
>
> A state which does not like to see its citizens read back numbers of newspapers.

These negatives imply a positive, and that positive is a central lesson of contemporary history: the unity of socialism and democracy. To preserve democracy as a political mode without extending it into every crevice of social and economic life is to allow it to become increasingly sterile, formal, ceremonial. To nationalize an economy without enlarging democratic freedoms is to create a new kind of social exploitation. Radicals and liberals may properly and fraternally disagree about many other things; but upon this single axiom concerning the value of democracy, this conviction wrung from the tragedy of our age, politics must rest.

24

The New Left and Its Limits

Nathan Glazer

For the last few years I have looked with increasing skepticism on the analyses and the actions of the radical Left in America. By the radical Left I mean those who believe there is something fundamentally and irredeemably wrong with our society, and who think the chief way of righting it lies in mobilizing the power of all the disadvantaged groups among us behind a drive for radical change, change going to the roots. My own skepticism in the face of so much passion and indeed accomplishment often troubles me, and it will certainly annoy radicals. They may say that to have been radical or liberal in one's youth, and to become relatively conservative in one's middle years, is so common an experience that it needs hardly any explanation at all. However, just as I would not explain the radical mood or outlook on psychological or temperamental grounds, so I would hope that radicals might suspend such easy judgments on my own outlook. There have been, after all, young conservatives and old radicals, even if not as many as the other way around. And just as I would accord the radical outlook full respect—as a perspective on the world that has its own rationale, its own roots, its own great thinkers, its own successes—so I would hope that radicals might for a while consider the point of view that is skeptical of their analyses, their programs, and their hopes.

There are three principal areas in which the new radicalism expresses itself: the problem of the Vietnam war, and by extension the

SOURCE: Nathan Glazer, "The New Left and Its Limits," *Commentary* (July, 1968). Reprinted by permission of the author.

whole question of the role of the United States in world affairs, and in the development of the poorer countries; the problem of achieving equality for Negroes, which now centers in the crisis of the great urban ghettos; and the problem of higher education—in particular the role of youth in the administration of the campus and the shaping of the curriculum. In none of these three areas can we point to much to be happy about. I need not describe the sense of catastrophe that hangs over us whether we consider the war or the black–white conflict. I would not apply so grand a term as catastrophe to the campus situation, and yet there is a growing sense of the triviality of much of mass higher education; and while I would hesitate to go so far as to say that the hearts and minds of our young people are being destroyed, I think the crisis in the universities is as serious in its own right for American youth as are Vietnam and race for the larger society.

In all three areas, radicalism, true to the term, wishes to go to the roots because, it says, what is wrong in each case is wrong at the roots. To find a half million Americans in Vietnam, killing and being killed, burning villages and destroying crops, is sufficiently outrageous to make it plausible that there is a horror within the bowels of our society which has called these outer horrors forth. To find in the ghettos vast numbers of poverty-stricken people who have lost all faith in society, their fellow man, and their own power, who present a picture of disinheritance that no other advanced industrial society can show us; and to find on the other hand among many whites a ferocious hatred of these unfortunates that again no other advanced society can show us—this too is sufficient cause to assume that the roots are poisoned. To confront, finally, in the colleges and universities a host of petty demands and restrictions irrelevant to understanding and education makes it easy enough to believe that something very basic is the operative cause.

Faced with these evils, and the general sense that something fundamental is wrong, the radical chooses between two broad general approaches to getting at the roots. One is the whole grand scheme of Marxism, in its various modern formulations. Capitalism is too old-fashioned a term to arouse much interest—it is now replaced by imperialism. Similarly, the increasing misery of the working class is replaced by the increasing misery of the underdeveloped world, and by that of our own "colonials" at home, the Negroes and other minority groups. The machine presumed to be at the heart of the misery has also been modernized, but fundamental to it still is the selfishness of a ruling class which cannot or will not give up its power and which therefore must be smashed. The mechanisms of a better society are still not studied much—they fall under the ban Marx and Engels imposed on utopianism and reformism. Thus the Communist country where the most serious effort to establish such mechanisms has been made, Yugoslavia, is of no great interest to today's radicals. They are more concerned with Cuba and China, which still maintains a pre-institutional—or a post-institutional?—revolutionary vigor, in which the thought and decisions of the central leader of the revolution are capable of overturning the new and barely established social structures every other day.

The most attractive aspect of the new radicalism is that it has developed a second and more popular approach to getting at the roots —more pragmatic and empirical, more humanist, less mechanical and dogmatic. This is the approach suggested in the Port Huron statement of 1962, a document characteristic of the early spirit of Students for a Democratic Society (SDS). But the candid and open stance of the New Left in its first phase of development—that something deep was wrong but no one quite knew precisely what it was or what would change it—could not be maintained forever as a basis for action. Thus an explanation began to emerge. The simple analysis of the Old Left, that capitalism or imperialism is at the root of the matter, was not very satisfactory, if only because it was too easy to point to the example of capitalist countries like Sweden and England on the one side and Communist ones like Soviet Russia and East Germany on the other to prove that no necessary causal relation exists between oppression and the institutions of capitalism. Referring to real experience—"Where am *I* bugged? Where do *I* feel the pinch?" —the New Left began to decide that the problem lies not in the institutions of capitalism as such but rather in all types of fixed and formal institutions. The university administrator is not involved in the search for private profit, nor is the indifferent slum school teacher, the insensitive social worker, the hypocritical mayor, the technologically minded general. Rather—so goes the new argument —they are all small men trapped into serving big and powerful institutions that have grown hopelessly distant from immediate human needs and satisfactions. The institutions nevertheless draw on strong personal motivations to achieve their inhuman ends—the desire for money and power and advancement, for security, for a comfortable home-life in suburbia. In the view of the New Left, the minor and more benign motivations of men emerge as having greater potentialities for evil than the grander ones. It is the man who wants to do his best for his wife and children, keep up the mortgage and buy a new car—it is this man who also releases the gas in the chambers and who makes the napalm containers. He may even be a good union member and vote Democratic.

When one sees institutions themselves as the source of our present evils, and when one sees these institutions fed not by the limited and distorted motivations of rampant capitalism, but by such ancient and well-rooted human impulses as the drives for comfort, security, and family, then one has forged an analysis which is indeed powerful.

Nevertheless, the New Left has an answer—a conception of democracy in which our traditional mix of civil liberties and elected legislatures and officials is supplemented or supplanted by new rights and new forms of democratic intervention in the process of decision-making and administration. Thus attempts have been made to establish such rights as those of the poor to direct representation in the institutions that affect their lives, to financial support with dignity, to legal counsel. These new conceptions have already scored remarkable successes. We have seen formerly unshakable boards of education begin to bow to demands that only a year or two ago may have seemed extremist and irrational—for example, the demand for community control of ghetto schools. We have seen "student power" in higher education reach levels that were inconceivable four years ago. To be sure, the forging of foreign policy still appears to lie beyond the reach of New Left ideas. And yet is it? In recent demonstrations we have seen revolutionary techniques employed that are justified less by resort to the traditional rhetoric of revolution than by the argument that new forms of "representation" of minority points of view are required in a democratic polity.

The question of how enduring these new developments will be still remains open, but it is clear that they already serve as extremely effective weapons to advance the argument that something fundamental is wrong with American society. Of course, the argument that something fundamental is wrong leads easily to the conclusion that something grand and apocalyptic is required to set it straight. And indeed, the two positions reinforce each other: given the inclination toward some tremendous change, some tremendous flaw must be found to justify it (just as the reverse is true). But a powerful analysis of what is wrong with society may be too powerful. The radical Left explains what is wrong by the tendency of men to act within institutions which develop their own dynamic, and a dynamic which may become irrelevant or positively subversive of the ends they are set up to realize. As instances, they point to the tendency of educational institutions to act in such ways as to inhibit education, welfare institutions in such ways as to reduce competence, defense institutions in such ways as to increase the likelihood and the ferocity of war. When I say that this analysis may be too powerful, I mean to raise the question: what alternative is there to institutions designed to deal with problems, calling upon the more common and everyday motivations, and developing their own rigidities and blinders?

There is an answer on the New Left even to that—and the answer is to release man's natural creativity and spontaneity, whether through revolution or through participatory democracy or through the smashing of the old institutions, and to hope that these newly released forces will finally lead to the overcoming of ancient social dilemmas. For the New Left believes that man is good by nature, and corrupted by institutions, that the earth and its riches are sufficient to maintain all men in comfort and happiness, and that only human selfishness and blindness prevent the emergence of this ideal state. One can appeal to the early Marx, who is so popular today, and his vision of a society in which man can fish in the morning, work in the afternoon, and criticize the arts in the evening, just as he will, and entirely according to the rhythms of his own being. Some on the New Left believe that only a violent overthrow of the institutions of society can bring such a world to birth; others believe that a steady and determined and unyielding pressure on power elites and power holders, if applied long enough, ingeniously enough, unflinchingly enough, will force these groups to give up their power and their goods and to desist in their willful obstruction of those who wish to create a better and more beautiful world.

There are, in my opinion, three serious flaws in this position.

The first is the assumption that the problems of bringing a better society into being are fundamentally problems of power. This has become a matter of gospel, and not only with the New Left. Yet the fact is that only certain basic problems can be settled, and even those only to a limited degree, by direct clashes between conflicting interests; and in advanced societies, the number of such problems grows progressively smaller and smaller. The natural history of social problems seems to involve an initial stage in which a selfish power monopoly must be defeated or overthrown. But clear evils to fight against are rapidly succeeded by increasingly ambiguous evils, whose causes and solutions are equally unclear. The minute we move to this later stage, we confront one important limitation of the radical perspective.

Let me be concrete. In the South not long ago, the resistance to equality for Negroes was centered in an irrational and inhuman racist ethos that denied to Negroes the most elementary rights of man in a democratic society, such as the right to a fair trial, to the security of life and property, and to the vote. The task of confronting these evils was simply to fight them, to organize to fight them, to insist that the Constitution be obeyed—even, if one was heroic enough, to die or risk death in the process.

But this was the initial stage of reform, equivalent in its moral clarity to earlier battles like those aimed at extending the franchise, banning child labor, establishing labor's right to organize, setting up systems of unemployment insurance and social security. After the principle has been established, there comes a second stage, in which the problems are more complex, often more technical. It is in part for this reason that the administrators and the experts now take over, together with those whose interests are directly concerned, while the army of reformers moves off to issues in which the conflict between good and evil is still clear-cut. This is precisely what happened after the victories of the civil rights movement in the South and the shift of the movement to the North.

We are often very sympathetic to cynical explanations of human behavior, including our own, and we are thus attracted to the belief that when Southern whites only were affected by Negro demands, Northern whites could be staunchly militant in defense of Negro rights, but that when the Northerners themselves were affected, they fell silent or slunk off the battlefield. But something rather more important occurred as the battleground of the civil rights movement shifted from the South to the North. In the South, the issues were civic equality and the vote; in the North, because both these goals had long been attained, the issues became employment and upgrading in jobs, income, education, housing. These are all highly complex matters that no simple law can settle. It cannot be decreed that Negroes and whites should have the same income regardless of their skills and education, or that they should have the same education regardless of their home backgrounds, or that they should have the same home backgrounds, regardless of their history, their culture, their experience.

Of course it is possible, even in this later stage of reform when the key element has ceased to be the obdurate political power of a selfish interest group, to insist that nothing has really changed. Thus, many who argue that it is "white racism" which is keeping the Negro down—an idea strongly encouraged by the Report of the National Advisory Commission on Civil Disorders—are in effect trying to cast the enormous problems of creating a true and widespread equality for American Negroes in the pattern of the heroic battles to change the cruel social structure of the South. Yet this interpretation flies in the face of the fact that racist attitudes have been in steady decline in this country for two decades. And if "white racism" refers to practices, it contradicts the reality that most of the major institutions in American life—government, big business, higher education, the foundations—have been engaged for years in a variety of efforts to increase and upgrade Negro participation in every area of American life. Paradoxically, "white racism" has become a rallying cry precisely at a moment when it has never been milder.

The truth is that it is not white racism but the difficulty of the problems which has so far frustrated us in finding satisfying jobs for the hard-core unemployed or improving education and housing in the ghettos and slums. Not even the enactment of such legislative proposals as are being put forward by the Poor People's March on Washington would by itself settle matters—as, in its time, the enactment of the right to collective bargaining did. If the government were to become the "employer of last resort," there would still be thorny questions concerning rates of pay (certainly minimal wages would no longer be a solution, as they were with WPA in the depression), civil-service protection for these workers, and policies for dealing with incompetence and absenteeism—for after all we are speaking of people who cannot get jobs or will not take those which are available in a fairly brisk labor market.

If we consider education, no reform has yet been proposed or envisaged that can reasonably promise better education for ghetto youth, though we can passionately support community control of schools as a measure which *might* at least help to affect the tricky factor of the child's motivation. And even when we speak of housing and neighborhoods, where simple physical facilities alone are important, we have no easy solutions—as becomes evident once the question is raised of how much happier the poor have proved to be in public housing projects than in slums. In none of these major areas is there a major reform that can promise what social security or the right to collective bargaining promised. This is only an index to the increasing complexity of our problems, themselves the result of the increasing sophistication of social demands—not *any* job, but a good and meaningful job with security and promise of advancement; not merely free education, but education with certain effects; not just a minimally adequate dwelling, but one located within a network of social supports that we can often scarcely divine, let alone set out to create.

Even the demands for a guaranteed annual income, or a negative income tax, or a family allowance—demands that are, it is clear enough, pressed because there is no rapid and easy path to equality through good jobs—raise further technical questions that will not be solved by the passionate insistence that Congress decree an end to poverty or that communities do away with white racism. The guaranteed annual income or negative income tax would have serious and undetermined effects on those who work for rates or or near the legal minimum. If such workers (maids, messenger boys, janitors, hotel employees, restaurant employees, etc.) are to retain any incentive to work, the guaranteed annual income or negative income tax return must be set below the minimum wage—at which point we are back to welfare and the painful issues it involves (who qualifies, for how much, etc.). The family allowance is less problematic, but as generally proposed it is too small to permit the abolition of the welfare system; nor can we be happy over the inevitable support it entails for population growth at a time when for other good reasons we might want to discourage large families.

At the moment it is fashionable among radicals to ignore these details and to justify their indifference by an assault on the idea that work is necessary to society. But anyone who looks concretely at what human beings in this country want, and what radicals feel is the least they should have (good housing, good education, various social services, good health care, recreational opportunities, etc.), and then simply adds up what that requires in the way of material and human resources would soon be disabused of the notion that we can ignore the effects of various social measures on the incentive to work. Quite characteristically, the radical wants it both ways—he wants services that are enormously costly in manpower, and he wants social measures that will encourage fewer people to work.

If the issues become thus complex, when there are no simple slogans to proclaim—or, when such slogans are proclaimed, there are no visible routes to their immediate realization—then understandably the fervor and commitment of many reformers and radicals falls off.

This is in part what happened when the issue of civil rights for Negroes in the South was replaced by the issue of achieving effective equality for the Negro throughout the nation. We can trace much the same development in all the earlier areas of reform; indeed, the advancement of a society can almost be measured by the extent to which political issues are transformed into technical issues—when this happens, it is generally a sign that the central power struggle is over. In Scandinavia and England the provision of good medical care, for example, has come to involve such questions as how many doctors and nurses are needed, how they should be trained, how they can be kept from going to America or induced to move to small towns and distant rural areas, what kind of hospitals should be built, etc. Of course, politics enters into all this, with parties taking positions according to their class composition, their history, and their ideology. Yet such differences are relatively marginal, and only one element of many—among which they are by no means the most important—going into the framing of solutions.

To my mind, there are fewer and fewer major areas of American domestic policy in which the old-fashioned conflict between interests representing clearly reactionary forces and the interests of the society in general still remains central. One is the continued Southern resistance to legislation aimed at bettering the lot of the Negro; another is the continued resistance of organized medicine to an adequate program of medical care. In most other areas, I would argue, complex technical issues have superseded the crude power struggle between the forces of reaction and the forces of progress. This is not to deny that self-serving interests still operate throughout the political sphere, but so long as care is taken to pay them off, they do not constitute serious roadblocks in the way of improving our society. The drive for security is a massive one—in farmers, in businessmen, in workers—and I am not sure that our special interests are so much stronger than their counterparts in other societies which manage their problems pretty well, or in any imaginable future society.

A second argument against the perspective of radical leftism follows from this general point that in an industrially advanced society, whatever its background and history, social problems become more and more complex, more technical, and less political: because change is continuous in such societies, no solution is ever complete or final, and consequently there is no alternative to bureaucracies, administrators, and experts. Of course, certain issues are on occasion structured so that solutions really can have a once-and-for-all character—in particular, those issues which can be posed in strictly political or legal terms. Thus, the right to organize, when put into law and upheld by the courts, finally ended one great battle in American history. But most of the problems we face are not so simple and require continuous expert attention.

Consider, for example, public housing. No directly political measure, like a huge appropriation of money, could solve the problem of housing in this country; nor could the introduction of some new principle, like the once-new principle of public housing itself. For no matter what we might do on the political front, we would still have to decide what kind of housing to build, where to build it, in what size developments, and at what scale; we would need to know the effect of setting different income limits, of excluding or not excluding those with criminal records, of accepting this proportion or that from the relief rolls; and we would have to determine the further effect of these and many other decisions on the balance of integration and segregation. There is no way of reaching such decisions from any large political position, radical or conservative: indeed, these questions (and they are increasingly becoming the ones that any advanced society must settle) make those very distinctions irrelevant. A few years ago I visited Warsaw and spoke to researchers in the field of housing and other social services. The problems we spoke about, that troubled them, were not very different from those of anyone dealing with housing in New York or Chicago, or, I would hazard, in Stockholm and Moscow.

Public welfare is another example. In the 1930s the basic issue was raised: is the government responsible for providing subsistence to those unable to earn it themselves? And the answer, after a struggle, was given: yes. It was, as is common in this politically complex nation, not as good or sharp an answer as other nations have given, but in the more advanced states of the Union, at any rate, public services of a standard commensurate with that of northwestern Europe were established for the widowed and orphaned and abandoned and aged and disabled. The battle was over; reformers and radicals rested, or moved off to other fields. Twenty years later they were back, in force, denouncing the social workers, organizing the clients against them. What had happened? Had welfare services deteriorated or been cut back? Quite the contrary. More was being spent on them and they were probably being run more efficiently. Yet where it had once seemed the achievement of a generous society that those without income were no longer required to beg or to depend on private charity, but now received as of right some minimal level of subsistence, it seemed to the society of twenty years later an outrage that they were maintained on a dignity-destroying dole, that they were not rehabilitated, turned into productive and self-respecting citizens. Let me suggest that it is much easier to give someone money than to turn him into a productive and self-respecting citizen. The first task is also a much easier one to place on the banners of a political movement or to write into legislation than the second.

Or consider the poverty program. Within Congress, Left and Right both agree that something should be done about poverty and that training the unemployed or the not yet employed is a good idea; in consequence we have now developed a large range of training programs, of varying kinds, under varying auspices. When any one of these programs comes up for renewal, the technical people running it will always argue that theirs is the most important and should be maintained or expanded, and will try to convince their friends in Congress. Now it is true that congressmen, faced with conflicting expert opinion and pressure from differing interests, will tend to fall back on old prejudices and old political commitments—the liberals will generally say, spend more; the conservatives, spend less. But the combat takes place in a surprisingly restricted area. It is not yet as restricted as the area of political combat in England and Sweden, but it is much narrower than it was in this country twenty years ago.

Admittedly the overall scale of expenditures on housing or welfare or work-training programs is still an important political question in America, but this is not really what many on the radical Left are concerned about. For even if we were to spend twice as much in each of these areas as we do now, things would not really change that much, and no one—least of all the radical Leftists themselves—would believe that the millennium awaited by the radical Left had arrived.* But as a matter of fact, even the scope of politics as regards the scale of expenditure is remarkably restricted. In all advanced countries, taxes are very high and not easily increased; similar proportions of the GNP are devoted to social welfare; and the increasing competition among equally worthy programs—health, education, welfare, work-training, scientific research, and the like—poses similarly perplexing decisions. We may come to a better understanding of these matters, but scarcely by following the assumptions and perspectives of the radical Left.

---

* New York City spends twice as much per child in its public schools as most other large cities do, yet these schools hardly serve as a model for the solution of the problems of urban education.

If, then, the need for reform and change is continuous, and depends on the expert knowledge of technicians continuously applied, there can be no alternative to institutionalization, the permanent bodies devoted to permanent problem areas, with all its consequences. I do not see how any sensible man can still think, as Lenin did in *State and Revolution,* that institutions and the state will wither away to the point where they can be run on a part-time and unspecialized basis by —in his term—cooks. Yet this is the vague, if not always expressed, hope of the New Left. Knowing that institutions corrupt, they hope to do away with them. One of the major grounds for my skepticism is my belief that, even though they corrupt, there is no chance of doing away with them.

I am aware, of course, of the common wisdom that to put education in the hands of the educators, housing in the hands of the professional housers, welfare in the hands of the social workers is to ensure that traditional practices will become institutionalized, that reformers will be fought, and the difficulties will pile up and get worse. But the fact is that judicious, flexible, creative people are always in short supply. Not every problem can be placed in the hands of the best men in the society—though this often seems to be what we are asked to achieve when we are told that our doctors must be better, our teachers must be better, our social workers must be better. Where after all are we to find a place for the people in our society who are less than the most imaginative, the most energetic, the most effective? The great majority of men, whether or not they lead lives of quiet desperation, certainly hope to lead lives of minimal security and moderate gratification. While we take it for granted that this is a reasonable and humane objective for Vietnamese peasants or Indian city-dwellers, we consider it reprehensible that most American doctors, teachers, social workers, and the like are of the same sort. No doubt this common human tendency seems reprehensible when viewed in the context of the suffering we are called upon to alleviate. But what solution is there? As far as I can see, only the normal political one—when the problems become bad enough, and enough people get angry and protest, new programs are started, new men and new ideas flow in, and hopefully all this leads to a new level of achievement, itself to become institutionalized in its turn, and to require at some later time another infusion of ideas, money, and innovators from the outside.

The New Left's main answer to the problem of institutionalization is participatory democracy, a concept derived from the Paris Commune in which, according to Marx's account, the people, permanently politicized, permanently in arms, met every day to settle their fate. This is a grand vision and one which makes it possible to argue that all established institutions, even if formally democratic, are actually undemocratic because they do not reflect the desires of the people at any given moment. I cannot imagine, however, how one can ever overcome the danger raised by a direct dependence on the people, permanently in session. For it inevitably means depending on that part of the people that is willing, for one reason or another, to stay permanently in session.

Participatory democracy is suited to truly revolutionary movements and moments—but only moments. No people as a whole has ever been ready to make a primary commitment to political action over a long period of time. Those who assert that formal democracy cannot be true democracy because many do not vote, many who vote do not know, the candidates do not reflect the full range of opinion and possibility, etc., ignore the fact that this limited interest on the part of most people most of the time is actually among the greatest defenses of democracy. It means, as Aaron Wildavsky has pointed out, that there are always enormous reserves to be mobilized whenever significant interests are affected. Wildavsky contends that one of the most critical resources in politics is time—time for talking, electioneering, canvassing—and the poor have as much of this resource as anyone else. Perhaps money decides only unimportant things, such as which of two not very different candidates will carry an election. But if important issues arise, reserves are available that can be brought into battle. Is it not such reserves that the organizers in the slums are now trying to mobilize? If they fail, as they sometimes do, it may be because they have not correctly diagnosed what is really troubling people in the slums, because they have been unable to convince them that the potential gains are worth their sacrifice of time and energy. And if issues are indeed becoming increasingly complex, it also becomes harder and harder to isolate and sloganize action that, if demanded and then taken, will result in a clear improvement of conditions.

In response to all these realities, we find new and astonishing doctrines coming into vogue. Herbert Marcuse, for example, attacks democracy and tolerance as themselves being barriers to the actions required for the overthrow of a monstrous society. In the past, even the Leninists, whatever their actual practices—the suppression of free speech and the murder of political opponents—usually tried to cover them up with such terms as "people's democracy" and with such justifications as the paramount need to defend the revolution from the violence of others. But lip service to the virtues of democracy and tolerance are now, it seems, to be abandoned by radicals on the ground that democracy and tolerance only protect an evil society— protect it precisely because they can be displayed as its virtues! We have come to such twisted arguments as one recently given by an American professor against accepting a Fulbright fellowship: he agreed that he was free to attack American foreign policy abroad, but by so doing he would mislead his foreign audience into believing that the United States was a free society and worthy of support by men of good will.

In the universities, participatory democracy has now been replaced by a new doctrine which decrees that either when democratic procedures do not exist (as indeed they do not in many sectors of many universities) or when a democratic system fails to respond to deeply felt needs (as with the Vietnam war), then it is quite legitimate to engage in disruption and disorder to bring about change. This argument has attracted the support of substantial minorities of students and even of faculties, though it has been less effective among the American people at large.

The new doctrine, which we see exemplified at Nanterre and Columbia, is a far cry from the ideals of participatory democracy, especially in the early days of the New Left when meetings were open to all, when discussions to gain consensus went on endlessly, when there was deep soul-searching about the morality of engaging in activity that provoked the violence of political opponents and police. Under the auspices of the new doctrine, the rights of the majority are held in derision, and political opponents are prevented from speaking or being heard. Tactics are worked out to strip authorities of dignity through staged confrontations, to arrange matters so that violence will erupt for the benefit of the press and television, to win over basically unsympathetic students who, owing to their commitment to fairmindedness, will almost always be "radicalized" by exposure to police intervention. In effect, we have moved from the ideal of the politicized masses with direct control over their fate—an unlikely form of organization in any case—to the quite cynical manipulation of the masses by those who themselves object to "formal" democracy and to the public order and tolerance that are its foundation. That small minorities are able to get so far with these tactics is attributable to two circumstances: first, that they operate in an environment (the university) which is in fact undemocratic and which is also totally incapable of handling confrontation, disruption, and provocation; and second, that we have in the Vietnam war a case in which democratic processes most certainly do not work well, any more than they do in less explosive sectors of foreign policy in this country.

I think some good has and will come out of these tactics—university constitutions are being revised, and probably for the better—balanced by a good deal of evil. Alongside the wrong of university administrations which are unresponsive to faculty and student opinion, we now have the new wrong of groups of students who can impose their will on the university, regardless of what the majority of their colleagues and teachers want or think. Just recently, the students of Stanford University voted 70 per cent in favor of allowing the government agencies and Dow Chemical to recruit on campus—but on how many other campuses has policy been made by an aggressive minority, without a student vote to determine majority sentiment? The fact that our universities are not democratically organized has made it possible for small groups to instigate change and reform—and this is to the good. But the ultimate end of these changes and reforms will still have to be something on the order of formal democracy—universal suffrage, free discussion, free balloting, all of which seem remote from the affections of the passionate on the New Left. For when these democratic forms prevail, Leftists can claim no greater rights than others, regardless of how strongly they feel they are right.

Through these changes in attitude and tactics, an anti-institutional bias remains at the heart of the New Left position; and at the heart of my own critique of that position is my belief that there can be no substitute for institutions, even though they may become tired, bureaucratic, and corrupt. Yet no more, in my view, can there be any substitute for the organized and aroused people when the institutions become, as they ineluctably will, inadequate to their task. At that point, they must be supplemented or supplanted by new institutions, which will hopefully respond more sensitively to the needs of their clients. I think in the host of proposals and experiments of the past six or seven years there have been many good ones—but then they eventually will become part of the institutionalized system too. We now have neighborhood law firms, which some people around the poverty program saw as the guarantor of a determinedly antagonistic and suspicious attitude toward all institutions. But why? How can they escape becoming institutions themselves? They will have to recruit staff, set limits to their work load, accept some cases and reject others, arrive at a modus vivendi with the rest of the institutionalized world, give security to their employees. And would we want it otherwise? Do we want to devote, each of us, full time to every problem—welfare, education, housing, legal rights, and what have you—or are we prepared to accept the subdivisions of a complex society, leaving some of our resources in reserve, to be called out against the worst problems, the most serious scandals?

One does feel rather like a Scrooge in insisting that spontaneity and feeling can never replace the institutions, with their bureaucrats, clerks, secretaries, forms, computers, regulations, and—hopefully—appeal boards. But there are to my mind more serious reasons than any I have yet suggested for thinking that this dream of the New Left must remain a limited one, and this brings me to the third major failing of the radical perspective. As I look to the future, I see that the expectation of more freedom, of more spontaneity, must be disappointed. Kenneth Boulding has pointed to three factors pushing us inexorably toward a more rather than a less organized society: one is the existence of the terribly destructive atomic weapons, the second is the growth of population, the third the exhaustion of natural resources. To these three might be added a fourth: the pollution of the environment.

The interesting thing about all these problems is that they take on roughly the same character in all advanced societies, and in each case the answer seems to come down to greater controls. Thus, once the atomic weapons emerge, there is no way of sweeping them under the rug. They are a reality, and to deal with them involves a species of considerations which makes the radical perspective all but entirely irrelevant. Perhaps I am wrong. Perhaps one can envisage the masses raging through the streets of Moscow and Washington demanding the absolute destruction of these horrible weapons, and with full faith in the good will of the other side. But even if we were to get this far, can anyone imagine the same thing happening in the streets of Peking, or Tel Aviv, or Cairo?

The population explosion—and I assume we are all frightened at the projections—constitutes a similar trap, for it means that the most basic of all forms of human spontaneity will have to be subjected to elaborate institutional controls if the world is ever to arrive at anything like the good life, or the good-as-possible life, that radicals so mistakenly tie to the overthrow of organized society. So too the gradual exhaustion of natural resources—which we are less concerned about today but which we will soon be forced to worry about constantly—sets another inexorable limit to the kind of society in which freedom is maximized and controls put at a minimum. As to environmental pollution, it is a more immediate concern, and one ironically linked to higher standards of living, in the form of insecticides, soaps, fertilizers, automobiles. Here too we can only foresee greater and more intrusive controls being imposed—not only in America but in all advanced countries, and not only under capitalism but under Communism (as a glance at the Russian response to these same problems quickly reveals). The radicals have offered no alternative to these imperatives, except the return to smaller communities and lower standards of living. This I would regard as wholly consistent with their outlook, and one that makes sense in its own terms. Relatively few people, however, are willing to adopt it, and in the underdeveloped world it makes no sense at all.

My discussion up to now has concentrated solely on domestic affairs. Perhaps many might agree that our domestic problems are complex, require continuous and expert attention, and in large measure transcend or make irrelevant traditional political distinctions. But what about Vietnam? It is on this issue, after all, that the radical Left now principally expresses itself. Does not Vietnam point to some horrible illness in the American system—a sick reliance on technology as the solution to all problems, an outrageous view of the American role and prerogatives in the world, a suppressed violence which will out in the most grisly forms, an inhumanly narrow view of other societies and other peoples? I would agree that just as domestic politics stops at the water's edge, so my analysis in large measure is relevant only to our domestic problems. Many people look at the war and conclude, as I said at the beginning, that the roots are poisoned, that radical change is needed. Many other people—and this is a constant in the history of radicalism—begin with the idea that the roots are poisoned and take the war as proof of their original conviction. Like the Talmudic scholar in the old story, they once ran through the streets shouting, "I have an answer! Does anyone have a question?" But now Vietnam has given them a very good question, too.

Nevertheless, I cannot accept the idea that the fundamental character of American society, its political or economic life, is the prime cause of the horrors of Vietnam. In the end, I cannot help believing, the Vietnam war must be understood as the result of a series of monumental errors. The key point to me is this: *America would not have had to be very different from what it now is for some President to have gotten us out of Vietnam rather than deeper and deeper into it.* Was America so much different or so much better under Eisenhower than it has been under Johnson? And yet all it took was a simple decision by Eisenhower to keep us from intervening in Vietnam in 1954.

The Vietnam war does to my mind point to something basically wrong with the American political system, but it is less apocalyptic than the analyses of the radical Left suggest. I believe—along with Senator Fulbright—that foreign policy, which was relatively marginal for the United States until the late 1930s, has become, or has remained, too exclusively the province of the President and his closest advisers. Whereas in domestic affairs the President must answer constantly to Congress, he has become literally irresponsible in the area of foreign affairs, where he must answer only to the electorate and only once every four years. If he is stubborn or stupid or makes mistakes and insists on sticking with them—and his position as head of a political party gives him every incentive to do so—he can destroy the country before being called to account. Since, moreover, we are still relatively insulated in our day-to-day national life from the world outside, the President can deceive the people as to the extent of his errors in foreign affairs much more effectively than he can in domestic affairs. This is a very serious matter indeed, and the United States may be fatally damaged before we find a way out. But I cannot easily reconcile my own understanding as to how we have come to this terrible position with the basic perspectives and criticisms of the New Left. Nor are those perspectives particularly helpful in figuring out what we can do to repair the political system against a defect of this character and magnitude.

Ultimately, my disagreement with the radical Left comes down to this: I see no Gordian knot to be cut at a single stroke, the cutting of which would justify the greatest efforts (as in the past it has seemed to justify great horrors). Nationalizing the means of production, as socialist countries have discovered, is no all-embracing answer; nor is permanent mobilization of the people, which is in any case fantastically difficult to accomplish, and which, if it were to be accomplished, as it has for a time in China, would create a society that we would find repulsive; nor is the destruction of the upper classes—in the advanced countries at any rate, whatever value such destruction might yield in underdeveloped nations—for the upper classes now consist of the managers, the organizers, and the highly skilled professionals, whom we would inevitably have to re-create.

From the point of view of the heroisms of the past, it is a gray world we are entering, in which technicians and interest groups, neither of whom can be said to bear the banner of humanity in its noblest form, will be the determining forces. The best we can do is to ensure that as things go wrong—and they inevitably will—the people will have an opportunity to protest. They will rarely know, I am afraid, quite what to do to set things right, but their complaints and their occasional rebellious fury will be important "inputs," to use the dreary language of the future, in setting the matter right. The logic of the situation—the size of our population, the number of our organizations, the extent of our problems, the interrelations among the different parts of our society, the development of science and technology—all point to this outcome. Under the circumstances, even reform and its traditions become part of the system. How much protest do we need to keep the system straight and keep it correcting itself? At what point will protest wreck the institutions altogether and prevent them from functioning? The system is necessary; not this system exactly, but some system, and one which, given the external forces that govern our lives, will turn out to be not so significantly different.

I view radicalism as a great reservoir of energy which moves the Establishment to pay attention to the most serious and urgent problems, and tells it when it has failed. To a more limited degree, it is also a reservoir of potential creativity—a reaching for new solutions and new approaches. What radicalism is not, and what it can no longer be, is the great sword of vengeance and correction which goes to the source of the distress and cuts it out. There is no longer a single source, and no longer a single sword.

Part Five

Perspectives—Radicalism in American Society

The main topics of this concluding section—the role of the intellectual, the interchangeability of radical movements, and the phenomenon of conformity—provide an opportunity to view the preceding source materials and commentaries in a context broad enough to encompass both. The problems explored and positions taken by the three writers compel the attentive reader to relate his views of radicalism and antiradicalism, their meaning and consequences, to the larger society.

CONTRIBUTORS

Clarence B. Carson is professor of American history at Grove City College and a frequent contributor to *The Freeman* and other journals. He is the author of *The Flight From Reality, The Fateful Turn, The American Tradition,* and other works dealing with American history and contemporary politics.

Alan Westin is professor of public law and government at Columbia University. He is a member of the bar in the District of Columbia and has served on the national board of directors of the American Civil Liberties Union. His published works include *The Supreme Court: Views from the Inside, The Uses of Power, Privacy and American Community Life,* and *Toward the New American University.*

Robert M. Lindner is a psychiatrist and the author of many works, including *Rebel Without a Cause, Prescription for Rebellion,* and *Must You Conform?* His studies frequently deal with the clash between individual and society from a psychiatric perspective.

25

The Radical Intellectual

Clarence B. Carson

Two developments stand out on the canvas of the world scene in the twentieth century. Viewers may differ as to whether these two dominate the picture or not, but there should be no denying that they are there. The first is the tremendous surge of reform effort that has been going on in the world for most of this century and that is by now so pervasive that it could be called universal. In the United States hardly a day passes that some reform is not proposed, advanced, revived, or instigated. Speakers scurry about over the country describing the problems and offering the solutions. Newspaper columnists echo the sentiments of speakers or provide them, as the case may be. One day attention may be focused upon the need for reform of the bail system. On another, the system of trial by jury may be up for examination, and proposals may be forthcoming for discarding it. Or again, the decaying centers of metropolitan areas may be described as the background for some proposal to use government to renew them.

Nor is the United States alone in being the scene of a prevalent reform bent. Many other countries share the bent with Americans but greatly exceed them in their willingness to radically alter existing institutions to accomplish the reforms. Thus, in predominantly agricultural lands proposals for redistributing the land are favorite remedies for what ails the population. This panacea often has to share the spotlight, however, with plans for rapid industrialization. These economic measures are usually only the most well known of the reforms

SOURCE: Clarence B. Carson, "The Mind of the Reformer," *The Freeman* (October, 1964), pp. 23–35. Reprinted by permission of the author.

being undertaken, depending upon the country and what its particular "problems" happen to be. Some countries may be occupied with "crash" programs of school building, others with placating dissident racial or religious groups, others with providing various welfare programs, and so on.

This reform bent is not restrained, however, by national boundaries nor restricted to sovereign states. It has promoted the establishment of institutions in international organizations. For example, the United Nations has associated with it an International Labor Organization, a Food and Agriculture Organization, a World Health Organization, and others. There have been gatherings for regional planning, such as those that were promoted by the Marshall Plan. There is the more general phenomena of foreign aid, and there are international loan agencies to finance reform programs. Conceiving the matter most broadly, the drive to make over men and societies is in the ascendant today.

The Corrosives of Civilization

The second development cannot be so readily reduced to a phrase for purposes of description. Actually, this development has many faces. One of them, perhaps the most prominent, is disorder. There has been mounting disorder in the world in the twentieth century: disorder in the relations among nations which evinces itself in almost continuous tensions and erupts in sporadic catastrophic violence, disorder in relations among groups which manifests itself in violence between and among groups, disorder in families indicated by broken homes and juvenile delinquency, and disorder of personality manifested in widespread mental illness.

Another face of this development is violence. The volume in the *New Cambridge Modern History* which deals with the twentieth century is called "The Era of Violence." The textbook on the western world in the twentieth century by Frank P. Chambers has the interesting title, *This Age of Conflict*. Who has paused to consider how many kinds of violence have begun to assume regular forms and have even been institutionalized in this century? A few examples of institutionalized violence may refresh our memories. There are industrial strikes, concentration camps, purges, "nationalization" of property; and even street fights among juveniles have assumed the semiform of "rumbles."

Yet another face of this development is the decline of liberty and the removal of protections from around the individual. In some countries this has occurred rapidly, as in communist and fascist revolutions. In others, such as the United States, it has occurred by a process of attrition. The loss of liberty may occur in such an apparently innocuous manner as the zoning of city properties, or it may assume the most drastic proportions of being held in jail without a hearing.

The point, however, is that the circumscription of liberty is virtually a universal phenomenon in this century, though there have been some movements to and fro in this matter. Certainly, the one new kind of government to emerge in this century has been totalitarianism. The tendency of governments everywhere has been to adopt some of the features of totalitarianism, though the exigencies of war may be the occasion for such adoption.

The composite face this second development wears is the disintegration of civilization. For what is civilization but order, peace, settled and regularized relations among men and groups, and conditions of liberty among individuals? Disorder, violence, and aggression are the antithesis of civilization. To the extent that they become pervasive, civilization disintegrates in equal degree. In short, the corrosives of civilization have become dominant in many places on the earth, and they threaten to become pervasive everywhere.

Attempts to Reform Society Have Undermined It

The pressing question for all of us, of course, is why this turn of events occurred. Why have there been total wars, concentration camps, confiscations of property, circumscriptions of liberty, institutionalizations of violence in this century? So far as we know, there were few who expected any such turn at the outset of the century. The literary evidence suggests the contrary, for it contains visions of peace, prosperity, and triumphant civilization in the twentieth century. And those who would be leaders have continued to hold out such visions up to the present, even as violence mounted and wars became total. Indeed, the glowing pictures of the future which reformers still paint have hardly been tarnished by this untoward course of events.

Yet, it will be my contention that there is and has been a direct connection between the first and second developments described above. That is, reforms have resulted in disorder, violence, and the diminution of liberty. To put it briefly, the attempts to make over society and man have been made by the undermining of beliefs, the destruction of institutions, the uprooting of traditions, and the aggressive use of governmental power.

The framework of order and liberty has everywhere been greatly shaken by this course of events and in many places utterly shattered. A semblance of order has usually been maintained or restored in most places, but it has quite often been at the expense of liberty. To state it another way, the disorder resulting from the undermining of traditional morality and the unraveling of the bonds of social unity has been quelled by governmental power. The result has been the police state which has emerged everywhere in varying degrees in the twentieth century.

The Bent to Reform

Since it will be a part of the burden of the remainder of this work to show the connection between reforms and the disorder of these times, the matter can be left at this point with the assertion that the connection exists. The question can now be stated more directly. Why have men been bent upon reforms and used methods to achieve them which have resulted in varying degrees of disorder and tyranny? Why are men bent upon reforming everything in our time?

This would probably appear to be a silly question to anyone who knows no history before this century. Indeed, the bent to reform goes back at least into the nineteenth century, if not before. Ralph Waldo Emerson asked in 1841: "What is a man born for but to be a Reformer . . .?" Indeed, the bent to reform—the urge to change, to make over, to redo—was well established in the outlook of many considerably before this century got under way.

Even so, it should be made clear that this is not a usual attitude for most people. Quite likely, people have ever been inclined to prefer the well-worn path to the uncharted course, the familiar to the new, the customary to the innovative, and the established to the prospect of reform. So deep-seated is this inclination that peoples have often rebelled against radical change and welcomed the restoration of the old order after a radical attempt at change. At most times and in most places in the past, reforms and reformers have gotten short shrift. Innovation has been much too perilous a game for a profession of innovators to be established. In short, for the reform bent to become acceptable to great bodies of people required a reversal of outlook on a huge and probably unprecedented scale. Insofar as reform depended upon popular approval, a great transformation of outlook had to take place.

The Intellectuals

The prime movers both of reform and of the changed outlook have been those who may be identified as intellectuals. This brings us to a third development of the nineteenth and twentieth centuries: the vast proportional increase in the number of intellectuals. They could not actually be counted, for the question of who is an intellectual has to be answered by definitions; opinions will differ, and the application of the most precise definition would be exceedingly difficult.

Nonetheless, there should be no doubt that the number and sway of intellectuals has greatly increased, probably in some direct proportion to the triumph of the reformist orientation. They teach school, profess at universities, write speeches, provide the material for the mass media of communication, advise businessmen and politicians, and so pervade societies today. Government leaders are quite often accredited intellectuals, or so one may judge by the number of them (particularly in Latin countries) who affect the title of "Doctor."

It will be my contention, then, that the reorientation of populaces in the direction of continuous reform has been the work of intellectuals. And, it may be incidentally noted at this point, the proposal and fostering of reform quite often provide intellectuals with their work.

It is in order at this point to make some distinctions which will help to focus attention upon the valid historical connections among the above developments. There are reforms and reforms, reformers and reformers, intellectuals and intellectuals. Not all reforms promote disorder; not all reformers have been instrumental in instituting tyranny; not all intellectuals have contributed to the circumscription of liberty. The species involved must be distinguished from the genus.

Individual Reform

There are at least four levels or kinds of reform. The one that has been most universally appealed to and most generally recognized as beneficial has been *individual reform*. Prophets, preachers, and teachers have ever exhorted their hearers to repent and to reform. They have usually meant that the individual should regroup and integrate the forces within him, that these should be brought to bear upon some worthwhile object or end, and that he should act morally and responsibly in the course of his life.

Advocates of this kind of reform differ as to how it may be achieved. Some hold that such inner reform can only be wrought by the grace of God. Others hold that it can be done by acts of the human will. Idealists usually hold that it is accomplished by focusing upon some worthy ideal. But they all agree that inward reform is possible and desirable. Such reforms and reformers need not detain us for long. They have been with us for as long as there are records, and they have certainly not wrought the contemporary predicament. We need only pause to wish them well, and move on.

Institutional Reform

The second level may be called *institutional reform*. Such reform is concerned with changing, creating, or disposing of organizations. Examples of this kind of reform would be the writing and amendment of constitutions, extension or restriction of the suffrage, changes in the modes of the selection of officials, the abolition of trial by jury, the creation of boards and commissions, and so forth.

Since institutions are means to ends, their reform does not necessarily entail movement in any particular direction. Thus, institutions may be reformed so as to create a balance of power in government and enhance liberty. Reform may even give formal recognition to traditional but unestablished institutions. It can be so radical, however, as to disrupt the tenor of political life. And reform can be used to destroy or undermine the institutions which protect liberty and maintain order within society. It all depends upon the methods used and the end that is in view as to the tendency of such reform.

Liberal Reform

The third kind of reform is much more difficult to name. It should be called *liberal reform,* despite the semantic difficulties involved. Liberal reform is that which removes legal restrictions upon the individual and thus enhances his liberty. There was a great deal of such reform in the eighteenth and nineteenth centuries in Europe and America. Examples would be the abolition of slavery, the removal of mercantile restrictions upon the economy, the disestablishment of churches, the abolition of primogeniture and entail, and the revocation of class privileges. It was these kinds of reform that gave reform a good name in the nineteenth century and helped to establish the reform bent.

It should be noted, however, that the method of reform is very important even if the end can be universally acclaimed. Thus, the abolition of slavery could be carried out in such a way as to respect the property values involved, or it could be carried out so as to amount to the confiscation of property. The latter was the method used in America; hence, it was accomplished by aggression and accompanied by deep rents in the fabric of society. In general, though, where liberal reform was accomplished by appropriate means, it was conducive to order, liberty, and prosperity.

Ameliorative Reform

The fourth kind of reform is *ameliorative reform*. This sort of reform involves the use of governmental power to improve people or the conditions of their lives. It is what is ordinarily meant today by social reform, though strictly speaking both institutional and liberal reforms are social reforms. Examples of ameliorative reform can be given that range all the way from a compulsory social security tax to the wholesale confiscation of property. The advocates of such reform are usually called "liberals" in twentieth-century America, but they have worn many labels in the world: democratic socialists, social democrats, communists, revolutionary socialists, fascists, and so on.[1]

Method is important, of course, and peoples bearing these names subscribe to a great variety of methods. It is better to have one's purse stolen than to have his life taken. It is better to be put into prison, other things being equal, than to be shot in the back of the neck. It may even be better to have a moderate redistribution of wealth accomplished by parliamentary means than to have a dictator proclaim the confiscation of all private property. But all varieties of meliorists appear to share many common objectives in the contemporary world. They want to make over man and society by political means so that they will conform to some version they have in mind. Such reforms, when they have been undertaken, have resulted in widespread disorder, suffering, violence, and loss of liberty.

It would take us too far afield from the present inquiry to enter

---

[1] Technically, Marxist revolutionaries are not reformers. In fact, however, they have not destroyed governmental power, as they were supposed to do, but have seized it. They then use it to effect their ends. That is, they become reformers.

into extensive proofs of the connection between ameliorative reform and the resultant disorder and tyranny. Let us be content, then, with an axiomatic statement of the reasons for the connection. To wit: men live their lives within a framework of customary relations and patterns for achieving their ends and solving their problems. In the absence of positive force, they have worked out and accepted these patterns voluntarily, or they submit to them willingly. Any alteration of these by government involves the use or threat of force, for that is how governments operate. The old order must be replaced by a new order for the reform to be achieved. The result of the forceful effort to do this is disorder.

Theoretically, the new order replaces the old order; in fact, it does not. It is, at best, an uneasy peace maintained by the presence of armies, as it were, for these may be only an augmented police force. Men may adjust to the new *dis*order, resume the course of their lives as best they can, and submit more or less to conditions. In time, they may even forget that the system is maintained by force, or that things could be otherwise. After all, most peoples at most times have lived under varying degrees of oppression. Nonetheless, ameliorative reform introduces violence into life. The force charged with keeping the peace becomes the disturber of the peace. Traditional relationships are disrupted. Liberty is restricted and reduced.

Reform Creates Suffering

The amount of suffering depends upon the kind and degree of reforms. In communist lands, actual starvation often follows the attempt to make over society. More moderate reforms may only lead to the decline of investment in industry, to the deprivation of those on fixed incomes, to the loss of spontaneity in human relations, to a desultory conformity to the establishment, to the rigidity of conditions, and so on. A considerable literature now exists detailing the consequences of ameliorative reform efforts by governments; anyone not convinced by theoretical proofs should avail himself of it.[2]

The blueprints for ameliorative reforms (and revolutions which have eventuated in reform) have been provided by intellectuals. They run the gamut from Saint-Simon to Karl Marx to Eduard

---

[2] It is not my contention that all disorder and suffering are caused by governmental intervention or that they would disappear if it did. On the contrary, suffering and disorder—both individual and social—have always existed for human beings and, so far as I know, will continue to do so. My concern is with that portion of suffering and disorder *caused* by planning and executed by collective endeavor.

Bernstein to Georgy Plekhanov to Karl Kautsky to George Bernard Shaw to Sidney and Beatrice Webb to Eugene Debs to Lester Frank Ward to John Dewey. These, and many others, have made analyses, drawn plans, described utopias, provided visions, and, in short, have supplied the ideological ammunition in the battle for ameliorative reform. There is a sense, then, in which it can be said that intellectuals have caused the reform effort.

Intellectualism Defined

Certainly, it would be valid to say that the initiative for such efforts has come from reformist intellectuals under the sway of ideologies. This fact has brought forth from some the conclusion that the attempt to make man and society over results from some inherent trait in *the* intellectual, or that the real villain of the piece is something that may be called *intellectualism*. Undoubtedly, "intellectual" can be defined so as to refer only to those who want to make the world over, and "intellectualism" can be defined as the inherent outlook which promotes such reformism.

This is a dubious use of language. It does not conform to contemporary conventional usage nor does it take into account the etymology of the words. In the current parlance, an intellectual is one who works mainly with ideas. The *American College Dictionary* defines "intellectual" as "appealing to or engaging the intellect . . . , of or pertaining to the intellect . . . , directed or inclined toward things that involve the intellect . . . , possessing or showing intellect or mental capacity, esp. to a high degree. . . ."

Such definitions apply equally as well to those who oppose reform as to those who favor and advance it. It may be that those who work with ideas are more likely to make mistakes in the realm of ideas than those who do not, in something of the same way that those who construct tall buildings are more apt to die from falling than those who stay on the ground. At the same time, those who are at home in the realm of ideas should be least likely to use them wrongly. If that is not the case, the matter requires explanation, not definition.

A Pithy Question

The question can now be framed which will bring us to the heart of the inquiry. Why have so many modern intellectuals been devoted to ameliorative reform and/or revolution? Why have they (and do they) promote reforms which, when put into effect, result in disorder, violence, and oppression? Is it because they love disorder? Is it because they are violent men by nature? Is it because they despise liberty and long to see oppression introduced? There may be intellectuals of such a character, but most of them certainly are not. Probably, no group of people has ever been so devoted to the ideas of peace, harmony, freedom, and plenty as have modern intellectuals. Their works are replete with references to these words, and contain numerous plans for the realization of the goals that are implicit in them.

There have been explanations from those who perceive that many intellectuals are actually at war with that which they profess to seek. One of these stems from the conspiracy theory of history. According to some versions of this view, intellectuals are "dupes" of the conspirators, notably those in the Communist conspiracy, or else they are part of the conspiracy. This view is given a certain plausibility by the existence of a Communist conspiracy, and by the attraction which communism has had for intellectuals over the years.

But it must be noted that Communism was an idea before any conspiracy existed, that it too was a product of intellectuals. Moreover, there have been and are many anti-Communist intellectuals who are wedded to melioristic reform. Most reformist ideas have been openly advocated or presented, quite often long before any conspiracy existed. Conspiracies have to do largely with the destruction or seizure of governmental power, though this is sometimes advanced by ideological subversion, which may also be covert. It should be noted, too, that some intellectuals have been taken in, or so they claim, by "front" organizations.

But after everything has been said for this theory, there are too many facts, and too many intellectuals, which it does not account for. Why, for instance, are intellectuals so readily attracted to Communism? Since they are supposedly adept at ideas, they ought to be the first to perceive errors in them. Instead, intellectuals are the one group in a country from which the largest contingent sympathetic to Communism can be drawn. This must mean that many intellectuals are already committed to the idea of reconstructing the world before they accept any particular ideology, or, to put it another way, that they are prone to ideologies which contain plans for remaking the world. Conspiracies are not causes of ideas, but effects; they may be used to promote particular causes, but they are creations, not creators.

There is another explanation, not quite a formal theory, for accounting for the reformist predilections of intellectuals. It goes something like this: Intellectuals want power and prestige. Reformism offers opportunities for them to achieve these, for they can draw up the plans and to some extent direct the execution of them. To put it baldly, intellectuals do not care how much destruction they wreak so long as they can achieve their own personal power objectives. To anyone who has known or read the works of many reformist intellectuals, this view should be incredible.

Of course, none of us knows the hidden motives of another, but such a view does not square in many instances with what we do know. The theories of most reformists have not been power theories at all. Earlier reformers quite often envisioned a condition in which all political power had been destroyed, when relations among people were free and spontaneous, when the last vestiges of the exploitation of man by man had been removed from human relationships. This thesis can have only limited application at most.

The Great Disparity

My thesis [is] that the gross disparity between the visions of the intellectuals and the realities which they help to create and perpetuate has resulted from limitations in their conception of reality. They visualize freedom and create oppression. Assuming their good faith and sincerity, this can only mean that they have misconceived the materials with which they are working. Many intellectuals are indeed deluded, but it is no simple delusion such as is imagined when they are described as "duped." It is a delusion rooted deeply in the contemporary outlook, supported by voluminous research, propagated by a prodigious educational effort, and developed by a steadfast attention to an aspect of reality. It has an extensive history and has been developed by some of the best minds of the last century.

The centerpiece of the delusion is the belief that there are no limits to man's creativity. Reality can be endlessly shaped and reshaped to suit the purposes of men. In effect, man has no fixed nature; the universe contains no unalterable laws. Stated so bluntly, many intellectuals might hedge at subscribing to these premises. Yet these are substantially the premises upon which reformist intellectuals have based many of their programs. They have, as R. R. Palmer said of Napoleon Bonaparte . . . "regarded the world as a flux to be formed by . . . [their] own mind[s]."

The Phenomenon Recognized

The flight of the intellectuals from reality has not gone entirely unremarked. In the following quotations, each taken from a different contemporary writer, the phenomenon is recognized, though the intellectuals are characterized by different names by each writer. Thus, Thomas Molnar calls them "progressives," but he is talking about the reformist intellectual:

> ... It [his description] points to the basic attitude of the progressive, his contempt for the structure of life, its given situations and hard data; and it evokes the impatience with which he presses for the social, political, economic, international pattern that his ideology dictates him to favor.... The envisaged and blurred picture of what would be the opposite of life's actual imperfect conditions has a great fascination for him, and he is apt to denounce as cynics those who call him back from the nowhere-never land to reality.[3]

Eric Voegelin calls the phenomenon "gnosticism," but he, too, is describing the attitude of the reformist intellectual in the following:

> ... In the Gnostic dream world ... nonrecognition of reality is the first principle. As a consequence, types of action which in the real world would be considered as morally insane because of the real effect which they have will be considered moral in the dream world because they intended an entirely different effect. The gap between intended and real effect will be imputed not to the Gnostic immorality of ignoring the structure of reality but to the immorality of some other person or society that does not behave as it should behave according to the dream conception of cause and effect.[4]

Calling them "liberals," and getting down to specifics, James Burnham says:

> ... The liberal ideologues proceed in a manner long familiar to both religion and psychology: by constructing a new reality of their own, a transcendental world, where the soul may take refuge from the prosaic, unpleasant world of space and time. In that new and better world, the abandonment of a million of one's own countrymen and the capitulation to a band of ferocious terrorists become transformed into what is called "liberation." ...
> A crude imperialist grab in the South Seas or the Indian subcontinent becomes a clearing up of the vestiges of colonial-

---

[3] Thomas Molnar, *The Decline of the Intellectual* (Cleveland: World Publishing Company, A Meridian Book, 1961), p. 132.
[4] Eric Voegelin, *The New Science of Politics* (Chicago: University of Chicago Press, 1952), pp. 169–70.

ism. The failure to retaliate against gross insults and injuries to envoys, citizens and property becomes a proof of maturity and wisdom.[5]

The Quest for Truth

But this view has to be seen to be believed. It must be set forth in its complexity and depth, with an understanding that the quest for truth is not undertaken in a well-lighted room. It is undertaken by men who see only in part, and to the extent that they concentrate their attention upon the most illusory part, to that same extent they may be drawn farther and farther from the object of their search. None of us is immune from this partiality of sight. Thus, it is necessary that we repair to the concrete realities of history, in humility submitting assertions to the test of fact and reason. We must relive, if only in the imagination of the recreation that is history, the sojourn of the reformist intellectual before we can understand him and the delusion into which he has been ensnared.

The reformist intellectual, then, has been caught up in a flight from reality.

---

[5] James Burnham, *Suicide of the West* (New York: John Day, 1964), p. 302.

26

Deadly Parallels: Left and Right

Alan Westin

Last spring, most Americans, including most of the nation's political leaders, had never heard of the John Birch Society, or its kissing kin such as We The People, the Liberty Lobby, the Christian Crusade of the Reverend Billy Hargis, the Circuit Riders, or Freedom-in-Action. Today there are some twenty-five major national organizations and over one hundred local or regional groups in this camp of the Radical Right. Its terrain lies between the right wing of American conservatism—which the Radical Right considers "soft"—and the frank "hate groups" in the Gerald L. K. Smith pattern—which the Radical Right avoids as "bigotry."

Radical Right organizations have by now attracted over 300,000 members; their annual budgets run to more than $20 million; and they have won priceless national publicity by featuring extremist charges in their literature, films, and indignation rallies.

While everyone now agrees that the Radical Right exists, there is far from universal agreement as to its origin, its prospects, or its meaning for American politics. At least three main analyses of the Radical Right have been suggested by leading commentators.

The first and most unruffled view, typified by the columnist William S. White, is that the Radical Right is a temporary boil on the body politic, like earlier fringe groups in American history. War fevers of 1960–61 brought the infection to a head and it is clearly an irration. However, the healthy, conserving processes of American life

---

SOURCE: Alan Westin, "The Deadly Parallels: Radical Right and Radical Left," *Harper's Magazine* (April, 1962). Reprinted by permission of the author.

will push the sore off if only the sensation-seeking press and what White calls "ultra-Liberals" will cease spreading the infection by overexcited rubbing.

A second, more anxious reaction, typified by comments in *The Nation* and in some leading foreign newspapers, views the Radical Right as a classic protofascist threat. Supported by reactionary big business, Southern racists, fundamentalist religious leaders, and angry military men, the Radical Right is crying "betrayal of the nation" and is attacking the capacity of democracy to cope with the Cold War. It is thus a kind of French "ultra" movement, lobbing ideological plastic bombs into the national marketplace.

A third analysis, and probably the most widely held one, sees the Radical Right as a regrouping of the old McCarthyite forces. Between 1950 and 1954, these forces used the charge of "internal Communist conspiracy" not to expose real Communists in government but to harass liberals within the Democratic and Republican parties, to discredit social reform, and to advance a neo-isolationist position in world affairs. Today, the same forces are seeking to regain influence by capitalizing on national unrest over Cold War setbacks.

While each of these analyses can be forcibly argued, none of them seems to me to capture the basic significance of the Radical Right's appearance in the 1960s. Nor do they provide the most compelling analogy with which to expose the dangers of the Far Rightists to the general public and to those conservative political figures inclined to flirt with the Radical Right camp.

What the Birchers and their compatriots really represent, I submit, is the second great surge of opposition to this nation's bipartisan policies for resisting Soviet imperialism abroad and Communist ideological penetration within our own nation.

The first challenge to this post-1945 anti-Communist consensus came in 1946 to 1948 from the Radical Left when the Communists and the "Progressives"—as the Radical Left liked to call itself, to distinguish its cause from that of American liberals—raised the cry of "fascist conspiracy" to attack our emerging containment position. How strikingly similar the present campaign of the Radical Right is to the Radical Left's drive in the late 1940s can be seen by comparing the ideology, program, strategy, and tactics of these two movements.

I

The Radical Left of 1946–48 and the Radical Right today both derive, of course, from the stream of American fundamentalism which goes back to the Know-Nothings of the 1850s, the Populists of the 1890s, and the Coughlinites of the 1930s. All these movements share a common belief in betrayal of the American dream by hidden conspiracies and the possibility of total solutions by the aroused masses of the nation. The two contemporary groups, however, must be seen in the unique setting of our contemporary situation. Since 1945, for the first time, the United States has consciously accepted leadership in international affairs. For the first time, the United States must live with the undeniable possibility of physical destruction by a self-declared enemy nation. For the first time, the American public has developed a high concern for foreign policy in "peacetime," though most Americans are still unskilled in the realities of international relations. It is against this backdrop of public instability that the two great challenges to the national anti-Communist consensus of our era should be examined.

Parallel Ideologies

In 1946, the Radical Left saw its wartime hopes for a perfect world—for total disarmament, an economy of abundance, a harmonious United Nations, and fraternal U.S.–Soviet relations—shattered by the rise of severe tensions between the United States and Russia. The cause of these tensions, the Radical Left concluded, was not Soviet imperialism or the "natural" conflicts of nation-states but a "fascist conspiracy" within the United States. The danger was basically *internal*. "Nazis are running the American government," Henry Wallace declared at one passionate moment in 1948. Our two major parties had "rotted," and Wall Street, the military clique, labor "misleaders," "red-baiting" intellectuals, and even the churches had become part of a program to "betray" peace and progress. Unless "the people" rose and shook off this conspiracy, the Radical Left warned, the country faced an imminent fascist take-over and American foreign policy would serve only dictator regimes and the former-fascist nations.

Compare this ideological image with that of the new Radical Right. Its dream of perfection was that a Republican administration in 1952 (preferably led by MacArthur or Taft rather than Eisenhower) and a green light for Senators McCarthy and McCarran would bring an end to the "appeasement" and "defeats" of the "Yalta–Acheson" decades. (This attitude was of course shared by many Democrats at the state and local levels who rejected the party's New Deal and Fair Deal leadership.) American prestige would soar upward, the Soviet empire would be pushed back to the borders of Russia, and the Soviet regime itself would probably collapse. All this would be accomplished while we were "restoring free enterprise" at home, erasing the "Socialist" measures of the New and Fair Deals, and balancing the budget.

However, when Soviet power rose rather than fell in the middle 1950s, when the forces of nationalism and neutralism increased, and when "Socialist" measures like TVA and social security remained and were even extended, the Radical Right exploded. Beginning about 1958, when the Birch Society was organized and other Radical Right groups began to expand, the cause of our troubles was perceived: a vast "Communist conspiracy" at home, even under the Eisenhower administration. Our major parties, with their "left-wing tendencies" and reliance on "minority groups," the "Socialist" unions, Communist-infiltrated churches, even leaders of American business—all had been saturated with Communist ideas and were in the hands of Communist conspirators.

Parallel Programs

The Radical Left attacked the basic international programs of the United States in the late 1940s as *too* "anti-Communist." It opposed American policy toward the UN as based upon Cold War power politics, and demanded that we abandon the regional "war pacts" in which we were supposedly engaging as contrary to the UN charter. The Radical Left opposed what it called the "Martial Plan" for Europe—as well as military aid to Greece, Turkey, and Iran—warning that we were shoring up decadent regimes and that "the people" in these countries would not be bought for our "Cold War mercenaries." Defense spending and rearmament were violently denounced as warlike, costly, and the death knell for domestic reform. To meet the might of Soviet power, the Radical Left urged us to rely on our overpowering moral example as a peace-loving nation and to trust the prospects of Soviet reasonableness at the conference table.

In its own terms, the Radical Right is mounting an identical attack on the nation's international position today. Now our policies are not "anti-Communist" enough. Our participation in the UN is rejected because we cannot use the world body as a Cold War spear. The Radical Right rejects American alliances and friendly relations with all governments which are not "firmly anti-Communist," a list which includes Mexico, India, Ghana, Burma, and others which are "playing along with the Communists." Foreign aid is bitterly assailed as "pouring money down Communist ratholes," wasting hard-earned and heavily taxed American dollars which should be given back to private enterprise at home. Balanced defense programs and overseas military establishments are regarded as "useless" measures which could be replaced by far smaller expenditures for "massive retaliation"; if the Soviets only were taught that we meant business, that would solve the problems of the arms race. That, after all, is the Radical Right's basic key to American foreign policy: Mean business! Really mean business! After that, the UN, foreign aid, NATO—all would be unnecessary, and a resolute America would turn back the Sino-Soviet tides by the stern announcement of our will to be Dead Rather Than Red.

When Radical Left and Radical Right are compared in their attacks on basic domestic programs, the parallels continue to mount. Both Radical Left and Radical Right put a hostile investigation of the State Department high on their agenda as the way to correct our foreign policy "mistakes"—the Radical Left because it saw the Department as honeycombed with "reactionaries" and "British Empire types," and the Radical Right because it sees our present Department as under the dominance of "Communists," "Nehru-lovers," and "pro-Soviets."

Both would destroy the centrist economic programs which the nation has followed since the rise of the Cold War. The Radical Left saw our policies as a Wall Street plot to make us an "arms economy" and save a decadent capitalism; they demanded "butter, not guns"—which meant no military spending and a massive increase in federal welfare expenditures. The Radical Right tells us that the Soviets are tricking us into national bankruptcy: their prescription is to abolish federal and state welfare programs; and their demand for abolition of the income tax would obviously mean the end of our defense expenditures as well.

Both groups opposed the internal-security measures of 1946–48 and 1960–62: the Radical Left because it found the pre-McCarthy measures of the Truman administration against Communist subversion to be wholly unnecessary police-state tactics; the Radical Right because it thinks that Communist agents are still nestled everywhere in our national government and at the switches of industry, and that the Supreme Court itself has become "part of the Communist apparatus."

Both Radical Left and Radical Right add a muted chord of prejudice to their positions, clear enough to draw the money and support of some of the bigoted but not loud enough to open the groups to charges of being full-dress "hate movements." The Radical Left in 1946-48 attacked the "Vatican conspiracy" which was pushing us toward a "holy war" against Russia. A Radical Left magazine, *The Protestant,* said that Catholicism wanted "a fascist world hegemony." Later, when the Soviets began to denounce "Zionism" and "cosmopolitanism," *The Protestant* denounced "American Zionism" for selling itself to the imperialists.

On the Radical Right some well-known anti-Semitic spokesmen have already appeared, such as Allen Zoll, a staff member of the Christian Crusade, and Merwin K. Hart, a chapter leader of the Birchers. The presence of powerful anti-Semitic currents in the audiences of the Radical Right's public meetings has been noted by careful observers from the Anti-Defamation League. Openly segregationist and anti-Negro positions are evident in the Christian Crusade, and the White Citizens Councils in the South have close ties with many national Radical Right groups. Leading anti-Semitic publications such as Gerald Smith's *The Cross and the Flag* and Conde McGinley's *Common Sense* are recommended in Radical Right literature.

Plus Similar Strategies

In terms of basic strategy, the Radical Left's top leadership in 1946-48 aimed at winning influence within two key sectors of American civic life which were considered to be ripe for penetration—the labor movement and organized liberalism. Communists and Progressives had secured important positions in the union movement between 1935 and 1945; they hoped to operate outward from unions controlled by the Radical Left such as the United Electrical Workers, the International Longshoremen's Union, and the Mine, Mill, and Smelter Workers to bring the "left-leaning" unions such as the United Auto Workers and then the CIO itself into the "Progressive camp."

The Radical Left had control of Communist-front groups such as the Joint Anti-Fascist Refugee Committee. Within organized liberal groups such as the American Veterans Committee, the Radical Left was already attempting to secure positions of influence, and a conscious drive was planned to move into liberal peace groups, farmer-labor movements, and university organizations.

Radical Left strategists reasoned that control of the CIO and organized liberalism would give them access to power in the Democratic party. At the least, the Radical Left would exercise a veto power in the formulation of foreign and domestic policy by the Democrats; with luck, the Radical Left could replace the "Truman Cold War" leadership of the Democrats with old New Deal figures who shared some of the Radical Left's perspectives.

Such a figure was soon found in a first-term New Deal Cabinet member, a former Vice-President under Roosevelt, and a man who left the Truman Cabinet because of disagreement over the national anti-Communist consensus—Henry A. Wallace. It was Wallace who gave the Radical Left its respectability in 1946–47 and it was Wallace who led the Radical Left to found the Progressive party in 1948 and break openly with the "two old parties."

While the Radical Right is still in its "1946" rather than its "1948" phase strategically, its basic objectives are clear enough. It is aiming at the "soft" areas of the business community and organized conservatism. The newer groups of the Radical Right, such as the Birch Society and We The People, and older organizations such as the National Economic Council and Constitutional Educational League already have influential business figures in their ranks and as their financial patrons. And as we shall see, the support of the business community has been increasing in recent months.

As for the established conservative groups, the themes of the Radical Right have been echoing in such conservative strongholds as the National Association of Manufacturers, the National Association of Real Estate Boards, the American Legion, and the Daughters of the American Revolution. Other conservative groups, such as the American Medical Association, American Bar Association, and American Farm Bureau Federation, are now facing ideological penetration.

If it can rally enough business and conservative group support, the Radical Right can look forward to influence in the Republican party. At the least, it could push Republicans in a Far Right direction, and it might lead the Republicans to nominate a Rightist in 1964 or 1968. If this is not possible, there is the distinct possibility of a third-party campaign by the Radical Right, as some of its leaders have already demanded. Obviously Senator J. Strom Thurmond, a nominal Democrat, would be delighted to lead this movement, just as he led the Dixiecrats in 1948.

. . . And the Same Old Tactics

Unlike Senator McCarthy and the loose apparatus of "McCarthyism," the Radical Right is fervently organizational today. Once people attending Radical Right rallies have been alarmed by tales of Communist betrayal in Washington and imminent collapse of the nation—as those of the Radical Left were alarmed by tales of impending fascism—the organizers carefully follow up by leading the new recruits into a total "life-way" apparatus. Followers are put to work in "Americanist" cadres. In the Birch Society, there are home "study groups" where tape recordings and films are played; Radical Right books and pamphlets are assigned and discussed under the careful direction of a chapter leader; members report on their activities and are given regular assignments to conduct pressure campaigns against their community's "Communists"—*e.g.,* local ministers, schoolboard members, library committees, and newspaper editors.

In a lovely parallel with the American Communist party, there are now bookstores throughout the nation which serve as nerve centers for local Radical Right activity: the Betsy Ross Bookshop in Los Angeles, the Pro-Blue Patriotic Book Store in Torrance, California, and the Anti-Communist Bookstore in Fort Lauderdale, Florida, are only a few of the dozens now in existence. The functions of such places were recently described by a *New York Times* report on Radical Right bookstores in California: Radical Right books and pamphlets are sold, speakers' names listed, rallies advertised, petitions left for signing, and membership and mailing lists traded among various local groups.

Like the Radical Left, the Radical Right knows how to manipulate the appeals of martyrdom. The Radical Right begins with Senator McCarthy, the patron saint driven to his death by the Communists, and moves on to "Americanists" such as General Edwin A. Walker who are "hounded" from positions in the military, the colleges, the communications media, and government because they dare to tell "the Truth." Thus a leading article in *American Opinion,* the Birch organ, could have cribbed a paragraph from a Radical Left organ of 1946 in its lament that today America sees "witch-hunting of patriots . . . , character assassination, and wild accusations against anybody who dares ask questions and insist upon answers." It is also an article of faith for both movements that all of these powerful persecuting forces can be wiped out in a flash by revealing "the Truth" to an "angry people." The Birchers will triumph, and soon, *American Opinion* states, because it is the movement of "the revolted, misinformed, deceived, abused, angry American. . . ."

These are some of the deadly parallels of ideology, program, strategy, and tactics between the Radical Left in 1946–48 and the present

Radical Right. One further element is a common one. Both are movements of the disaffected fringes within the middle class. The Radical Left had its base in middle-class elements in the urban centers of the East and West coasts, especially professionals, drawing heavily on segments of the Jewish and Liberal-Protestant communiters of the East and West coasts, especially professionals, drawing class adherents, and virtually no farm or business response.

The Radical Right draws on another part of the middle class. Its followers are predominantly business and professional people who live in rural and suburban areas and in the "inner cities" of the Midwest and South—such as Wichita, Nashville, Houston, or Columbus, Ohio. They are also strong in coastal cities like Miami and Los Angeles which have had heavy migrations from the Midwest and South in recent decades. There is no working-class ground swell in the Radical Right, virtually no Jewish and Negro support, and its farmers are well-to-do entrepreneurs.

II

Two things should be said immediately about this comparison of the Radical Left and the Radical Right.

First, I am not suggesting that the two movements are identical. History provides complex and suggestive analogies at times, but no photographic reproductions, and obviously, there are great differences. Most important of these is the fact that no hostile nation and its puppet party within the United States are guiding the Radical Right, as the Soviet Union and the American Communist party came to dominate the Radical Left. There is no secret espionage and infiltration apparatus linked to the Radical Right, despite Robert Welch's airy pledges to set up Birch "front groups" such as the Committee Against Summit Entanglements or College Graduates Against Educating Traitors at Government Expense. And there is less unity and single-mindedness on the Radical Right than there was on the Radical Left, for all the efforts of Billy Hargis and Kent Courtney to establish a national Anti-Communist Federation. Yet, in its own way the Radical Right does present a unified and pointed danger to the national consensus.

Second, I hope it is clear that I do not regard departures from the "national anti-Communist consensus" as automatically putting all critics in the Radical Left or Radical Right. Nor is this an argument that national progress comes only from "moderate" and "unvisionary" ideas. Obviously there can be legitimate, far-reaching criticisms of our internal-security measures, welfare programs, alliance policies, military strategy, disarmament position, UN policies, and the like. Thus Norman Thomas and the Committee for a Sane Nuclear Policy are legitimate participants in our national debates, as are Russell Kirk and the American Enterprise Association. The all-important distinction is that their criticisms are made within the framework of rational discourse and civic responsibility. They do not rest on cries of grand hidden conspiracies, allegations of traitorous leadership, and dangerously millennial proposals. Nor do they include bullying tactics in the civic marketplace, whether Communist or Birchite. With this as a guide, it should be clear that talk of Americans for Democratic Action or the NAACP as the "Radical Left" today is absurd.

The Purge That Worked

Having made these distinctions, what insights can we draw . . . from a comparison of Radical Left and Radical Right in the post–World War II era? First, it should be clear that neither of these movements—despite their grandiose plans—has had any practical prospects of winning the Presidency, capturing a national party, or having its panacea policies enacted into law. Each has viewed the other extreme as already "running the nation," but the fact is that the American political system is too vital to allow these antidemocratic movements to become dominating national political forces in their own right: the traditions of the center are too powerful in our society, and the influences of reformist civic and religious groups too pervasive.

However, someone who stops with this comforting realization and dismisses the Radicals as political mosquitoes makes a serious error. The Radical Right poses the same kind of threat to the democratic process today that the Radical Left did in the forties: It threatens the freedom of action of the national administration in its efforts to formulate realistic anti-Communist programs and to demonstrate the maturity of American democracy to the world. It threatens to muddy the terms of debate on sensitive but central issues—from Katanga to school reading programs. And it threatens the integrity of the groups it has marked for penetration.

In addition, the Radical Right presents a special threat—the destruction of civic freedom in local communities by broadside charges of "Communism." Each of these threats from Radical Left and Right deserves to be examined carefully.

Between 1946 and 1948, after a pitched battle marked by a few misadventures for liberalism (such as the Alger Hiss case), American labor and the American liberal community thoroughly repulsed the Radical Left. The CIO expelled the Radical Left unions, eliminated powerful Radical Left staff members such as the CIO's general counsel, Lee Pressman, and pressed "left-leaning" union chiefs such as Mike Quill and Joseph Curran to break loose from the Radical Left. Liberal organizational leaders such as Mrs. Eleanor Roosevelt, Reinhold Niebuhr, Walter Reuther, and Arthur Schlesinger, Jr., formed Americans for Democratic Action to focus the opposition of American liberals to the Radical Left. And, by a painful process, the American Veterans Committee showed that liberals could save their organizations from Radical Left infiltration.

On the Far Left itself, there were a number of vocal, if small, anti-Stalinist groups which fought the Progressives—*The New Leader* magazine, for example, and Norman Thomas' Socialist party, and many of the writers and intellectuals who had been supporters of Trotsky in the thirties. By 1948, after some earlier flirtation with the Radical Left by influential Democrats such as Senator Claude Pepper and Secretary of the Interior Harold Ickes, the New Deal Democrats and the Democratic party both unequivocally repudiated the Radical Left.

The result of these various actions was that the Radical Left was isolated from either political or civic respectability in the nation. The Truman administration was able to execute the Marshall Plan, create NATO, and meet the explosion of the Korean War without hindrance from the Radical Left. And American liberalism emerged from the 1945 to 1948 period purged of the misunderstandings of Soviet Communism which marked the thirties.

Where the Money Comes From

How is the response to the Radical Right progressing? When publicity about the John Birch Society first appeared and Robert Welch's fantastic allegations about Eisenhower, Dulles, *et al.*, were revealed, there was widespread condemnation from conservatives as well as liberals. That was in the spring of 1961. Then the Birchers began to recover from the first wave of criticism and began to organize effectively throughout the country, proclaiming themselves the "toughest" anti-Communist group around. The Christian Crusade, Project Alert, the National Indignation Rallies, Freedom in Action, the Cardinal Mindszenty Foundation, the Circuit Riders, the Conservative Society of America, and other Radical Right groups caught the crest of public alarms about Berlin, bomb shelters, the Soviet fifty-megaton explosion, the Congo, and Laos. Suddenly they found themselves packing in thousands of Americans at rallies in Garden City, Long Island; Miami, Florida; Houston, Texas; or Los Angeles, California. The Radical Right swiftly became "hot news" and press, radio, and television were filled with accounts of Radical Right charges and activities. Money began to flow in heavily.

At that time, the response of the business community, conservative organizations, and the Republican party—the target groups—was not altogether reassuring. In the business community there were a disturbingly large number of corporations and corporate leaders who embraced the Radical Right. For example:

• The Birch Society has sixteen corporate executives on its twenty-five-member council, including the presidents of H. Masland and Sons, Cherokee Mills, the A. B. Chance Company, and the Rock Island Oil and Refining Company.
• Coast Federal Savings and Loan Company in California, one of the five largest savings-and-loan institutions in the nation, distributes Birch literature and a steady stream of Radical Right materials.
• Project Alert has had its extremist rallies sponsored on television by the Carnation Milk Company and Southern California Edison.
• "Communism on the Map" is a film produced by the National Education Program in Searcy, Arkansas. Written by a Birch Society coordinator, it incorporates large chunks from the Birch Society's *Blue Book*. According to the National Education Program, this film has been purchased by companies such as Goodyear Tire and Rubber, Boeing Aircraft, Minnesota Mining and Manufacturing, Revere Copper and Brass, and Aluminum Company of America.
• The National Education Program itself lists officials from such corporations as Swift and Company and Monsanto Chemical on its Freedom Forum Advisory Committee, and it has claimed support from high executives of General Electric, The American Iron and Steel Institute, Olin Mathieson, Lone Star Cement Company, and dozens of other blue-chip corporations.*

This is only a sampling. A cautious estimate—based on recent surveys of annual corporate donations and the published gifts of compa-

---

* This claim of support was stated in a letter dated March 25, 1961, signed by Howard W. Bennett, vice-president of the National Education Program, and made available by Mr. Irwin Suall, author of "The American Ultras" (New York: New America, 1962).

nies to the Radical Right—would show that the business community contributed about $10 million to the Radical Right last year.

Within organized conservatism, there has been a sharp rise in Radical Right speakers at chamber of commerce, junior chamber, Lions Club, American Legion, medical association, bar association, and women's club meetings. A Lions Club in New Jersey was told recently that leaders of the community could fight Communism and serve America best by founding a Birch Society chapter. In Flint, Michigan, the junior chamber of commerce educated itself on the Communist menace by inviting a popular Radical Right speaker who said Secretary of Labor Arthur Goldberg was a Communist and is still sympathetic to the Communists, and that the major Jewish groups in this country are heavily penetrated by Communists. The Miami Board of Realtors recently conducted a course in anti-Communism at the national realty convention which heard Senator McCarthy extolled and played the National Education Program's latest slanted films. Such speakers are not presented as one side of a disputed issue —they are offered as responsible purveyors of the Truth About Communism in America.

As for the Republican party, there seemed to be a period when the party's leaders hoped that the following of the Radical Rightists could be channeled into Republican ranks. Much of the money and energy which the Radical Right was expending could normally have been "Republican resources." In addition, some Republican officeholders, such as Congressmen Hiestand and Rousselot of California, were open members of the Birch Society, and some candidates for Republican nomination leaned to the Radical Right. Loyd Wright, former president of the American Bar Association and a candidate for the Republican Senate nomination from California, announced, "I wish we had ten thousand or ten million more members like those I know in the John Birch Society."

* * *

Threats in the Night

The recent criticisms of Robert Welch and the Birch Society are welcome actions. But cutting Welch adrift and issuing general denunciations of "extremism" will not solve the problem of the Radical Right. A stronger cure is required and has not been forthcoming. The top leadership of the business community has not yet launched the kind of clear ideological counterattack which would both separate free-enterprise advocacy from the nihilistic propositions of the Radical Right, and also educate careless corporate executives against financial support—and verbal endorsement—of Radical Right activities.

Nor has there been sufficient awareness within conservative organizations of the dangers created by many of the alarmist anti-Communist speeches on the Radical Right. These speeches may start by denouncing Moscow or Peiping, but they usually wind up as campaigns to fire a town librarian who has "pro-Communist" books on the shelf, or to prevent the Foreign Policy Association from conducting local "Great Decisions" courses.

When the business community, conservative groups, and the press do not oppose such activities, the Radical Right is free to poison the prevailing climate of debate. The result has been the erosion of the democratic process in dozens of communities by a variety of bullying tactics. For example:

- Anonymous and threatening phone calls are being made to liberal teachers, ministers, and school principals; to dentists who support fluoridation; or to Quakers supporting disarmament.
- Private meetings of churches, civic groups, and community forums are being packed by Radical Rightists who harass the speakers and provoke violence.
- On the eve of liberal gatherings, anonymous telephone calls are warning that a bomb is planted in the hall, thus causing the police to cancel the meeting.
- Vicious falsehoods are being circulated from the platform and in print about such responsible groups as the National Council of Churches of Christ, the Foreign Policy Association, and the Anti-Defamation League.

To restore these communities to the climate of free debate, to turn the concern of Americans over the dynamics of Communism into constructive channels, businessmen, conservatives, and the Republican party must rise to defend the basic ideals of American democracy, as labor, liberal groups, and the Democratic party did in the late forties.

27

The Curse of Conformity

Robert M. Lindner

... I intend to reveal the truth about adjustment, to show it for what it is—a mendacious idea, biologically false, philosophically untenable, and psychologically harmful. Together with a gradually increasing group of psychologists and scientists from other fields, I regard it as perhaps the single great myth of our time, and one to be exposed to its roots lest it continue to sap human vitality and exhaust the energies which men require to build the better society they seek.

Those of us who reject adjustment as a prescription for living, who believe that it is a concept that disregards many if not all of the pertinent facts of human nature, who feel that it is an untruth that is rendering man impotent at a time when he needs the fullest possible mastery over his creative abilities, are in a sad minority. Ranged against us is an entire world, committed to the concept despite the fact that it is founded on fallacy. For there is perhaps no idea so ubiquitous as the idea of adjustment. Latterly, to adjust—or to be adjusted, or to make an adjustment—has come to be deemed the highest good and the goal of every effort. At every turning the Commandment—"You must adjust"—confronts us. Monotonous and persistent, the phrase is repeated over and over at all levels of our society and for every conceivable purpose. It is offered to us as medicine when we are sick, as hope when we are unhappy, as faith when we are perplexed. There is no escaping from it. Woe to him who does not adjust! Upon him will fall every imaginable kind of ill and, what is more, he will deserve what he gets, for there is no crime so great

SOURCE: Reprinted by permission of Harold Ober Associates Incorporated. Copyright © 1952 by Robert M. Lindner.

as the crime of unadjustment. To violate this Eleventh Commandment is to court social ostracism and to invite a pariah's destiny. Nor is there any acceptable compromise. You adjust—or else!

* * *

. . . Remarkably, there actually exists today neither creed, organization, nor ideology not devoted to the myth of adjustment. If our institutions and philosophies differ in all else—and they obviously do—here is the point of their unity: that the only acceptable way of life is the way of conformity. On this diverse philosophies agree; on this political Left and Right unite; here Churches meet and Schisms join; at this place even Religion and Science embrace. All—regardless of their differences—find in the concept of adjustment a meeting ground. Commonly, all of them—although each does so in its own interest—regard protest as unforgivable and believe—covertly if not openly—that the flame of rebellion that burns in every human breast must be gutted.

* * *

Now, partisans of causes, criers of ideologies, makers of philosophies, and servitors of religion will, of course, deny the thesis here stated: that all of them aim, by exploiting the adjustment fallacy, to enslave man. Each proclaims its heartfelt desire only to free man, to ensure for him a permissive and expansive existence, to unchain him—providing, naturally, that he first makes his surrender and adjusts. Significantly, those who more loudly proclaim such good intentions are the most insistent on reducing him initially to the status of an obedient and unprotesting automaton. Their denials to the contrary, the fact remains that, without exception, they endorse the adjustment idea. With fervor and persistence they spread the concept abroad. With enthusiasm they lend their influence to the propagation and enforcement of the Eleventh Commandment. And in the doing of these things they disclose themselves; for the no longer inescapable truth about adjustment is that it has an aim: the reduction of the variability of man to an undistinguished formlessness, a sameness, an amorphous homogeneity so that dominion over him can more easily and more completely be established.

* * *

With all the weight of this history behind it, entrapped and stultified by the collusive efforts—. . .—of science, religion, and philosophy, it is not to be wondered at that ordinary men uncritically accept the myth of adjustment as truth. The notion is, in a sense, bred into them. In any case, from the cradle forward they are schooled in renunciation. From babyhood they are rewarded only when they conform, made comfortable only when they surrender, given love only when they relinquish what gives them satisfaction. By the time of their presumed maturity—or at least their physical adulthood—their lessons have been learned well. Their senses inform them continuously that protest and rebellion are fruitless and, if expressed, are met with immediate and severe reprisals. Their minds are pinioned by an imperative from which there is no escape. The things they crave must be bought with the coin of resignation. Forced thusly to suppress the most vagrant protestant urge, they are ever tormented by disquiet and unease. This, then, must be the real source of that anxiety which has been the outstanding characteristic in the psychology of mankind, and the wellspring of that abiding guilt all men feel particularly in our time. For the best that an individual can do in a world dominated by such a fallacy is to turn inward his revolt, either upon himself as illness or as vague and restless longing from which he fabricates his dreams and fantasies, sometimes his hallucinations and delusions. And to his children he passes on the heritage of suppression and its techniques. In this way the denial of instinct proceeds apace, meeting nowhere more than the shade of resistance. In its wake lie human wreckage, tumbled civilizations, countless generations of potentialities unrealized, the whole sorry gamut of disease, frustration, and despair.

* * *

The propagation of adjustment as a way of life is leading inexorably to the breeding of a weak race of men who will live and die in slavery, the meek and unprotesting tools of their self-appointed masters. This, so it seems, is the goal of almost every ideology, creed, and philosophy to which we have been asked or forced to subscribe not only today but for ages past. This is why we are literally commanded to adjust and . . . are threatened with disbarment from the human race if we do not. The unspoken aim, it appears, is to make of all of us Mass Men, beings who will be alike to each other in every aspect of form and feature, in thought, desire, feeling, and expression. In such a condition we can be ruled. To realize this aim the injunction to adjust has been laid upon the planet.

* * *

... From almost the moment of a child's birth forward, the single aim of most parents is to discourage its innate rebelliousness and to find techniques to bury deep within that child its every protestant urge. Supported by the authority of all institutions, parenthood has come to amount to little more than a campaign against individuality. Every father and every mother tremble lest an offspring, in act or thought, should be different from his fellows; and the smallest display of uniqueness in a child becomes the signal for the application of drastic measures aimed at stamping out that small fire of noncompliance by which personal distinctness is expressed. In an atmosphere of anxiety, in a climate of apprehension, the parental conspiracy against children is planned. By the light of day the strategies and tactics that have taken form in whispered conclaves during the dark are put into operation. Few children can survive the barrage: most develop that soft rottenness within, that corruption which forms the embryo of their coming Mass Manhood. And like some hereditary disease of the body, generation after generation proliferates a sickness which can be fatal to our culture.

* * *

Beneath the verbiage of description and classification of human types there remains a simple but significant dichotomy. Mankind largely divides itself, on the one hand, into a great mass of pawns, prisoners of conformity, and those who are untroubled in mind and spirit, having signed a treaty with tractability; and, on the other, into the nonconforming, the protesting, and the rebellious. The fashion this day—a fashion dictated by the increasing preoccupation with regimentation evident on all sides—is to praise and encourage the former. The neurotic is scorned, on the maladjusted we heap abuse, and the different we vilify. But when the dominant illusion of our era is subjected to a closer scrutiny than that usually accorded it, a surprising truth emerges. This truth is that those who don a coat of many colors to set themselves apart from the uniform drabness that clothes the rest of us are the objects of our envy and the victims of our own frustrations. For there is no escaping the recognition that those whom we are wont to deride with the derogation of the label "sick" may well be the really healthy among us and the potential instruments for the salvation of the species.

Suggestions for Further Reading

ABCARIAN, GILBERT, "Radical Right and New Left: Commitment and Estrangement in American Society," in W. J. Crotty (Ed.), *Public Opinion and Politics, A Reader*. (New York: Holt, Rinehart and Winston, 1970), pp. 168–83.

ADORNO, T. W., AND ASSOCIATES, *The Authoritarian Personality*. (New York: Harper and Row, 1950).

AMERICAN POLITICAL EXTREMISM IN THE 1960's," *Journal of Social Issues, 19* (April, 1963), entire issue.

AVERILL, L. J., "Political Fundamentalism in Profile," *The Christian Century* (August 24, 1964), pp. 1009–1012.

BELL, DANIEL, *The Radical Right*. (New York: Doubleday and Co., 1963).

BITTNER, EGON, "Radicalism," *International Encyclopedia of the Social Sciences*, Vol. 13. (New York: Macmillan and the Free Press, 1968), pp. 294–300.

———, "Radicalism and the Organization of Political Movements," *American Sociological Review, 28* (December, 1963), pp. 928–940.

BOTTOMORE, T. B., *Critics of Society: Radical Thought in North America* (New York: Pantheon Books, 1968).

BUNZELL, J. H., *Anti-Politics in America*. (New York: Alfred F. Knopf, Inc., 1967).

FROMM, ERICH, *Escape From Freedom* (New York: Avon Books, 1966).

HOFFER, ERIC, *The True Believer* (New York: Harper and Row, 1951).

JACOBE, PAUL, AND SAUL LANDAU (Eds.), *The New Radicals* (New York: Random House, 1966).

KOPKIND, A. (Ed.), *Thoughts of the Young Radicals* (*New Republic,* 1966).

LASSWELL, H. D., *Psychopathology and Politics* (New York: Viking Press, 1960).

LINDNER, R., *Prescription For Rebellion* (New York: Rinehart and Co., 1952).

MCCORMACK, T., "The Motivation of Radicals," *American Journal of Sociology* (July, 1950), pp. 17–24.

MARMOR, JUDD, "The Psychodynamics of Political Extremism," *American Journal of Psychotherapy, 12* (October, 1968), pp. 561–568.

"THE NEW RADICALISM" (symposium), *Partisan Review* (Spring-Fall, 1965; Winter, 1966), entire issue.

ROKEACH, MILTON, *The Open and Closed Mind.* New York: Basic Books, 1960.

SCHOENBERGER, R. A. (Ed.), *The American Right Wing* (New York: Holt, Rinehart and Winston, 1969).

SHILS, EDWARD, "Authoritarianism 'Right' and 'Left,' " in S. Ulmer (Ed.), *Introductory Readings in Political Behavior.* (Chicago: Rand McNally, 1961), pp. 27–33.

TOCH, HANS, *The Social Psychology of Social Movements* (Indianapolis: Bobbs-Merrill, 1965).

TOMKINS, S., " 'Left' and 'Right': A Basic Dimension of Ideology and Personality," in R. W. White (Ed.), *The Study of Lives* (New York: Atherton Publishing Co., 1966), pp. 389–411.

WOLFINGER, R. E., AND ASSOCIATES, "America's Radical Right: Politics and Ideology," in D. Apter (Ed.), *Ideology and Discontent* (Glencoe: The Free Press, 1964).

ZINN, H., "The Old Left and the New: Emancipation From Dogma," *The Nation* (April 4, 1966), 385–389.

Footnotes to *Democracy is a Fraud*

[1] Our Liberal critics would have you believe that this statement, for an American, is practically heresy. This is because these same Liberals have been working so long and so hard to convert our republic into a democracy, and to make the American people believe that it is *supposed to be a democracy*. Nothing could be further from the truth than that insidiously planted premise. Our founding fathers knew a great deal about history and government, and they had very nearly a clean slate on which to write the blueprint for our own. They gave us a republic because they considered it the best of all forms of government. They visibly spurned a democracy as probably the worst of all forms of government. But our past history and our present danger indicate that they were right in both particulars.

[2] The folly of the two-sides-to-every-question argument is emphasized in a brief story we have told elsewhere and often. The minister had preached a superb sermon. It had moved his whole congregation to a determination to lead nobler and more righteous lives. Then he said: "And that, of course, is the Lord's side. Now for the *next* half hour, and to be fair, I'll present the devil's side. You can then take your choice."

[3] The whole theme of these several paragraphs, and the monolithic structure of the Society, have of course been seized on by the Liberals (and worse) as the basis of vicious and persistent attacks against the Society and myself. Their criticism is about as slippery and phony as everything else the Liberals turn out today under the label of argument.

Our members are told specifically and emphatically in our bulletins, about once every three months, never to carry out any of our requests or to do anything for the Society that is against their individual consciences or even contrary to their best judgement. If they find themselves too constantly and continuously in disagreement with our activities, then probably they do not belong in the Society and may wish to resign. But it is only a real troublemaker that we put out of the Society ourselves.

So far, with many thousands of members and two years of experience, we have dropped less than a dozen. (We have had a total of about one hundred resignations in the two years). One of the two dropped directly by the Home Office was a lonesome widow who did not have the slightest interest in, or idea of, what The John Birch Society was all about. She simply wanted companionship and a place to go, and she constantly bogged down her chapter meeting with her personal affairs. The other turned out not even to be a member. But he had been going regularly to the meetings of one of our chapters, posing as an important member of our Home Chapter, and turning the meetings more and more—before we knew about it—into sessions in advanced anti-Semitism. We simply asked this man to stay away from our meetings, straightened out the chapter, and have had no further trouble from that source.

We have refused to accept just one chapter since the Society was founded, and this was because of the extreme racist views of some of its prospective members. How little we go along with such views is shown by the fact that we have two all-Negro chapters, of which we are very proud, and several chapters in northern states with good citizens of both white and colored races who meet together. We are bitterly opposed to *forced* integration, in schools or *anywhere else,* but on far sounder grounds than the "racial superiority" arguments. It is because, according to the Constitution, the Federal Government has absolutely nothing to do, legally, with public education; because every American, white or black, should have the right to select his own associates for every enterprise and occasion; and because all of the trouble over integration—which is doing inestimable damage to both the black and white races—is Communist inspired, encouraged, and implemented for Communist purposes. And while these remarks may appear to be of a rambling nature, it seems well worth while to get them down on paper at this point to avoid misunderstandings in the future.

When we were viciously attacked in one of the Midwestern papers a few months ago, on the basis of the monolithic structure of the Society, our members came to our support with a veritable flood of letters to that paper, quoting passage after passage from the Blue Book to show how unfounded were the charges advanced. Our members themselves are fully aware, from actual experience as well as from study of our materials, that the monolithic structure is purely for the sake of *efficiency, effectiveness,* and *steadfastness* of purpose within the Society itself—from which anybody can resign, with our good will and good wishes, at the drop of a hat. Our members themselves soon find that there is absolutely no reason to object to this protection of the Society internally against infiltration, splintering, and inside fights.

And you our critics frequently and vehemently charge that we are a *fascist* organization, far more dangerous and tyrannical than the Communists themselves. We don't know how they attempt to justify any such charges, but in any event we should like to call to their attention *one* difference between the Communists and ourselves. You join the Communist Party, and you are told what to do. You refuse to do it enough times, and you are shot in some dark alley or pushed off a subway platform in front of a moving train. You join The John Birch Society, and you are asked to do certain things, *if you agree.* You refuse to do them enough times—and we give you your money back! Somehow it does seem to us that there is a difference.

A B C D E F G H I J   5 4 3 2 1